I0813216

Chai Noon

WISCONSIN FILM STUDIES

Patrick McGilligan, series editor

Chai Noon

Jews and the Cinematic Wild West

JONATHAN L. FRIEDMANN

THE UNIVERSITY OF WISCONSIN PRESS

The University of Wisconsin Press
728 State Street, Suite 443
Madison, Wisconsin 53706
uwpress.wisc.edu

This book will be made open access within three years of publication thanks to Path to Open, a program developed in partnership between JSTOR, the American Council of Learned Societies (ACLS), University of Michigan Press, and The University of North Carolina Press to bring about equitable access and impact for the entire scholarly community, including authors, researchers, libraries, and university presses around the world. Learn more at https://about.jstor.org/path-to-open/

Printed in the United States of America
This book may be available in a digital edition.

Library of Congress Cataloging-in-Publication Data

Names: Friedmann, Jonathan L., 1980- author.
Title: Chai noon : Jews and the cinematic Wild West / Jonathan L. Friedmann.
Other titles: Wisconsin film studies.
Description: Madison, Wisconsin : University of Wisconsin Press, 2025. | Series: Wisconsin film studies | Includes bibliographical references and index.
Identifiers: LCCN 2024039498 | ISBN 9780299352103 (hardcover)
Subjects: LCSH: Jews in motion pictures. | Western films—History and criticism.
Classification: LCC PN1995.9.J46 F74 2025 | DDC 791.43/65878089924—dc23/eng/20250203
LC record available at https://lccn.loc.gov/2024039498

Contents

Illustrations

Chai Noon

Introduction

Books on Westerns often begin with childhood memories. Authors wax nostalgically about seeing their first Western on the big screen or being glued to Western series on their TV sets.[1] Writers warmly recall playing cowboys and Indians in their backyards or staging battles between plastic five-and-dime cowboys and Indians.[2] These musings hearken to an era, usually the 1950s and early 1960s, when Western films, novels, comic books, advertising, clothing, toys, attractions, tchotchkes, television series, and radio shows mutually reinforced collective myths and memories of the Old West. As a California city kid growing up in the 1980s and 1990s, I cannot claim this Western-saturated Americana as my own. Unlike South Dakota–raised historian Josh Garrett-Davis, author of *What Is a Western?* and associate curator at the Autry Museum of the American West in Los Angeles, who was born the same year as me, I was not exposed to "real cowboys, real Indians, and real pretty landscapes."[3] All I had was the facsimile ghost town of Knott's Berry Farm, the faux-rustic decor of Claim Jumper restaurants, and a week-long family trip to a Wyoming dude ranch, which in retrospect was probably inspired by *City Slickers* (Columbia, 1991).

By the time I was a TV junkie, Saturday morning cartoons and sci-fi space Westerns were the pop culture vernacular. This was about a decade after film critic Pauline Kael had declared the Western dead—although, to be fair, Westerns had more properly transitioned into a postpopularity "afterlife" phase.[4] The same year Kael made her pronouncement, *Blazing Saddles* (Warner Bros., 1974), Mel Brooks's raucous jab at contemporary racism, became the highest-grossing Western to that point.[5]

Westerns had been pronounced dead before. A 1911 article from the *Nickelodeon* opined, "There seems to be prevalent a sentiment that the Western photoplay has outrun its course of usefulness and is slated for an early demise. The old thrills are exhausted and the people want something new."[6] As strange as this statement reads in hindsight (Westerns comprised between 20 and 35 percent of U.S. annual releases between the 1930s and 1950s), it accurately foretold the end of "eastern Westerns."[7] Major motion picture companies were in the process of relocating from the East Coast to Southern California, where picturesque vistas awaited a cinematic revival.

After a multidecade run that regularly saw more than one hundred Westerns per year, production declined by roughly 80 percent between 1970 and 1980.[8] Between 1971 and 1982, the genre's share of film rentals fell from 12 percent to just 1 percent. *Variety* figures for 1983 and 1984 listed the U.S. market share for Westerns at zero.[9] This absence was partly offset by the persistence of Western television series, among them the martial arts adventure *Kung Fu* (ABC, 1972–75) and the historical drama *Little House on the Prairie* (NBC, 1974–83), as well as the cultural impact of Italian Westerns. During the 1960s, European studios made more than five hundred Westerns, while American studios made just two hundred, and the decline has continued unabated "with no promise of return to the previously high production figures."[10] Putting it positively, film historian Andrew Patrick Nelson argues that the genre shifted from "a popular to a specialty form," with occasional prestige Westerns still attracting critical acclaim and financial success—for example, the Coen brothers' *True Grit* (Paramount, 2010), Quentin Tarantino's *Django Unchained* (Weinstein, 2012), and Alejandro G. Iñárritu's *The Revenant* (20th Century Fox, 2015).[11] Recent years have also seen a renaissance of prestige Western series and miniseries, including *Deadwood* (HBO, 2004–6), *Hell on Wheels* (AMC, 2011–16), *Longtime* (A&E and Netflix, 2012–17), *Strange Empire* (CBC, 2014–15), *Westworld* (HBO, 2016–22), *Godless* (Netflix, 2017), *The Son* (AMC, 2017–19), *Yellowstone* (Paramount+, 2018–present), *Wild West Chronicles* (INSP, 2020–23), *1883* (Paramount+, 2021–22), *That Dirty Black Bag* (AMC+, 2022), and *Lawmen: Bass Reeves* (Paramount+, 2023). Even so, with well over eight hundred thousand titles currently available on traditional and streaming platforms, Westerns are only a miniscule drop in the bucket.[12] In fact, the twenty-first century has given us more academic books on Westerns than actual films.[13]

The Western's fall from pop culture dominance is allegorized in *Toy Story* (Disney, 1995), Pixar's debut animated film. Woody the cowboy sheriff loses his favorite toy status to sci-fi hero Buzz Lightyear, signaling the replacement of the American frontier with the new frontier of outer space. The 1990s also gave us mainstream, family-oriented genre critiques, such as *The Indian in the Cupboard* (Paramount, 1995), which deconstructed the cowboy-and-Indian mythos through plastic figures that came to life, and *Addams Family Values* (Paramount, 1993), which demolished the myths of Thanksgiving and westward expansion through a play orchestrated by Wednesday Addams.[14] Futuristic Nerf guns, Super Soakers, and laser tag took the place of frontier battles. Comic book and trading card manias, fueled by ill-fated speculator booms, had little room for cowboy lore save for DC Comics bounty hunter antihero Jonah Hex and a few baseball cards with pitcher Nolan Ryan on horseback and in cowboy attire. I had some monochromatic plastic cowboy and Indian figures, but they were toy chest filler, mixed in with diminutive dinosaurs, zoo animals, and green army men. These grocery store acquisitions took a backseat to my coveted action figures: G.I. Joe, Transformers, Star Wars, and Marvel superheroes. I was aware that Gene Autry, a retired singing cowboy, owned the California Angels baseball team. I recognized the Marlboro Man as a vestige of the cowboy's former glory, but he was drowned out by aggressive antismoking campaigns. Iron Eyes Cody, the Italian turned crying Indian of the Keep America Beautiful commercials, had been replaced by Woodsy Owl, the U.S. Forest Service mascot who told us to "Give a hoot, don't pollute." My introduction to Iron Eyes Cody came via his role as Chief St. Cloud in *Ernest Goes to Camp* (Buena Vista, 1987)—among my earliest encounters with Native American stereotypes.

To be sure, cowboys and Indians had not entirely disappeared from popular consciousness. But for the most part, they were updated, repurposed, remixed, and recontextualized. A boy my age was more familiar with helicopter pilot Wild Bill or Indigenous infantryman Spirit on the *G.I. Joe* animated series (Sunbow, 1983–86) than with the Lone Ranger or Tonto, let alone Wild Bill Hickok or Geronimo. My exposure to film and television Westerns was sporadic and usually indirect: Bugs Bunny's nemesis Yosemite Sam; the *American Tail* sequel *Fievel Goes West* (Universal, 1991); occasional cartoon episodes, memorably the "Pest o' the West" segment of *Beetlejuice* (ABC, 1989); Laurence Fishburne's Cowboy Curtis on *Pee-wee's*

Playhouse (CBS, 1986–90); *The Frisco Kid* (Warner Bros., 1979) shown in Sunday school; *Three Amigos* (Orion, 1986) played at the local movie theater; and a few cowboy-fantasy mashups, including *Back to the Future Part III* (Universal, 1990), the animated series *BraveStarr* (Filmation, 1987–88) and *Wild West C.O.W.-Boys of Moo Mesa* (ABC, 1992–93), and the live-action series *The Adventures of Brisco County, Jr.* (Fox, 1993–94). Equally vivid are memories of switching channels whenever reruns of *Bonanza* (NBC, 1959–73) or *Little House on the Prairie* came on.

When film professor Ray Merlock showed John Ford's *The Searchers* (Warner Bros., 1956) to a class in the early 2000s, he was surprised that many of his students had never before seen a Western.[15] I was an undergraduate at the time, and this does not shock me at all. Had it not been for a film analysis course I took in high school, I would not have seen *The Great Train Robbery* (Edison, 1903), *High Noon* (United Artists, 1952), *Butch Cassidy and the Sundance Kid* (Twentieth Century–Fox, 1969), or Sergio Leone's trendsetting spaghetti Western *A Fistful of Dollars* (United Artists, 1964). As high school led into college, I became infatuated with Leone's other films. But when I rented Howard Hawks's *Rio Bravo* (Warner Bros., 1959) after reading a recommendation from Tarantino, I fell asleep during the viewing. The same thing happened years earlier when I was taken to see *Dances with Wolves* (Orion, 1990). Yet although I was born into a post-Western milieu, I had a cowboy-themed birthday party when I was young—an aberration inspired more by Knott's Berry Farm than anything else.

Growing up in concrete-covered Southern California, I never considered that the streets I walked were once the (Far) Wild West. The closest we came to learning state history in school was the obligatory (and by today's standards problematic) fourth-grade California mission project. I was unaware that many Westerns were filmed within driving distance of my house.[16] My maternal great-grandfather, Ukrainian-born merchant Harry Millman, had a department store in Reseda, nestled against the Western film backdrops of the San Fernando Valley. He outfitted Western movie actors from the 1940s until his death in 1956. Around the same time, Nudie Cohn (Nuta Kotlyarenko), another Ukrainian-born Jewish valley resident, was adding glamour and rhinestones to Western wear sported by Roy Rogers, Dale Evans, Johnny Cash, Elvis Presley, and many others. Little did I know that both Lorne Greene and Michael Landon, stars of shows I habitually avoided (*Bonanza* and *Little House on the Prairie*), were Jewish; that *Bonanza*'s creator, David Dortort, used his Jewish immigrant father as the basis for the show's patriarch, Ben Cartwright (Greene); that Ed Spielman and Herman Miller, two of the three creators of *Kung Fu*, were Jews; or that *Gunsmoke* star James Arness, a non-Jew, gave his 950-acre ranch to the Brandeis-Bardin Institute in Simi Valley, California—the largest gift of land to a Jewish institution in the state's history.[17]

Reviewing my fragmented relationship with Westerns, I started noticing Jewish contributors behind the things I had seen. Beyond the obvious examples of the rabbi-centered *Frisco Kid*, the Jewish mice of *Fievel Goes West*, and the Jewish sensibility of *Blazing Saddles*, there was Eli Wallach stealing the show as Tuco in Leone's *The Good, the Bad, and the Ugly* (United Artists, 1966). My plastic cowboy and Indian figures were copied from ones popularized in the 1950s and 1960s by Jewish toymakers Herbert and Harold Rosenberg (Giant Plastics) and Louis and David Marx (Marx Toys). *City Slickers* and *Three Amigos* featured white-collar urban schlemiels roughing it in the West. Yosemite Sam was modeled on creator Friz Freling and voiced by the inimitable Mel Blanc. *Pee-wee's Playhouse* was created by Paul Reubens (Pee-wee Herman), whose father, Milton Rubenfeld, was a founding pilot in the Israeli Air Force. Max Aronson had bit parts in *The Great Train Robbery* and later became the first Western movie star, Broncho Billy Anderson. *High Noon* was written by Carl Foreman, was directed by Fred Zinnemann, and featured Dimitri Tiomkin's Academy Award–winning score and song. *Butch Cassidy and the Sundance Kid* won Academy Awards for screenwriter William Goldman and composer Burt Bacharach and co-starred Paul Newman, who once said, "I'm half Protestant, half Jewish. But I've always thought of myself as a Jew because it is harder."[18] Even Frank S. Nugent, writer of *The Searchers* and ten other screenplays for John Ford, had a Jewish mother and an Irish father.

All of these experiences and revelations, from boyhood to the present, have shaped my interactions with and interpretations of this book's subject matter: Jews in the cinematic Wild West.[19] My memories serve as a "primary data set" and jumping off point.[20] In large part, this book focuses an unlikely Jewish lens (mine) on an underexplored aspect of the genre. I am an outsider to Westerns looking for outsiders within the genre: Jewish characters on screen and Jewish sensibilities behind the scenes. Rather than a hindrance, my outsider's perspective allows me to engage with fresh and inquisitive eyes, unclouded by nostalgia.

Where Are the Jews?

Overtly Jewish characters and subjects are rare in Westerns and even rarer in films that aficionados hold up as essential viewing. There is, for example, nothing obviously Jewish about *Stagecoach* (United Artists, 1939), *Shane* (Paramount, 1953), or *The Man Who Shot Liberty Vance* (Paramount, 1962), which is perhaps unsurprising in a genre that has been called "white-supremacist entertainment."[21] Film scholar Scott Simmon begins *The Invention of the Western Film* by acknowledging the genre's inherent racism and outdated social views, arguing that younger viewers avoid Westerns because of a "dislike of the retrograde cultural attitudes carried by Western films, not only their treatment of non-European races but also their ways of representing gender."[22] To a great extent, the Western's peaks and valleys are linked to Americans' self-perceptions: frontier fantasies, glamorized expansionism, and a near-religious devotion to individualism appealed to viewers grasping for hope during the Great Depression or imbibing the optimism of an ascendant post–World War II superpower. As time went on, growing social unrest and foreign policy malaise made the genre's triumphalist message passé. By the late 1960s, frontier violence had lost its redemptive value, strict gender roles had been challenged, distinctions between white-hatted heroes and black-hatted villains had become muddy, and Indigenous Americans were no longer seen as obstacles to divinely ordained settler colonialism.[23] The era's revisionist or anti-Westerns, exemplified by Sam Peckinpah's *The Wild Bunch* (Warner Bros., 1969), Ralph Nelson's *Soldier Blue* (Embassy, 1970), and Robert Altman's *McCabe and Mrs. Miller* (Warner Bros., 1971)—and a trio of films explored in this book: George Roy Hill's *Butch Cassidy and the Sundance Kid*, Brooks's *Blazing Saddles*, and Arthur Penn's *Little Big Man* (National General, 1970)—interrogated these themes, chipped away at recycled myths, and flipped untenable plot points on their head. Anti-Westerns' critical approach to "traditional representations of history or myth, heroism and violence, masculinity and minorities" spoke to a youth culture jaded by the Vietnam War and clamoring for racial justice, gender equality, and economic fairness. Indeed, while revisionist Westerns have been read as correctives of the Wild West mythos—unearthing multiracial, multiethnic, and violently colonizing realities of the frontier—they also shape their own fantasies to suit the needs of the present.[24]

Yet the old guard did not step aside quietly, nor did classic Westerns simply disappear. Compounding the offense were quotes from John Wayne, the genre's most iconic performer, whose real-life attitudes blurred art and artist. In an infamous 1971 *Playboy* interview, Wayne stated, "I believe in white supremacy until the blacks are educated to the point of responsibility," adding, "I don't feel we did wrong in taking this great country away from [Native Americans]. There were great numbers of people who needed new land, and the Indians were selfishly trying to keep it for themselves."[25] Ronald Reagan, a fellow cowboy actor who later starred as a cowboy president, remarked during his second term in office, "Maybe we made a mistake in trying to maintain Indian cultures. Maybe we should not have humored them in that, wanting to stay in that primitive lifestyle. Maybe we should have said: No, come join us."[26] During the 1980s, the burgeoning right wing kept the mythic West alive even as the myth-making films had faded to the sidelines.[27] In 1992, Universal Pictures chair Tom Pollock referred to both John Wayne–esque conservative lessons and lessons in the revisionist mold when he stated that the company was not "rushing out to make Westerns, because audiences find history lessons an immediate turnoff."[28]

Like any long-lived art form, Westerns mirror the eras in which they are made, presenting the "essence of what the audience wants to believe is reality."[29] American studies scholar Richard Slotkin describes how "presentism"—interpreting the past through modern values—is reflected across the decades in Western film violence: racial violence through vigilantism; violent masculinity through marshals and gunfighters; violence of alienation through the outlaw; violence of conquest through destruction of Native Americans; violence of fascism through the cavalry; and the futility of violence through revisionist critiques.[30] Others have similarly tracked changing depictions of Native Americans in ways that appealed to younger and better-educated audiences: early portrayals of "primitives" coincided with positivist racial theories; World War II analogies of cavalrymen as overseas soldiers and Native Americans as foreign enemies; and the 1960s use of Native Americans as stand-ins for persecuted Blacks and ostracized white hippies.[31] More recently, *Killers of the Flower Moon* (Paramount, 2023), Martin Scorsese's interrogation of the murder of Osage Nation members for their oil-rich land in 1920s Oklahoma, has been criticized for adopting a "self-flagellating white gaze" despite directly addressing atrocities committed against the Osage people.[32] Native American scholar Ted Jojola observes that with each iteration, Natives are merely projections of how whites see themselves: "The Hollywood Indian is a mythological being who exists nowhere but within the fertile imaginations of its movie actors, producers, and directors. The preponderance of such movie images have reduced native people to ignoble stereotypes."[33] Even the misnomer *Indian* is an Anglocentric category evoking the religious, economic, and nationalistic interests of American colonialism.[34]

Westerns have also mirrored public sentiments regarding other nonwhites and women, most often denigrating, demonizing, or downplaying them but at other times countering these negative portrayals. The ups and downs of these depictions are explored in Juan Alonzo's *Badmen, Bandits, and Folk Heroes: The Ambivalence of Mexican American Identity in Literature and Film*, Sue Matheson's *Women in the Western*, and Mia Mask's *Black Rodeo: A History of the African American Western.*[35]

The subject of Jews and Westerns has not previously received equivalent treatment—probably for good reason. Westerns have historically made little room for Jewish characters, who, despite their mostly European ancestry, are either rendered invisible or much less commonly (and with few exceptions) Otherized as stereotypical fish-out-of-water peddlers and merchants. Both of these options—nonexistence and ill-suitedness—fall outside the historical record.

Although Jews reside on the margins of the mythos, Jewish contributors have significantly shaped the cinematic genre. Since Hollywood's earliest days, Jewish actors, directors, producers, writers, editors, composers, costumers, casting directors, sound designers, cinematographers, and others have made major contributions to Western films. The index to Michael R. Pitts's guide to 5,105 Western features has more than 220 key Jewish directors, screenwriters, and actors accounting for more than 800 films. These players include director Sam Newfield, who made 125 B Westerns; screenwriter Bennett Cohen, who penned over 50 Westerns; and actors who include William Shatner and Leonard Nimoy, Phil Silvers and Walter Matthau, Madeline Kahn and Lainie Kazan, and postconversion Marilyn

Monroe and Sammy Davis Jr.[36] Donn J. Moyer's *Cowboy Cliffhangers*, an encyclopedia of Western serials from the 1930s to the 1950s, has several recurring Jewish names, including producers Nat Levine and Sam Katzman, screenwriter Sol Shor, and composer Lee Zahler.[37]

Yet as important as these contributions are, they reveal an underrepresentation in an industry known for its Jewish movers and shakers. Back in 1976, Jon Tuska claimed to have seen eight thousand Westerns—a number comprising A and B features, talkies and silents, short films, serials, and likely some exaggeration.[38] That Jews are absent from prominent roles in the overwhelming majority of these films results largely from the Jews' perceived lack of character traits driving those tales: rugged masculinity and rural individualism. Indeed, unless Jewish actors were conventionally attractive leading men, like Kirk Douglas or Paul Newman, they were much more likely to play Native Americans—both chiefs and cavalry fodder—than cowboy heroes.

Jewish self-perceptions also contributed to the paucity of representation. According to historian Hasia R. Diner, "The main currents of American Jewish culture in the twentieth century have posited the city as the Jews' natural habitat and New York in particular as the city that most suited the Jewish temperament."[39] As late as the 1970s, East Coast Jewish literary critic Leslie Fiedler wrote that the "the notion of the Jewish cowboy is utterly ridiculous."[40] Largely because of such assumptions, the close association of Jews with other film genres, notably musicals, comedies, and science fiction, did not translate to the Wild West. In fact, the few Westerns with identifiably Jewish characters, either named or coded, generally show them as urban peddlers and merchants trying to make it as cowboys and pioneers, often with comic results. These depictions perpetuated the nebbishy Jewish cowboy that originated on the vaudeville stage.

Beyond these genre-specific factors were self-imposed regulatory guidelines known as the Hays Code or the Motion Picture Production Code, which began in 1934, waned through the 1960s, and ended in 1968. Particularly during the 1930s, the Code was embraced by Hollywood executives fearful that antisemitic fervor—stirred by industrialist Henry Ford, radio broadcaster Father Charles Coughlin, film censor Joseph Breen, and their like-minded ilk—would lead to even stricter censorship.[41] In addition to prohibiting profanity, realistic violence, and sexual "perversion," the early years of the Code—and the studio system that supported it—essentially put an end to onscreen multiculturalism and filmmakers' freedom to "portray ethnic groups unapologetically."[42] A few pre-Code Westerns showcase overtly Jewish characters, both comic and tragic. But after the Code was instituted, these characters were sanitized, coded, or most frequently removed altogether.

The near-invisibility of Jews in Westerns reflected largely assimilated Hollywood Jews' market-driven avoidance of controversy, desire for mass appeal, and aversion to Jewish subjects. Although the industry had in large part been created by Jewish immigrants, studio heads were more interested in shedding their old identities than seeing them onscreen, especially after the film industry relocated from the East Coast to Los Angeles. The studio founders went from Poland to polo in one generation, consciously rejecting their pasts and wholeheartedly adopting their new country and the reinvention it afforded them.[43]

This process continued even as the great retreat from Jewish representation in the 1930s gave way to Jewish themes and characters in films such as Jewish director Ernst Lubitsch's *To Be or Not to Be* (United Artists, 1942), about a troupe of actors in Nazi-occupied Poland; *Gentleman's Agreement* (Twentieth Century–Fox, 1947) and *Crossfire* (RKO, 1947), the first Hollywood films to confront antisemitism in the United States; and a number of philosemitic movies dealing with the Holocaust and Israel, including *The Search* (MGM, 1948), *Sword in the Desert* (Universal, 1949), *The Juggler* (Columbia, 1953), *Me and the Colonel* (Columbia, 1958), *Judgment at Nuremberg* (MGM, 1961), and *Cast a Giant Shadow* (United Artists, 1966). The liberalizing of the film industry during the 1960s brought a number of socially and politically relevant Jewish-made films, like Stanley Kubrick's controversial Cold War satire *Dr. Strangelove* (Columbia, 1964), Sidney Lumet's *The Pawnbroker* (American International Pictures, 1964), the first U.S. film to explore the Holocaust from a survivor's perspective, and Arthur Penn's *Bonnie and Clyde* (Warner Bros., 1967), which was accused of glamorizing crime and mocking law and order.

What Is a Jewish Western?

This book examines around fifty Westerns that have Jewish content—a tiny sum in a genre totaling upward of eight thousand. This modest total includes a few borderline cases along with more than a dozen television episodes that resurrected the Jewish peddler to teach viewers lessons in tolerance (and Judaism 101). As an exercise in mining the margins, the search for relevant content raises the question *What is a Jewish Western?* This question, in turn, contains two others: *What is a Jewish movie?* and *What is a Western?*

An expansive approach to defining Jewish cinema embraces any film that happens to have a Jewish star, writer, director, producer, composer, cinematographer, and so forth, regardless of content. This is a variation of "Jewhooing," named for a now-defunct website, Jewhoo.com, where visitors typed in celebrity names to find out whether they were Jewish. As explained in David Kaufman's *Jewhooing the Sixties*, the process entails "naming and claiming" famous Jews and projecting group identity onto them.[44] Yet if a movie becomes Jewish by virtue of a Jew working on it in some capacity, then nearly every Hollywood film (and television show) would qualify. As Lawrence J. Epstein cautions in *American Jewish Films*, "Given the role of Jews in Hollywood, [such a broad definition] is not very helpful because there are Jews involved in an extraordinary number of important motion pictures."[45]

The expansive approach becomes even more maximalist if we consider the viewer's perspective via response theory: the individual's reception and interpretation in the meaning-making process.[46] A viewer-directed understanding appreciates the activity of Jews watching movies as a cultural practice independent of what is being watched. In other words, self-consciously Jewish eyes and ears can make anything Jewish.[47] In *Coming Out Jewish*, Jon Stratton similarly discusses "Jewish moments": references in film and television that Jews are more likely to pick up on than are non-Jews.[48] Valid as this may be in terms of understanding how Jews individually and collectively consume popular entertainment, it distracts us from the question of what constitutes a Jewish movie.

A stricter definition looks only at films with Jewish characters that also comment on aspects of Jewish life. This shrinks the pool of possibilities significantly, particularly as Judaism—the lifeways and worldviews of the Jewish people—is rarely a subject onscreen. Epstein adds caution here as well: "When the subject is Jews (a film about the Holocaust or about Israel), rarely is there a discussion about what it means to be Jewish."[49]

This definition may in fact be too narrow, as the Jewish experience involves more than ritual and is lived out in sometimes unstated ways. Few would argue with the Jewishness of the Marx Brothers or Three Stooges or with the thinly veiled Jewish subtexts of many film musicals. One could even interpret Steven Spielberg's *E.T. the Extra-Terrestrial* (Universal, 1982) as a parable of a Jewish immigrant who arrives in America and longs to return home.[50] This broadens the notion of Jewish film to include Jewish *sensibility*: the presence of a recognizable (or at least arguable) Jewish attitude, reference, or experiential lens. Teasing out these qualities requires what Cantor Gabrielle Newman terms "Yiddishkeiteria"—or criteria used to determine the Jewishness of something.[51] The Yiddishkeiteria employed in this book embrace explicitly Jewish content and/or characters as well as examples where Jewish sensibility is particularly pronounced.

What constitutes a Western is also less straightforward than it seems. A basic definition might be any film that takes place in the American West between the 1850s and 1900 and presents the frontier as a borderline and battleground between civilization and wide-open land as well as films that challenge this narrative. Western pulp author Frank Gruber reduced Westerns to seven plots and their primary characters: (1) journey—wagon train/stagecoach/railroad versus raiders or Natives; (2) ranch—ranchers versus rustlers or cattlemen versus sheepmen/settlers; (3) empire—an epic ranch plot; (4) revenge—the wronged man versus the truly guilty; (5) cavalry—cavalry versus Natives; (6) outlaw—outlaws versus lawmen; and (7) marshal—lawman versus outlaws.[52] Others have proposed a variety of subcategories: anti-Western; border conflict; comedy; eco-Western (resource scarcity); feminist; historical; modern West; musical; Native Americans; railroad construction; and singing cowboys.[53] Pitts's guidebook is less rigid, going beyond shoot-'em-ups to incorporate "north woods dramas, south of the border action films, outdoor adventures and foreign titles that either deal with the American frontier or have plots indigenous to the Western" as well as films with science fiction, supernatural, and horror elements.[54] Larry Langman's guide to silent Westerns likewise includes tales about Mexico, various Native tribes along the eastern seaboard, and the search for Yukon gold, and lists borderline cases in an appendix.[55]

As these classifications suggest, little genre consensus exists. For example, not everyone places film musicals with cowboy trappings in the Western category. The Autry Museum, for example, does not mention *Oklahoma!* (RKO, 1955) outside of a Polish movie poster for the film adaptation (made by Jewish director Fred Zinnemann, Jewish screenwriters Sonya Levien and William Ludwig, and the Jewish songwriting team of Rodgers and Hammerstein). According to Garrett-Davis, the museum, like several other western history institutions, dismisses the musical as "regional," ignoring its "tangle of Western, folk regionalism, and cutting-edge art."[56] Beyond illustrating the recurring phenomenon of East Coast Jews imagining a western locale, what is perhaps most Jewishly relevant about the film *Oklahoma!* is peddler Ali Hakim (Eddie Albert), a comic Persian peddler whose caricatured Orientalism may have a "whiff of anti-Semitic stereotype." Historically, the peddler was often a Jew who, like Hakim, was portrayed as "foreign, conniving, and other."[57] On the positive side, Hakim might be considered a predecessor to *The Frisco Kid*'s Avram Belinski (Gene Wilder), with both characters alluding to complex demographic realities rarely seen in Wild West entertainment.[58]

What qualifies as a Western is further stretched when considering films that began as Westerns and turned into something else but never completely left behind the Old West. John Carpenter's *Big Trouble in Little China* (20th Century Fox, 1986), for example, was originally pitched by Jewish screenwriters Gary Goldman and David Z. Weinstein as a turn-of-the-twentieth-century Western set in San Francisco and centered on gunslinger Jack Burton. Unsure of the financial viability of a Western, producers handed the script to W. D. Richter, director of the mind-bending cult classic *The Adventures of Buckaroo Banzai* (Twentieth Century–Fox, 1984), who adapted the trite story into a contemporary supernatural action-adventure comedy set in San Francisco's Chinatown. The filmed version, starring Kurt Russell as truck driver Jack Burton, lampoons Hollywood's exoticized depiction of Asian villains and subverts the white savior cowboy hero. Burton's self-confident boasting in a hammy John Wayne accent is repeatedly exposed as empty rhetoric; the real heroics belong to his martial artist sidekick Wang Chi (Dennis Dun) and his Asian teammates. By shedding its Western origins, *Big Trouble in Little China* became a revisionist Western without being a Western at all.[59]

Westerns are among the earliest and most flexible film types: they can be set in earlier or later periods and/or occur outside the geographic West. For example, B Westerns from the 1930s introduced automobiles. Encounters between motorists and a horse-riding John Wayne in *Somewhere in Sonora* (Vitagraph, 1933) and *Paradise Canyon* (Monogram, 1935) may seem anachronistic but remind us that more land was taken through the Homestead Acts in the first two decades of the twentieth century—the automobile age—than during the nineteenth century.[60] Filmed versions of *The Last of the Mohicans* (1920, 1932, 1936, 1965, 1977, and 1992, plus a Mascot serial, animated version, BBC television series, and more) are set during the French and Indian War in 1757 around Lake George, New York, a frontier of its era. Because the story involves Indigenous Americans and accumulated more and more Western signatures as the interpretations piled on (for example, Sierra Nevada shooting locations and covered wagon chases), these movies are regularly filed as Westerns.[61] Similarly, *Smoke Signals* (Miramax, 1998), a film set in the 1990s, is considered a contemporary Western—and an important one at that: it was the first movie written, produced, directed, and acted by Native Americans, and it depicts "contemporary and complex American Indian characters in a contemporary and complex Indian world that exists both within and outside of the larger American culture."[62] A less groundbreaking film with more Jewish content is *Sioux City* (IRS Media, 1994), starring and directed by Lou Diamond Phillips as a young Lakota doctor who was adopted by a wealthy Jewish couple in Beverly Hills. After receiving an amulet from his biological mother, he travels to the Lakota reservation in South Sioux City, Nebraska; discovers that his mother has died in a fire; investigates her mysterious death; and learns about tribal customs in the process. More recently, *Little Bird* (Crave, 2023), a Canadian television series created by Jennifer Podemski and Hannah Moscovitch, follows a First Nations woman who was adopted into a Jewish family during the Sixties Scoop, a period of mass removal of Aboriginal children into the child welfare system, and tries to reconnect with her birth family and heritage.

The neo-Western *Brokeback Mountain* (Focus Features, 2005), exploring the conflicted emotional and sexual relationship between two cowboys, was a landmark in LGBTQ cinema and earned a slew of accolades, including the GLAAD Media Award for Outstanding Film and Oscars for directing (Ang Lee), adapted screenplay (Larry McMurtry and Diana Ossana), and score (Gustavo Santaolalla). *Nope* (Universal, 2022), a present-day, racially aware science fiction/horror film from Black director/writer/producer Jordan Peele, is considered a neo-Western due to its California horse ranch setting, stoic cowboy-like hero Otis "OJ" Haywood Jr. (Daniel Kaluuya), and other variations on Old West themes. Jewish writer/director David Jacobson's neo-Western *Down in the Valley* (ThinkFilm, 2005), set in the modern-day San Fernando Valley, centers on Harlan Fairfax Carruthers (Edward Norton), a mentally unstable cowboy impersonator who, it turns out, is the estranged son of Hasidic parents.

As with any genre, the Western is an inherently hybrid form, absorbing and interacting with multiple styles and elements. In *The Afterlife of the Hollywood Western*, Pete Falconer argues for the Western as a context, not a fixed category: "I treat the Western primarily as a pool of flexible conventions, which can be adapted to different contexts, but which still require some degree of recognition and understanding in order to function." Falconer warns against conflating individual films with "the Western," which is not just a descriptive but also a constructive label. Calling a film a Western (or anything else) forces us to identify aspects that align with what the category conventionally entails. Genre categories start out as adjectives and only later congeal into broad designations—mostly for marketing and promotional purposes. Western tropes and themes have been used and reused in multiple (sub)genres: melodrama, romance, action-adventure, thriller, noir, mystery, comedy, epic, sci-fi, fantasy, steampunk, war, martial arts, and more. With each contribution, Falconer reminds us, the Western remains "open-ended, never arriving at a final, definitive genre identity," an instability that has led some to call for the "death of genre."[63]

Yet for there to be Jewish Westerns, both Jewish films and Western films must exist in some recognizable way. There is an old adage about folk music: "You know it when you hear it." U.S. Supreme Court justice Potter Stewart used a similar dictum to define pornography: "I know it when I see it."[64] This applies to Westerns as well: you can sense it, even if it defies, stretches, or combines conventions. As derivative, recycled, and commercially motivated as Westerns can be—especially when reduced to archetypes and stereotypes—they are not simply one movie with many faces. A Jewish Western, then, is a film with a distinctly Jewish face, either in terms of content (text) or sensibility (subtext), situated in the open-ended cinematic Wild West.

Overview

The films and television episodes surveyed in this book reveal a number of recurring Jewish tropes and motifs: masculinity (puny versus macho), personality types (schlemiel versus rugged individualist), occupational niches (merchant/peddler versus cowboy), residential preferences (urban versus rural), survival strategies (brain versus brawn), antisemitism, intermarriage, and marginalization. Related issues of American Jewishness and whiteness, race relations, and identity formation also appear, as do interactions of Jews with other Others of the Western genre: Blacks, Native Americans, Asians, Mexicans, and so forth. Rather than applying broad theoretical or analytical strokes, these themes are explored through case studies, with each example assessed and contextualized based on its own elements and merits. As much as possible, I avoid jargon and overanalysis to preserve the structure, narrative flow, and salient points. My aim is to be informative, entertaining, and descriptive, providing something of a handbook or guide to Jews and Westerns rather than a theory-heavy treatise.

Readers interested in locating the stories and depictions in this book within larger discussions of identity and representation would do well to consult Werner Sollors's *Beyond Ethnicity: Consent and Descent in American Culture*.[65] Movie-specific explorations, such as Lester D. Friedman's *Unspeakable Images: Ethnicity and the American Cinema* and Marsha J. Hamilton and Eleanor S. Block's *Projecting Ethnicity and Race: An Annotated Bibliography of Studies on Imagery in American Film*, are also helpful, as are books dealing with portrayals of specific groups, such as Charles Ramírez Berg's *Latino Images in Film: Stereotypes, Subversion, and Resistance*, Peter X. Feng's *Screening Asian Americans*, Michael Boyce Gillespie's *Film Blackness: American Cinema and the Idea of Black Film*, and Joanna Hearne's *Native Recognition: Indigenous Cinema and the Western*.[66]

Chapter 1 of this book offers an overview of Jewish vaudeville and silent film cowboys, the role of Jewish moguls in selling the imaginary West during Hollywood's golden age, a profile of early cowboy star Gilbert "Broncho Billy" Anderson, and a look at Jewish composers who shaped the Western soundscape. Chapter 2 excavates both silly and sentimental Jewish representations in pre-Code silent and sound films from 1909 to 1931. Chapter 3 examines the coding of Western Jewish identities during the Motion Picture Production Code era (1934–68), how both negative and positive stereotypes are reflected in these portrayals, and how Jewish trappings were subdued in even outwardly Jewish characters during that period. Chapter 4 documents the appearance of Jewish peddlers and merchants in television Westerns from 1960 to the early twenty-first century, with a mix of out-of-place caricatures, important social commentary, sincere lessons in tolerance, attempts at historical accuracy, and plenty of anachronisms. Chapter 5 explores a few examples of Jewish Westerns in the post-Code period, starting with the standout picture *The Frisco Kid.* Chapter 6 uncovers a Jewish comedic sensibility in Western spoofs, satires, and parodies from the 1930s to the 1990s. Finally, chapter 7 evaluates revisionist Westerns made by Jews, highlighting the socially critical outsider lens of Jewish filmmakers who interrogate the genre while also contributing to it.

CHAPTER 1

How the West Was Made

In 1958, the Manischewitz company released a six-minute Passover record narrated by Harold Stern, "a real honest-to-goodness Jewish cowboy" from Centerville, Texas.[1] Anticipating giggles and incredulity from his urban Jewish listeners, Stern remarks, "Frankly, there's nothing so unusual about being a Jewish cowboy." It was a history lesson pressed onto a novelty record, alternating between Stern's folksy monologue and musical interludes by Israeli singer/accordionist Avram Grobard. The mashup was hardly accidental. Israeli mythmakers (and filmmakers) recognized American Westerns as a useful symbol for their own Zionist project, reimagining the cowboy as a *chalutz* (pioneer) or Sabra (native-born), the Western town as an agricultural community (moshav or kibbutz), rifles as machine guns, denim jeans as khaki pants, Stetsons as tembel hats, boots as sandals, and Native Americans as Arabs.[2] The album jacket bio touts Stern's combination of physical skills and mental aptitude, an image in line with Israel's "new Jew":

> He's 6 ft. tall—20 years old—and single! When he isn't helping his Dad on their 1300 acre ranch, Harold treks to Austin to study history and pre-law at the University of Texas. He can ride with the best of them—and he's as fast on the quip as he is on the draw! Thanks to Manischewitz—thousands of Eastern folk have come to know that there really is a hard-riding Jewish Cowboy—and that he observes Passover the same as they do.[3]

Historically, there really is nothing unusual about a Jewish cowboy. Jewish settlers and pioneers on the American frontier worked as merchants, miners, farmers, tradespeople, industrialists, ranchers, bankers, law officers, innkeepers, gamblers, prostitutes, madams, and more. The California Gold Rush attracted thousands of mostly German-speaking Jews to fill business and civic roles in San Francisco, up north in the gold country, and down south in Los Angeles.[4] Beginning in the late nineteenth century, a number of Jewish organizations and individual donors—most famously Baron Maurice de Hirsch—helped form Jewish agricultural colonies across the United States, including several in the "unsettled" West. These enterprises relocated Eastern European immigrants from crowded urban centers, although most of the farms failed as a consequence of unsuitable land and a lack of farming experience.[5] Lithuanian-born Robert Lazar Miller arrived in Colorado in 1881 and became Denver's "dean of cattle buyers."[6] Isaac Raboy's Yiddish novels *Herr Goldenberg* (1923) and *Der Yiddisher Cowboy* (1942) drew from his experiences as a North Dakota ranch hand in the 1910s.[7] Some Jews had significant contact with Native Americans as traders, translators, and U.S. government agents.[8] Those who helped create the "cowboy aesthetic" included blue jeans creators Levi Strauss and Jacob Davis, ten-gallon hat popularizer Max J. Meyer, Polish-born western attire designers Bernard "Rodeo Ben" Lichtenstein and Nathan Turk, farm and ranch supplier Nathan Kallison, and Nathan's daughter-in-law Frances Rosenthal Kallison, who is honored in the National Cowgirl Museum and Hall of Fame.[9]

Since the mid-twentieth century, accounts of Jews in the pioneer West have been a fertile subtopic of American Jewish history, filling journals like *Western States Jewish History* and an assortment of nonfiction books both critical and celebratory.[10] For example, Natalie Ornish's *Pioneer Jewish Texans* notes that "not every Jewish cowboy became a cattle baron, and not every Jewish peddler became a merchant prince, but a surprising number, by industry and perseverance, made enviable names for themselves in the new land."[11] Other accounts list ranching among the trades and professions taken up by Jewish settlers in Texas and their descendants.[12]

Whereas earlier literature highlighted Jewish success stories, proudly proclaiming "We lived there, too," current research increasingly interrogates how Jewish immigrants, with their European backgrounds and light skin tone, wittingly or unwittingly benefited from the settler-colonial apparatus.[13] In both cases, efforts to correct the historical record anticipated and build on the New Western History, which emerged in the 1980s and (re)introduced voices previously absent or distorted in frontier stories of the trans-Mississippi West: women, lower classes, Indigenous Americans, and diverse races and ethnicities.[14] Amanda Kinsey's documentary film *Jews of the Wild West* (Electric Yolk, 2023) occupies a middle ground between triumphalist and hypercritical, offering positive vignettes of successful Jewish pioneers while acknowledging the devastation wrought on the environment and Native Americans as a result of westward expansion.

Despite the now well-documented presence of Jews in the early American West, historians of the region still find themselves admonishing Jewish studies colleagues to look "beyond New York" and to abandon the view of New York as "typical" for all American Jews.[15] Even those familiar with Jewish life in the pioneer West tend to have a metropolitan bias, as historian William Deverell observes: "Our attention as scholars of the Jewish American experience, if it has come West at all, has tended to focus on urban areas: places such as Denver, Salt Lake, and, especially San Francisco and Los Angeles. There are good reasons for this, of course, with demography leading the way: these were centers of Jewish life, commerce, and culture, and historians are right to focus on them." Deverell reminds us that Jews also found their "*haim afen* range," as musician Mickey Katz called it in his 1947 Yiddish parody of "Home on the Range." Jewish settlement was far-flung, decentralized, and "diasporic," extending well beyond bustling cities.[16]

The cinematic Wild West was imagined and codified long before historians of American Jews began looking westward. Concerned more with "rousing stories" than with reality, Westerns habitually ignore the presence of Jews and other "outliers" on the western frontier.[17] History in general is not a major concern for a cinematic genre that, according to Jane P. Tompkins, author of *West of Everything: The Inner Life of Westerns*, "doesn't have anything to do with the West as such."[18] Westerns have been labeled a "fantasy genre" comprising many "imaginary Wests," where the Hollywood Indian is a "mythological being" and heroic cowboys are products of "myths that have accumulated through the years."[19] On rare occasions when Jewish characters appear in Westerns, they are usually cinematic Jews, popping up in the wrong time and place: Eastern European Hasidic (or Hasidic-adjacent) immigrants associated with turn-of-the-twentieth-century New York. Shaina Hammerman complains that these immediately recognizable types—whose customs, dress, and accents reflect a tiny minority of actual Jews—are stereotypical Others, foreign to both the Christian-dominant milieu and to the Jewish (or non-Jewish) actors playing them.[20] For these reasons and others, an examination of Jews and Westerns must set aside real Jewish pioneers, turning instead to the history of entertainment that gave rise to the mythic West.

Yiddish Cowboys and Hebrew Indians

Closer to the period of westward expansion, Jewish immigrants arriving in the United States during the 1880–1924 wave were largely oblivious to the Jews' participation in settling the frontier. Huddled together in working-class East Coast neighborhoods—with Manhattan's Lower East Side as their megashtetl—what little exposure these predominantly Eastern European Jews had to cowboys, prairies, or Native Americans came from dime novels, Wild West shows, silent movies, and occasional tales in Yiddish- and English-language newspapers. Taken together, the stories impressed on these urbanized political and economic refugees that life in the Wild West was unsuitable for them.

Dialect comedians on the vaudeville stage poked fun at the seeming incongruity of Jewish cowboys and their fictional adversaries, Jewish Native chiefs. For Eastern European immigrant Jews, who largely portrayed these characters and were their main audience, these caricatures warned of barriers to becoming fully American: acculturation and Americanization were attainable and commendable but should not be taken too far.[21] For non-Jews, who would laugh at and occasionally donned the cowboy Jew persona, the stage characters embodied prejudices and insecurities about Jewish Others, most of whom had European skin tones but could nevertheless only imitate whiteness. In both cases, the message was clear: "A Jew cannot function as a real cowboy."[22]

The satirical Jewish cowboy was a subcategory of "Jewface," one of the many racial and ethnic stage types populating variety shows from the late nineteenth to early twentieth centuries. During that era of massive immigration and its associated anxieties, race humor played an outsized role in American popular entertainment. Vaudeville bills featured Jewface, blackface, and stock Irish, Dutch/German, Chinese, and Native American types. What set Jewish caricatures apart was that they were performed mostly by

Jews and for Jewish audiences, who self-effacingly laughed at bumbling, money-obsessed "Cohens" with pushcarts, pawnshops, disheveled prosthetic beards, putty-enhanced hook noses, tattered overcoats, and protruding ears under derby caps. Jewface performers failed at romance, botched business schemes, and got beat up by Irishmen—all in broken Yinglish (a dialect of English with Yiddish constructions and loan words).

Vaudeville's popularity coincided with the arrival of more than twenty million immigrants to the United States between 1880 and 1924, a group that included more than two million Jews, most of them Eastern European. Vaudeville remained the preeminent form of American theatrical entertainment until the early 1930s, when sound films took over.[23] Variety show bills presented an eclectic assortment of affordable light entertainment for America's rapidly diversifying populace. More than a thousand theaters seating as many as thirty-five hundred patrons popped up in big and midsize cities across the United States between 1900 and 1925, playing host to some twenty-five thousand performers.[24] Vaudeville theaters used racial categories to identify all sorts of acts, as cultural historian David Nasaw explains: "Singers, sketch artists, dancers, comedians, and acrobats were on the 'bills' as Irish, Hebrew, colored, blackface, or German. The designation referred not to the performers' ethnicity but to the 'type' of act they presented. Each 'type' spoke its own language, dressed in readily identifiable costumes, and had its own routines. The Irish knockabout comics engaged in a particularly physical brand of comedy, tough-guy routines, dances, and songs. Dutch and German comics dressed in peaked cap, short pants, and large wooden shoes. The 'Hebrews' sang and told their stories in 'stage' Yiddish."[25]

Perhaps the best remembered Jewface song is Irving Berlin's "Cohen Owes Me Ninety-Seven Dollars" (1915). The song tells of a dying businessman who gives his son a list of debtors to collect from. When all the money is retrieved, the man makes a miraculous recovery, declaring, "It's all right to pass away, but when people start to pay, that's no time for a businessman to die!" Other notable examples include "The Original Cohens" (1905; unknown composer), "Under the Matzos Tree" (1907; A. Carr and F. Fischer), "It's Tough When Izzy Rosenstein Loves Genevieve Malone" (1910; G. Kahn and G. Le Boy), "Marry a Yiddisher Boy" (1911; A. S. Brown and G. Botsford), and "Jake, Jake (The Yiddisha Ball Player)" (1913; B. Merrill and I. Berlin).[26]

These songs and most others like them were written by Jews and/or published by Jewish companies.[27] Although the stage Jew was initially introduced by xenophobic non-Jews who Otherized the newcomers with mean-spirited acts inspired by Shakespeare's Shylock, Jews quickly took the satire into their own hands. By the turn of the twentieth century, Jewface was mainly a product of Jewish actors, agents, and theater managers and mostly aimed at Jewish audiences. Some of the acts were so full of Yiddish and culturally specific references that outsiders could not understand them. Jewish critics of the phenomenon, many of whom were descendants of those who had come to the United States from Central Europe earlier in the nineteenth century and had already gained acceptance into the Anglo mainstream, not only feared that the acts would exacerbate antisemitism but also warned that they siloed Jewish performers.[28] A 1913 opinion piece by American-born critic Rabbi Tobias Schanfarber chides a performance of the Avon Comedy Four, a quartet of dialect comics headed by Joe Smith (Joseph Sultzer) and Charlie Dale (Charles Marks): "The actors must not forget that the Yom Kippur reference has no meaning whatsoever for the non-Jews in the audience, when they refer to some Jewish curse words used only by Russian Jews they are wholly without meaning to the other Jews in the audience who have never heard them and do not know what they mean."[29]

While some of this self-mockery can be chalked up to vaudeville's "anything goes" atmosphere, it was also a strategy for assimilation.[30] Jewish immigrant audiences striving to Americanize embraced songs and skits that ridiculed Jewishness as a means of distancing themselves from their Old World past. To laugh at these caricatures meant that they no longer applied to people who were in on the joke. In much the same way, immigrants of all kinds enjoyed seeing native-born hicks and hayseeds spoofed on stage: no matter how green the audiences were or how humble their conditions, they were more sophisticated than the bumpkins.[31] Versatility was also an asset on the vaudeville stage. Many Jews who wore Jewface also inhabited other types, changing from Jew to Black to Irish, sometimes within a single show. Such efforts did not always go well, as when Harry Jolson (Al Jolson's brother) played an Irish role but mistakenly delivered his lines in "Yiddish-American gumbo."[32] Yet however clumsy the execution, the performers' chameleonlike "ability to become someone else with a simple change of costume," as Andrea Most observes, modeled a way to "negotiate the perilous landscape of American ideology" that stood in the way of Americanization.[33]

If ethnic sendups demonstrated rapid adaptation in America's multicultural landscape, the cowboy subtype warned about limits of self-transformation. Such caution was epitomized in "Yonkle the Cow-Boy Jew" (1907; W. J. Harris and H. I. Robinson), a song with illustrated slides describing Yonkle Finkelstein's abysmal attempt at living a clichéd cowboy lifestyle.[34] In the chorus, Yonkle quotes from a letter he wrote to friends:

Western life is fine and dandy,
I have got no kick.
When I think of the pawn shop bus'ness,
Oy, it makes me sick.
Ev'ry time I see some Indians
I just kill a few.
So I've changed my name from Finkelstein
To Yonkle, the Cow-Boy Jew.[35]

Musicologist Aaron Manela explains that despite Yonkle's boasting, the slides show his persona dissolving from faux-macho Native hunter to fretful tenderfoot.[36] As the song unfolds, Yonkle's hat reverts from a heroic Frederick Remington–like Stetson to a ranger hat to a bowler more typical of Jewish caricatures, accentuating the mismatch of Jewish and cowboy types. In part, such portrayals played on traits and expectations developed in urban centers of Jewish Europe, where verbal skills were valued more than physical prowess or outdoorsmanship.[37]

While the Yonkle caricature used long-standing stereotypes and Jewish self-understandings—which would resurface in Eddie Cantor's *Whoopee!* (United Artists, 1930) and later in Billy Crystal's *City Slickers* (Columbia, 1991)—not everyone was satisfied with the accepted limitations. For example, Sigmund Shlesinger, a Hungarian Jew who arrived in Philadelphia in 1864, fought as a teenage scout against Native Americans at the Battle of Arikaree Fork in Colorado. His superior, General George Forsyth, initially questioned Shlesinger's masculinity, believing that Jewish men were unassimilable to the West as a consequence of their smaller frames and effeminate tendencies—tropes exploited by the diminutive Three Stooges in their

Western shorts. Undeterred, Shlesinger proved his manhood and patriotism through violence against Indigenous people.[38]

Another satirical song, "I'm a Yiddish Cowboy ('Tough Guy Levi')" (1908), has a greenhorn-turned-cowboy protagonist marrying a "blue blood Indian maiden" in a union of immigrant newcomer and original American.[39] "I'm a Yiddish Cowboy" was later featured in the Krazy Kat cartoon short *Rough Dough* (Columbia, 1931), which has Krazy Kat singing the song as a Jewface rodeo clown and which was written, directed, animated, and produced by Jews.[40] In "Big Chief Dynamite" (1909), the titular chief is a Jewish pawnbroker who becomes a Native American revolutionary and sworn enemy of the Yiddish cowboy.[41] The song may have been inspired by pseudohistorical tales of a Jewish Native chief that circulated in Yiddish- and English-language Jewish newspapers at the time. Originally written by J. Fuchs for New York's *American Hebrew* (1909–10), the sketches told of "Nahum Blanberg, Indian Chief," who left Russia, arrived in New York by way of Germany, headed west, became a business success, joined a New Mexico tribe, learned English and the tribal language, paternalistically "civilized" the Natives, and defended them against a U.S. agent and exploitative bosses. In *Members of the Tribe: Native America in the Jewish Imagination*, Rachel Rubinstein describes Blanberg as "a curious amalgam of conquistador, Moses, Horatio Alger hero, and labor union organizer."[42]

Rubinstein posits that Blanberg was based on Solomon Bibo, a Prussian immigrant who established a mercantile business in New Mexico with his brothers, opened a store in the Acoma Pueblo, learned the Acoma language, was elected governor of the pueblo in 1885, instituted "civilizing" policies of assimilation and modernization, and, like Tough Guy Levi, married a Native woman. By the time the Blanberg stories and parody song were written, Bibo and his family had already left the Acoma Pueblo for San Francisco, likely in response to traditionalist tribal factions' opposition to his assimilation policies.[43] But the idea of a Jewish Native chief continued to resonate with immigrants longing for a fast track to becoming fully American, however far-fetched the possibility. Literary critic Leslie A. Fiedler sums up the Native American's immigrant appeal: "Descendants of East European Jews or Dublin Irish, at home and abroad, everyone who thinks of himself as being in some sense an American feels the stirrings in him of a second soul, the soul of the Red Man."[44] In much the same way, Jewish performers wore

“Big Chief Dynamite,” sheet music illustration (Chicago: Piantadosi, 1909).

blackface in part to identify with Blacks, whom they viewed as "true Americans."[45] And although there is a lack of evidence that Jewish immigrants had widespread knowledge of the erroneous idea that Indigenous Americans were descendants of Israel's Lost Tribes (a theory popularized during the seventeenth century that mostly petered out with the passage of the 1830 Indian Removal Act), it may have had a lingering effect.[46]

Another factor motivating Jewish "redface" performers was sympathy for the "vanishing Indian," a concept that resonated among Jewish immigrants struggling to preserve their own customs against racism, assimilation, and modernization, the same forces that erased Indigenous folkways. This sympathetic feeling yielded a Yiddish translation of *The Song of Hiawatha* (1910) and can be heard in Fanny Brice's Yiddish-accented rendition of "I'm an Indian," written by Leo Edwards and Blanche Merrill for the musical *Why Worry?* (1918), as well as Irving Berlin's "I'm an Indian Too," introduced by Ethel Merman in *Annie Get Your Gun* (1946).[47]

An important distinction thus existed between how Jewface entertainers portrayed cowboys and Native Americans. While the clumsy cowboy represented barriers to whiteness, the Native embodied an imagined kinship and promise of Americanness. Whether or not a direct line can be drawn between the Native American's immigrant appeal and the frequency with which Jews would portray Natives onscreen (casting choices mostly based on the actors' ethnic physiognomies), being a "pretend Indian" had ennobling qualities.[48] Again, the creators and consumers of these types were largely unaware of earlier European-born pioneer Jews, primarily from Central Europe, who actually traversed and often succeeded in the Old West. From a New York, Eastern European, greenhorn, and greenhorn-descendent perspective, frontier Jews were an oddity or perhaps an impossibility.

Invisible Jews of Hollywood's West

Like their vaudeville predecessors, Jewish architects of the motion picture industry were largely ignorant or dismissive of real-life Jewish settlers and pioneers. Instead, these filmmakers were drawn to the heroic cowboy, an archetype they saw as a projection of themselves. Carl Laemmle, the Jewish German-born founder of Universal Pictures, was infatuated with cowboy dime novels, identifying with their aspirational, individualistic, rags-to-riches narratives. Westerns comprised nearly a third of his studio's output.[49]

Hollywood's first feature-length film was a Western, *The Squaw Man* (Lasky, 1914). The directorial debut of Cecil B. DeMille, who had some Jewish forebears but was raised Episcopalian, the movie centers on a British officer who takes the blame for his cousin's embezzlement and journeys to the American frontier to start a new life. Coproduced by Jewish San Francisco–born Jesse L. Lasky and his Warsaw-born Jewish brother-in-law, Samuel Goldwyn, for the Lasky Feature Play Company, which later morphed into Paramount Pictures, the movie signaled the rise of Hollywood's film industry and its Jewish moguls. It also set an enduring framework for Western romantic adventures.[50]

Other Jewish executives of Hollywood's golden age—notably Adolph Zuker (Paramount), William Fox (Twentieth Century–Fox), Harry Cohn (Columbia), Louis B. Mayer (MGM), and the Warner Brothers (Harry, Sam, Albert, and Jack)—likewise projected their American dreams onto

Carl Laemmle (suited) at his horse ranch, Universal City, with cowboy star Jack Hoxie and other movie cowboys, ca. 1925 (Western States Jewish History Association).

the screen, seeing the romance and rugged determination of the cowboy hero as an allegory for their scrappy perseverance in a strange new land. They, too, had gone west, escaping miserable conditions in Europe, navigating exclusion from WASP-monopolized fields, fleeing Edison's oppressive movie monopoly, and finding a niche in popular entertainment.[51] Arriving in a still underdeveloped and largely untapped region, they created an industry in their own grandiose image.

The optimistic Americanism embodied in the movie cowboy might explain the existence of a 1940 Yiddish-language Western. It might also explain why Will Rogers, America's "cowboy philosopher," spent six weeks learning Yiddish for a speech honoring fellow vaudevillian turned movie star Eddie Cantor, a feat that not only earned laughs from the predominantly Jewish crowd but also pandered to their affinity for the cowboy.[52] However, the mass-market-driven films and censorial Motion Picture Production Code prohibited overtly Jewish themes and characters in studio films, an invisibility especially pronounced in the "quintessentially white genre" of the Western.[53] Cohn, whose reputation as a self-hating Jew was embellished by accounts of him smoking in synagogue, working on Yom Kippur, and admiring Benito Mussolini, bragged of hiring Jewish actors only to play Native Americans.[54] The Coen Brothers' 1991 film, *Barton Fink* (20th Century Fox), references this incident when Jewish producer Ben Geisler tells Fink, an aspiring left-wing Jewish screenwriter, "Think about it, Fink! Writers come and go; we always need Indians!"

While Cohn's views and antics were extreme, they were also indicative of broader tendencies among Hollywood's Jewish moguls, who started out in retail and fashion, set up nickelodeons in ethnically diverse urban areas, expanded into theaters, and by the 1920s centralized production, distribution, and exhibition as the Big Five (Twentieth Century–Fox, Warner Bros., MGM, Paramount, and RKO) and the Little Three (United Artists, Universal, and Columbia).[55] Lasky hid his Jewishness from his children, hiring a cross-wearing Catholic governess to raise them, and Louis B. Mayer enhanced his all-American, white-passing credentials by claiming that his birthday was the Fourth of July.[56] According to Neal Gabler, author of *An Empire of Their Own: How the Jews Invented Hollywood*, these founders "wanted to be regarded as Americans, not Jews; they wanted to reinvent themselves here as new men."[57]

For some, this attitude suggests that studio heads were Jews in name only—or in some cases, Jews with names changed to mask their lineage. They consciously pushed their Jewishness aside or into their private lives, outwardly identifying with the whitewashed aesthetics presented in their films and particularly in their Westerns. More properly, they were a specific type of American Jew who lacked nostalgia for the Old Country that had rejected them, abandoned their inherited Otherness in favor of a "ruthless assimilation," mostly married non-Jews, and aspired to have more in common with America's moneyed Gentiles than with their own people. These American Jews' self-transformation was directly linked to the industry's formation. In addition to luck and timing, they inherited a cultural dexterity that came from being a stateless people in Europe. They were also urbanites at a time when most immigrants (and most Americans) had rural backgrounds, and they were adept at navigating exclusion from established fields and seizing opportunities on the economic margins. Coming from retail, they knew how to gauge the market and public taste; coming from foreign lands, they knew the hopes and experiences of the immigrants and members of the lower classes who comprised the majority of moviegoers.[58]

When it came to Westerns, Jewish studio heads presumably saw themselves as latter-day exemplars of the self-made man and packaged stories for audiences similarly drawn to adventurous, social-climbing stories. Like the dime novel publishers who had played a major role in shaping the imaginary West from 1860 to 1915, moviemakers sided with capital over labor.[59] Their upward mobility and assimilationist impulses led them to imitate America's aristocracy, aligning with the Republican Party when most Jews were Democrats, living in palatial estates modeled on those of the East Coast Anglo elite, and consciously avoiding overtly Jewish displays in both their lives and their films (where they surrendered to both internal and external pressures). But they also democratized high-quality entertainment, marketing their films to the masses. They sensed that everyone wanted what they had achieved: a share of the American dream, which, according to novelist Jill Schary Robinson, was really the Jewish American dream.[60] Warner Bros. was especially notable in this regard. The studio was not only known for films celebrating "working-class heroes" but was also more courageous than others in taking on the Nazis: *Confessions of a Nazi Spy* (1939) was the first Hollywood film to confront Hitler's Germany.[61]

Even with the studio heads' commercial triumphs and notoriety, age-old anxieties were never far from the surface. Patriotic symbols onscreen were simultaneously expressions of immigrant gratitude and apprehensive overcompensation at a time of heightened nativism and antisemitism. Gary Baum, a senior writer at the *Hollywood Reporter*, describes how Jewish anxieties and Americanization often collided:

> The consistent xenophobic assault on a group anxious about its own precarious position within national life shaped the industry's leadership. A reactionary conservatism prevailed among many of the moguls. They proactively implemented the Motion Picture Production Code, a puritanical set of guidelines that not only put limits on sex, skin and violence but also symbolism or storylines that it deemed anti-patriotic or amoral. Later, they'd release the Waldorf Statement, which blacklisted the so-called Hollywood Ten—producers, directors and screenwriters who refused to answer questions regarding their political affiliations before the House Un-American Activities Committee. A candid assessment of Hollywood's Jewish founders must tangle with this record, along with their more personal failings.[62]

Allying themselves and their product with conventions of patriotism and implicit whiteness, these moguls' films unsurprisingly followed the path of least resistance.[63] Specific to Westerns were three overlapping themes: Theodore Roosevelt's emphasis on racial battles over land, foregrounding Native American wars and white victors; John Fiske's view of manifest destiny, justifying white imperialism in the Americas; and Frederick Jackson Turner's frontier thesis, arguing that egalitarianism and democracy were fostered in the "free land" of America's frontier. These late-nineteenth-century notions were mainstays of both film and popular history well into the 1960s. Despite challenges from revisionist Westerns and new historicism—some of which came from Jewish authors and filmmakers—they remain fixtures of America's hard-to-shake Old West mythology.

A major theme in Roosevelt's four-volume *The Winning of the West* (1889–96) is the "eternal border warfare" between white expansionists and Natives on the American frontier. According to Roosevelt, "war with savages" was the "most ultimately righteous of all wars": "I don't go so far as to think that the only good Indians are the dead Indians, but I believe that nine out of ten are, and I shouldn't inquire too closely into the case of the tenth."[64] For Roosevelt, the acquisition of territory and spread of (white) democracy were inevitable outcomes of a "favored race" exerting its rightful dominance over lowly savages.[65] This ideology was prevalent in A Westerns from the 1930s, such as Raoul Walsh's *The Big Trail* (Fox, 1930), featuring John Wayne in his first starring role, and *Stagecoach* (United Artists, 1939), John Ford's first sound Western and first collaboration with Wayne. Scott Simmon characterizes Native Americans in these films as "an unindividualized horde, war-whooping, seldom speaking, swooping en masse from ominous hilltops, and then gunned down with godlike accuracy from long distance in uncountable numbers."[66] A biting retort to the presumed bravery of sharpshooting white men comes from the revisionist *Little Big Man* (National General, 1970), directed by Arthur Penn, the son of Russian Jewish immigrants. Protagonist-narrator Jack Crabb (Dustin Hoffman), who was rescued by members of the Cheyenne Nation as a boy, recalls a one-sided battle between cavalry guns and Native arrows: "I never could understand how the white world could be so proud of winning with them kind of odds."

In an 1885 book, *American Political Ideas Viewed from the Standpoint of Universal History*, philosopher-historian Fiske added God to this deterministic image, championing the belief that European advances across the continent were divinely ordained.[67] Like Roosevelt, Fiske had a conception of manifest destiny influenced by Herbert Spencer's social Darwinism, wherein purportedly natural laws favored the survival of the fittest racial group. Onscreen, this idea not only fed into depictions of heroic white settlers and cavalrymen taming the vast and wild landscape (where Native Americans were functionally wild animals) but also served as "conscience-cleaning cinema," ameliorating or suppressing viewers' guilt over the nation's dark history of Indigenous removal and extermination.[68] This "colonizer mentality" began as a conscious cinematic choice more than a collective myth but became a shared narrative through filmic reiterations.[69] The plight of Native Americans in this divine plan was sometimes shown sympathetically, as in the 1925 silent film *The Vanishing American* (Paramount).[70] But more often than not, cinematic depictions of manifest destiny meant rationalizing and celebrating the stealing, clearing, and development of "empty" land. The preposterousness of sanctioned brutality as altruistic violence is lampooned in Mel Brooks's *Blazing Saddles* (Warner Bros., 1974), when Taggart (Slim Pickens) learns that the town of Rock Ridge has a Black sheriff: "Now if that don't beat all. Here we take the good time and trouble to slaughter every last Indian in the West, and for what? So we can appoint a sheriff that's blacker than any Indian. I am depressed."

Whereas Roosevelt and Fiske are rightly criticized for dehumanizing Indigenous Americans, Turner is faulted for ignoring them. His frontier thesis, presented in 1893 at the World's Columbian Exposition in Chicago, claimed that the American frontier was more than just a physical space: it was the sociopolitical location where individualism, democracy, and free enterprise blossomed irrespective of one's national origins (at least as long as one's skin was a European shade).[71] For Turner, the dispossession of Native Americans was a necessary prelude to this grand experiment on "free lands," where people prospered or failed on the basis of their wits, work ethic, and ingenuity; where prior status or pretentions meant little; and where ethnic differences were nonissues.[72] Twentieth-century historians of Jews in the West freely adopted the frontier thesis. Ray Allen Billington, Turner's devoted student, wrote in his foreword to Rabbi I. Harold Sharfman's *Jews on the Frontier* (1977), "This is a book that Frederick Jackson Turner, pioneer historian of the American frontier, would have loved."[73] Yet Jewish novelist Edna Ferber was among the first to poke holes in Turner's thesis with her 1930 novel *Cimarron*. Adapted to film the following year, *Cimarron* tells a decades-spanning story of the settlement and development of Oklahoma. The film opens with a triumphalist text reminiscent of Roosevelt—"A nation rising to greatness through the work of men and women . . . new country opening . . . raw land blossoming . . . crude towns growing into cities . . . territories becoming rich states"—but the unfolding story challenges this declaration by critiquing unrestricted capitalism, exposing disharmony in multiethnic settlements, and portraying the female lead as a bigot, upending the cliché of the wholesome settler woman.[74]

The driving themes of border warfare, manifest destiny, and the frontier thesis make even subtle glimpses of Jewishness in the Western genre difficult to detect. Instead, as religion scholar M. Gail Hamner notes, the critical consensus is that Westerns, at least in their classic stage (before the 1960s), "are prototypically racist and are built on a Protestant redemption narrative and the logics and aesthetics of white male supremacy."[75] Andrew

Patrick Nelson observes that "the Western's ideological baggage includes racism and imperialism."[76] And Leah Williams writes in the *Atlantic* that the Western "draws from a well of cultural symbols meant to capture the essence of America, including the freedom and open frontier and the righteous self-determination of man. Standing tall inside this cinematic shorthand is the cowboy himself, a figure commonly understood to be an excellent shot who rides horses and who, above all, is white."[77] If anything, these observations attest to the Jewish movie moguls' success in projecting whiteness onscreen.

The Non-Jewish Cowboy Jew

Gilbert M. Anderson affirmed both the skepticism of Jewish vaudeville and the evasion of Jewish Hollywood. Born Max Aronson in Little Rock, Arkansas, in 1880, Anderson was the son of a traveling salesman of German Jewish descent and a woman from a Russian Jewish family. He was on the ground floor of the nascent Western genre, landing several roles in *The Great Train Robbery* (Edison, 1903), whose unprecedented popularity spurred the nickelodeon craze, turning movies from penny arcade novelties and vaudeville filler to a thriving stand-alone business. Aronson rode this crest over the next five years, transforming into Broncho Billy, the first cowboy star. Yet to become a cowboy, Aronson, an Arkansas-born Jew, hid behind the white mask of Anderson. Far from the impossible and over-the-top Jewface cowboy, Anderson gave no hint of his Jewish identity. He was in a sense the ultimate fulfillment of the Hollywood moguls' dream: the non-Jewish Jew.

In 1894, a year after Turner coined his theory, Westerns were introduced with a series of single-reel silents produced by the Edison Company. Drawing from stage melodramas and dime novels, these early efforts featured scenes that became staples of the maturing genre, such as gambling, drinking, and pistols. Within a decade, *The Great Train Robbery* constituted the first fully formed narrative Western. Directed by Edwin S. Porter for Edison, the twelve-minute silent follows a gang of outlaws who rob a steam locomotive, flee across a mountainous terrain, and are done in by a local posse. The film was inspired by an 1896 stage play by the same name written by Scott Marble for New York's Bowery Theatre as well as by the popularity of trains, Western landscapes, and accounts of real-life train robberies. Filmed in New York and New Jersey, *The Great Train Robbery* was an eastern Western, predating the genre's growth in the diverse terrains of Southern California. The geographical shift was gradual, with some Western productions beginning in California in 1908. By 1910, 213 of the 1,001 American-made movies were Westerns. According to David Lusted most of these films and many subsequent ones built on aspects of *The Great Train Robbery*: "Despite its lack of individual characterization and character development, its narrative structure is classical—crime, chase, retribution. Within that simple structure, there are familiar situations; effectively two hold-ups, two gunfights, a fist-fight, and a dance that includes a ritual humiliation of an Easterner by a Westerner. . . . Western types are also familiar, including criminal gunmen, lawmen, railroad workers, train passengers and townspeople. Perhaps most importantly, the gun and its uses (to threaten and harm) are central to the film's drama."[78]

Anderson's roles in *The Great Train Robbery* included playing a bandit, a passenger who gets shot, and a tenderfoot dancer. In 1907, he partnered with theatrical booking agent George K. Spoor in Chicago to form Essanay Studios, which took its name from *S* (Spoor) and *A* (Anderson). The following year, Anderson made a two-reel outdoor Western, *The Bandit Makes Good* (Essanay, 1908). Based on Peter Kyne's short story "Broncho Billy and the Baby," the film follows a bank robber who loses the stolen money to gamblers, retrieves it, returns it to the sheriff, and earns a pardon. Unable to find another actor for the lead, Anderson took the role, subsequently assuming the name Broncho Billy Anderson and becoming the first cowboy movie star—and the first actor whose career was attached to a single genre. From 1908 to 1915, Anderson produced, directed, and starred in more than 375 one- and two-reel Westerns and possibly as many as 500.[79]

The Broncho Billy series created a mold for others that followed. While Billy was always the main character, his personas varied from film to film. He might be a law-abiding cowboy in one, a ruthless villain in the next, die in a film's climax, and return again. Strung together, these ten- to twenty-minute shorts created complicated plots centered on action and melodrama. Anderson's onscreen presence also foreshadowed Wayne's: bulky, noble, rugged, independent, and courageous, with "paw-like hands and raw-hewn face."[80]

Anderson's popularity declined by 1915, owing to the rise of feature-length Westerns and his increasingly outdated, gesture-heavy acting style.

Gilbert M. "Broncho Billy" Anderson, publicity photo, 1914.

Anderson made only a handful of other films prior to his final starring role in *The Son-of-a-Gun* (William L. Sherry Service, 1919). The cowboy spotlight was taken over by William S. Hart, an actor, writer, director, and producer who embraced the newfangled feature-length format.[81] Anderson received an honorary Oscar in 1957 for his contributions to cinema and a star on the Hollywood Walk of Fame three years later. He made his final appearance in *The Bounty Killer* (Embassy, 1965) and was posthumously honored with a U.S. postage stamp (1998) and induction into the Western Performers Hall of Fame at the National Cowboy and Western Heritage Museum in Oklahoma City (2002).

Distancing from Jewishness was a prerequisite for Anderson's accomplishments as a cowboy actor. He was so successful at passing for white that critics have identified his films as "Christian," a quality sociologist Frederick Elkin cited as the genre's primary appeal: "The moral values are those of our Christian society. In the conflict of Good and Evil, the Good is invariably held up as right. On the side of Good are honesty, loyalty, sympathy for the oppressed, respect for the law, and, if it is occasional in the story, love of children and respect for religion."[82] For example, in *Broncho Billy's Christmas Spirit* (Essanay, 1914), a poor prospector has no money to buy Christmas presents for his two small children. In desperation, he steals Anderson's horse, sells it, and spends the money on toys. Anderson arrives at the prospector's home with a hanging posse, but when Anderson sees how the funds had been spent, he instructs the members of the posse to contribute money to the family.

In a biographical essay on Broncho Billy Anderson, Lane Roth and Tom W. Hoffer suggest that his "saintly virtues, bravery, celibacy, renunciation and sacrifice conform to the Christian ideals of the hero" and demonstrate "the tension inherent in the duality of the Christian cosmos, the vision of the material world as a battlefield for the forces of good versus evil in continual combat for the possession of man's soul."[83] These authors seem unaware that Anderson was born Jewish, further highlighting the achievement of his white American persona. Even sources that acknowledge his Jewish parentage, such as *The Encyclopedia of Jewish American Popular Culture*, add nothing beyond that fact; the same holds true for a historical marker in Little Rock that is dedicated to "Max Henry Aronson—The First Cowboy-Western Movie Star" and that was erected by the First United Methodist Church, the Niles Essanay Silent Film Museum, and the Jewish American Society for Historic Preservation.[84]

Scoring the West

A chameleon quality is likewise present in Jewish contributions to the Western cinematic soundscape. An entire volume could (and should) be devoted to exploring Jewish composers' imprint on the Western. Just as Jewish actors and filmmakers were instrumental in shaping the genre, Jewish composers were largely responsible for its musical architecture.

The "Hollywood sound," like Hollywood movies, can be called a Jewish invention. Since the earliest original scores, Jewish composers have dominated the industry. The career of Max Steiner, a Vienna-born composer whose filmography began in 1929, took off in 1933 with *King Kong* (RKO), the first sound film accompanied by an original, nondiegetic score that supported and enhanced the action onscreen.[85] Steiner introduced principles and techniques that continue to govern film scores, among them the employment of leitmotifs to represent characters, settings, emotions, and themes and click tracks to enable precise synchronization of music to film.

The development of sound in Hollywood film coincided with Hitler's rise to power in Germany, sending many European Jewish émigré musicians to Southern California in what musicologist Dorothy Lamb Crawford calls the German chancellor's "(unintentional) gift to American music."[86] These émigrés included golden age film composers Hanns Eisler, Erich Wolfgang Korngold, Ernst Toch, Franz Waxman, and Eric Zeisl. Whether from religiously observant or avowedly secular families (Steiner, for example, did not consider himself Jewish at all), these composers inherited a cultural affinity for integrating music and ceremony, a diaspora-informed and necessitated musical eclecticism, and an innate appreciation for music as a vital accompaniment to nonmusical objectives and events.[87] Of course, Jews were not the only ones with these musical-cultural tendencies, but being at the right place at the right time—and with the right connections—enabled Jewish composers to develop and define Hollywood music, including for Westerns.

Basic musical conventions for cowboy heroes, horses, and Native Americans had already been established in silent film cue sheets and musical encyclopedias in the 1910s. Ernö Rapée's *Motion Picture Moods for Pianists and Organists* from 1924 has a "Western Allegro," "Western Scene," "Indian Agitato," "Indian War-Dance," and "Sun Dance," and many of these themes spilled into early sound Westerns.[88] However, Steiner, the earliest "wall-to-wall" film composer, laid the motivic foundations for Westerns of the sound era, scoring thirty Westerns during his prolific thirty-five-year career.[89] With his score for *Dodge City* (Warner Bros., 1939), Steiner created a template for the archetypal "cattle theme" and "Indian theme."[90] A number of influential scores followed, beginning with *Santa Fe Trail* (Warner Bros., 1940), *Virginia City* (Warner Bros., 1940), and *They Died with Their Boots On* (Warner Bros., 1941). Steiner initially did not use folk sources in his Westerns, writing in 1937 that "familiar music, however popular, does not aid the underlying score of a dramatic picture" and that such themes "might cause an audience to wonder and whisper and try to recall the title of a popular composition, thereby missing the gist and significance of a whole scene which might be the key to the entire story."[91] However, he soon changed his tune, developing what became a Western convention of grounding the drama in well-known period music. Throughout *Virginia City*, for example, Steiner reworked the Confederate tunes "Dixie" and "Rally 'Round the Flag," and in *Santa Fe Trail* he prominently used "John Brown's Body." These extended quotations helped situate Steiner's march-heavy, tightly orchestrated sound and "classically formal structure of order, disorder, and eventual restoration of order" in the American West.[92]

Some observers found Steiner's compositional style too European. When Steiner complained that director John Ford had cut down his score for *The Searchers* (Warner Bros., 1956), producer C. V. Whitney responded that by doing so, Ford had created a "typically American" score.[93] Elmer Bernstein, the son of European immigrants, was part of a second wave of Jewish film composers whose Western scores were, in his words, "tinged with that Americana . . . to be differentiated from the sort of middle-European music that Max Steiner or Victor Young used in American western films. I'm talking about authentic Americana music."[94]

Bernstein, like other mid-twentieth-century Western composers, took his Americana cues from Aaron Copland, a fellow New York progressive born to Jewish immigrant parents. Bernstein did not study with Copland but nevertheless viewed him as a mentor and "biggest single musical influence," singling out *Appalachian Spring* (1944) as particularly important.[95] Copland's immediately identifiable rhythms, harmonies, and orchestration and impressionistic use of American folk tunes are clearly heard in Bernstein's iconic score for *The Magnificent Seven* (United Artists, 1960) and more than twenty other Westerns, including *The Tin Star* (Paramount, 1957), directed by Anthony Mann, and *The Scalphunters* (United Artists, 1968), directed by Sydney Pollack. Alfred Newman, who was the eldest of ten children of Russian Jewish immigrants and who was instrumental in crafting the Hollywood sound in the 1930s, drew inspiration from both Bernstein and Copland in creating the landmark score for *How the West Was Won* (MGM, 1962).

Jerome Moross, another Jewish New Yorker, claimed to have invented the modern Western score with *The Big Country* (United Artists, 1958). "This is the way to do a western now," he later recounted, "the way I did it in *Big Country* . . . a western with American rhythms, American tunes and a boldness and brashness to it."[96] Moross's score, while groundbreaking, is also highly reminiscent of Copland. Copland was, in fact, the first choice to score the film, and Bernstein had also requested the opportunity to score it.[97] Moross's relationship with Copland began when the eighteen-year-old Morros was included in Copland's Young Composers Group. In 1940, Morros helped orchestrate Copland's music for *Our Town* (United Artists). According to musicologist Mariana Whitmer, *The Big Country* was Moross's take on the trend of infusing Americanism into modern music as well as the Young Composers Group's cooperative interest in creating an American sound.[98]

Because of his direct and indirect impact on the genre, Copland, more than any other composer, was key to shaping the Hollywood Western sound. According to music critic Paul Griffiths, Copland's ballets *Billy the Kid* (1938), *Rodeo* (1942), and *Appalachian Spring* provided "a language for cowboy film scores, using traditional songs in a manner to suggest the open spaces of the American west and the excitement of pioneer life," notably through wide interval leaps, a melody carried by the upper strings, and a rhythmic ostinato underneath.[99]

The Brooklyn-born son of Russian Jewish immigrants, Copland devised his Americana sound while studying at the American Conservatory in Fontainebleau, near Paris. With the encouragement of his instructor, Nadia Boulanger, Copland constructed an American style based on the urban, jazzy, ethnic music of his native surroundings. At first, this resulted in avant-garde "city sounds," but as the Great Depression dragged on, Copland became convinced of the artist's responsibility to ennoble the populace and elevate the "common man."[100] He began incorporating folk songs into his orchestral works, first using Mexican sources in *El Salon México* (1936) and then writing a series of populist works rooted in American frontier folk songs, including ballets and *Fanfare for the Common Man* (1942). Copland also used his signature Americana idioms when scoring two John Steinbeck film adaptations, *Of Mice and Men* (United Artists, 1939) and *The Red Pony* (Republic, 1949).

Copland's lasting influence on the Western is especially remarkable considering that he lived almost his entire life in big cities. When he ventured west, his initial impression of the actual landscape, especially the deserts, contrasted negatively with images he saw in cowboy films and the European vistas he adored. However, he eventually came to appreciate the expansive spaces and diverse inhabitants.[101] "I suppose in one sense it's the feat of the imagination," Copland said. "But after all, a kid in Brooklyn would've seen movies with cowboys in them. As a matter of fact, I did go out to the southwest fairly early in my career. And, I don't know, every American kid grows up with a sense of cowboys and what the west must have been like."[102] Bernstein similarly remarked, "I was a boy brought [up] on the streets of lower middle class New York, and the West was always a great romantic place with big scenery. I never forget the time I drove across the country to California. I was thrilled by the sense of space."[103] More significantly, Copland's political and musical identification with the everyman and working-class hero attracted him to the romance of the Westerns and drew the Western romance out of him.

At the same time, Copland's leftist ideological positions, especially during World War II, connected him to his Eastern European Jewish roots. His knack for quoting and arranging folk music had begun in his youth, when he experimented with Jewish liturgical chants.[104] This proclivity stayed with him, even as the folk shifted from urban Jews to frontierspeople. Although Copland rarely discussed his Jewish identity or dealt with it in his work (outside of *Vitebsk: A Study on a Jewish Theme* [1929] and a short arrangement for a Jewish National Fund postcard initiative in the late 1930s), he made an interesting comment connecting his views on Jewish, jazz, and cowboy music: "It seems to me that my use of Jewish themes was similar to my use of jazz—Jewish influences were present in my music, even when I did not refer to them overtly. I have often been asked why I wrote 'cowboy' music rather than 'Jewish' music. I never thought about these things at the time, but it must have been partly because I grew up in the Eastern European tradition and there was no novelty to it."[105]

Arguably, there was something Jewish about the way Copland quoted melodies in his Western-themed ballets. In *Billy the Kid*, for example, source materials are so obscured, altered, fleetingly presented, and rapidly juxtaposed that many reviewers did not notice them at all. This style-defining approach might reflect Copland's unease with long-standing claims, anchored in Wagnerian diatribes, that Jewish composers were uncreative "rootless cosmopolitans" who mimicked and corrupted music of the host culture.[106] Sidestepping this antisemitic canard, Copland balanced his conviction that folk song was the true music of the people with an idiosyncratic use of that music, thereby creating a sonic template that was both utterly original and quintessentially American.

Russian-born Dimitri Tiomkin brought identifiably Russian flavors to his trendsetting score for *High Noon* (United Artists, 1952), whose Oscar-winning ballad, "Do Not Forsake Me, Oh My Darling" bears a strong resemblance to a Yiddish folk song, "Dem Milners Trern" (The Miller's Tears).[107] The song's popularity spurred the use of title songs in a range of A and B Westerns as well as numerous television series. (Tiomkin cowrote the theme to *Rawhide* with Ned Washington.) When discussing the Civil War drama *Friendly Persuasion* (Allied Artists/MGM, 1956) and its theme song, "Thee I Love," radio host Arthur Godfrey asked the composer, "Marvelous melodies you have in your mind, Mr. Tiomkin—old Russian melodies maybe?" Tiomkin replied in what his friends called "Tiomkinese": "I don't know—I don't think that, so much, stranger to say. Naturally, like Irish fella, he has some connection with Irish soil even when he living in America, do same thing, naturally, I, who was living all country, so of all country speaking—nothing to be shame about that."[108] A fuller appraisal of Tiomkin's Western innovations comes from Phillip Drummond's book on *High Noon*: Tiomkin's music has a pared-down sound with minimal orchestration, replaces the full-orchestra fortissimo with understated pianissimo, uses the ballad as an almost monothematic anchor for the entire film, and eliminates violins in favor of "darker, starker, de-glamourized" sonorities of lower strings, brass, wind, and piano.[109]

Jerry Goldsmith, a California-born composer of Romanian Jewish descent, helped define Hollywood's silver age (the late 1950s to the 1990s). Goldsmith's impressive output—spanning more than two hundred film credits, numerous television scores, and extracinematic works—began in

1957 with a mostly forgotten Western, *Black Patch* (Warner Bros.). Goldsmith introduced his trademark galloping rhythms and irregular themes to Westerns, a genre he considered a step down artistically but a necessary step up in his Hollywood career. Among his better-known Western scores are *Rio Conchos* (Twentieth Century–Fox, 1964), *Hour of the Gun* (United Artists, 1967), *100 Rifles* (Twentieth Century–Fox, 1969), and the genre comeback *Bad Girls* (20th Century Fox, 1994). Goldsmith won an Emmy for *The Red Pony* (NBC, 1973), a made-for-television remake of the 1949 film scored by Copland. The score seamlessly fuses Coplandesque flourishes with Goldsmith's techniques.

Goldsmith was also a musical architect of the space Western, reapplying the Old West soundscape to the final frontier of space cowboys, indigenous extraterrestrials, and cosmic manifest destiny. He sensed this genre legacy. Commenting on his score for *Star Trek: The Motion Picture* (Paramount, 1979), Goldsmith said, "When you think about it, space is very romantic. To me, it's like the old west. We're up in the endless universe. It's about discovery, new life. . . . I've treated all the *Star Trek* movies that I've done in this more musically romantic way, rather than getting very avant-garde and making strange noises."[110] This pioneer spirit, reminiscent of Copland's fanfares, is also heard in scores by Jewish *Trek* composers James Horner (*Star Trek II: The Wrath of Khan* [Paramount, 1982] and *Star Trek III: The Search for Spock* [Paramount, 1984]) and Leonard Roseman (*Star Trek IV: The Voyage Home* [Paramount, 1986]).

CHAPTER 2

Pre-Code Westerns

Before the 1934 Motion Picture Production Code put a lid on the industry's boundary-pushing elements, audiences saw "strong violence and stronger sexual content, candor about drug use and homosexuality, even nudity" onscreen as well as overt and unapologetic portrayals of ethnic groups.[1] Movie critic Kenneth Turan highlights examples of casual and over-the-top Jewishness in pre-Code films, as when Al Jolson's character in *Wonder Bar* (Warner Bros., 1934), released just before the Code went into effect, reads a Yiddish newspaper in blackface or when Jewish caricature comedian Max Davidson starred in the silent short *Jewish Prudence* (Pathé, 1927), a pun on *jurisprudence*.[2] Turan speculates that the disappearance of Jewish ethnicity and especially the Yiddish language—which even Irish American actor James Cagney used from time to time—might not have happened had the movie industry "stayed true to the New York and New Jersey roots of its earlier days." The East Coast was "the old country for Jews who moved to Los Angeles, the place where parents and possibly grandparents lived, and where leaving ethnicity behind could not even be imagined."[3] But California's sunshine bleached Jewishness from films and filmmakers alike. As historian Felicia Herman points out, the new locale made it possible for the Jewish men who built the film industry to minimize their backgrounds as "almost incidental to their lives and to their work."[4]

Still, the virtual erasure of Jewish themes and signifiers was not simply a willful escape from ethnicity. For decades, the Anti-Defamation League, the Reform movement's Central Conference of American Rabbis, and other national and local Jewish organizations had been working to eliminate negative Jewish images—both the Jew as Christ killer and self-mocking Jewface—

from stage and screen. Motion picture censorship in the United States began in Chicago in 1907, nearly thirty years before the Hollywood Code. Jewish lawyer and civic leader Adolf Kraus authored a law giving Chicago police the authority to ban any film that "portrays depravity, criminality or lack of virtue of a class of citizens of any race, color, creed or religion and exposes them to contempt."[5] In an effort to prevent onscreen caricatures, the Anti-Defamation League attempted to distinguish Jews from racial categories, defining Jews instead as a religious group with "no reasonable basis for comparison [with] the negro, the Chinaman, the Irishman or the Italian."[6]

Such efforts escalated as rising foreign and domestic antisemitism made even innocuous depictions of Jews or Jewish themes potential fodder for alarmist xenophobes who believed that "the Jews" controlled Hollywood and used movies to manipulate the American public.[7] Fueled by anti-immigrant sentiment, already pervasive since the immigrant influx that occurred between the 1880s and early 1900s, antisemitism took aim at movies with the rise of Jewish moguls in the 1920s. Jew hatred was a major factor when Protestant deacon Will H. Hays was hired to lead the newly formed Motion Picture Producers and Distributors of America in 1922, an organization that had a morals clause and was a precursor to the development of the Catholic-written and -enforced Code.

Publisher Martin Quigley and Jesuit priest Daniel Lord first proposed a code governing motion pictures and promoting "Roman Catholic values" in 1930.[8] Two years later, Joseph I. Breen, a devout Catholic who later became director of the Production Code Administration, told a colleague that Hollywood's Jews were "simply a rotten bunch of people with no respect for anything." These comments echoed Los Angeles Catholic bishop John J. Cantwell's call for Jewish executives to rid movies of offensiveness and an article in the *Churchman*, a Methodist paper, attacking "shrewd Hebrews" for "selling crime and shame" onscreen.[9] In 1934, the newly formed Catholic Legion of Decency collected ten million signatures from Catholics pledging "to refrain from viewing all objectionable movies or attending any theater that showed such films."[10] Responding to the hysteria, the Anti-Defamation League implored studios not to produce films that could be deemed immoral and thus avoid further inflaming antisemitism.[11] In this heated atmosphere, it made sense that studios would not only voluntarily adopt the Code but also actively avoid Jewish subjects—especially as movies had no First Amendment rights and any municipal, state, or federal authority could censor them.

While Code-enforced Jewish invisibility in New York street scenes was conspicuous, the Jews' disappearance from the Wild West was hardly noticed. As comedian Lenny Bruce later explained, "To me, if you live in New York or any other big city, you are Jewish. . . . If you live in Butte, Montana, you're going to be goyish even if you're Jewish."[12] Hence, the handful of identifiably Jewish characters in pre-Code Westerns faded without fanfare.

The soon-forgotten Jewish Western type began as a carryover from the vaudeville stage. As in the era's urban Jewish comedy shorts, most of the characters were male—complete with black coats, straggly beards, and exaggerated noses—and the plots concerned common immigrant themes of family struggle, earning a living, and interacting with whites and other ethnic types. Running from under a minute to just over ten minutes, the films mainly centered on the bumbling schlemiel (bungler, dolt) or, in more negative portrayals, the scheming merchant. The Jewish cowboy subgenre played up the incongruity of Eastern European Jews in the Wild West, exaggerating the juxtaposition by making the Jew an out-of-place loner.[13] This practice set a template for pre-Code feature films, both comedic and dramatic, where the Jewish peddler ventures West alone, is identifiably an outsider, struggles to acclimate, and faces intense local prejudices.

These elements departed from the prevailing narrative of real-life frontier Jewish peddlers. During the early phase of the pioneer-settler period, most of them had Central European origins, relaxed their ethnoreligious folkways, benefited from physical and social mobility, were often among the founders of towns and local institutions, and, despite some lonely, grueling, and emotionally taxing days, were connected to extended Jewish family and business networks. Jewish peddlers typically divided the countryside among themselves, avoiding direct competition, and had little daily contact with other Jews. But they were not the solo "wandering Jew" of medieval lore. As historian Hasia Diner explains in her book, *Roads Taken: The Great Jewish Migrations to the New World and the Peddlers Who Forged the Way*, "The entire new-world peddling experience depended upon the existence of webs of relationships that reflected the Jews' age-old connection to trade. Young Jews showing up in one place or another, no matter the country or continent, sought out other Jews, often, though not always, individuals with whom they shared ties back home. Those Jews already present in a place had likely spent time themselves on the road as peddlers and provided the newest arrival, the would-be peddler, with some basic place to stay, food, and, most crucially for the peddling experience, contracts to wholesalers, who then offered the goods to be sold."[14] But these realities rarely reached the cinematic Western Jew, who, much like the movie Native American, fit squarely in the "imaginary West."[15]

Silent Westerns (1909–1928)

In her study of Jewish films of the "primitive years," film scholar Patricia Erens suggests that comedies produced by Jewish-owned or -founded companies—such as Lubin (Siegmund "Pop" Lubin), Keystone (Charles O. Bauman and Adam Kessel Jr.), Essanay (Gilbert Anderson), Joker (Carl Laemmle), and Crystal (released through Laemmle's Universal Pictures)—avoided subjecting Jews to excessive ridicule and punishment. This was not the case for Gentile-produced films such as *Levi, the Cop* (Atlas, 1910), *Such a Business* (Royal, 1914), and *A Bad Day for Levinsky* (Precision, 1909), where Jews are disciplined for their cleverness. A review of *A Bad Day for Levinsky* complained, "There is too much malicious feeling expressed in the fun and one cannot but believe that this apparently holding up a certain people to scorn and making them the basis of certain species of fun—which is anything but funny." By contrast, Jewish-made comedies typically replaced comeuppance with fantasy: "In stories told by Jewish humorists, the Jew begins as a victim and through mental dexterity extricates himself from his predicament, like Izzy in *Foxy Izzy* [Lubin, 1911]." According to Erens, "No doubt such stories were also based upon a great deal of wish-fulfillment and served to ease the pain that resulted from the numerous real-life experiences in which no amount of cleverness could change the fact of their oppression. In stories told by Gentiles about Jews, the protagonist is depicted riding high on his ill-gained profits. The humor revolves around seeing him outsmart himself. The tale ends when the tables are turned and the Jew gets his 'just desserts.' In either case the Jew is depicted as intelligent, clever, and scheming."[16]

Jewish Old West comedies add a fish-out-of-water element. The image of a frontier Jew was hilarious to Eastern European immigrant audiences, who saw the West as a hopelessly foreign landscape. While the scheming merchant trope is still present, in most cases the Jewish cowboy prevails. He fumbles physically but perseveres mentally, simultaneously reinforcing perceptions of both unruggedness and cleverness and drawing laughs from the apparent absurdity of a peddler turned cowboy.

Yiddisher Cowboy (Bison, 1909) follows Levi, a peddler who falls asleep under a cowboy poster and dreams of performing daring feats. The film is lost, but according to one reviewer, it had some of "the funniest incidents ever chronicled in motion pictures"—no doubt referring to the inability of the stereotypically unphysical, self-conscious Jew to pull off the cowboy persona. Another film also called *Yiddisher Cowboy* (American Bank Flor, 1911) centers on Ikey Rosenthal, a peddler who moves to a Wyoming ranch and is harassed by the ranch hands and made to perform a "Yiddisher dance" at gunpoint. Rosenthal gets revenge when his tormenters ride off to town and he decides to start a pawnshop. The men return broke and are forced to sell Ikey their weapons, making him the gun-toting "monarch of all he surveys."[17]

In *Cohen and Murphy* (Powers, 1910), Jake Cohen and John Murphy are the comic Jewish and Irish proprietors of a hotel in Mudtown, Arizona, where a drunken man fires his gun erratically, killing Murphy. Cohen offers a large reward for the outlaw's capture. When no one takes up the offer, Cohen hides under the villain's bed, waits for him to pass out drunk, ties him up, and brings him back to town.

In *Tough Guy Levi* (Lubin, 1912), the title character, a Jewish peddler, is robbed and later steals back his money plus profits. In *Business and Love* (Lubin, 1914), Izzy Leopold accidentally shoots himself in the foot, thus winning the affection of the female lead, much to the chagrin of the Gentile cowhands. *The Old Cobbler* (Bison, 1914) tells of a shoemaker who goes West, befriends Wild Bill, and is reunited with his outlaw son. *Business is Business* (United Film Service, 1915) has Isadore Rosinsky capturing a bandit singlehandedly and receiving a $1,000 reward, with which he takes the cowboys out for drinks. They all get drunk and Rosinsky is forced to dance a "Yiddisher Kasatsky." As in *The Yiddisher Cowboy* (1911), Rosinsky turns the tables when the men run out of money and sell him their guns.[18]

Two silent feature melodramas from 1928 include cowboy heroes coming to the aid of Jewish merchants. In *The Rawhide Kid* (Universal), a lost ethnic Western directed by Del Andrews and written by Arthur Slatter, Irish American cowhand Dennis O'Hara (Hoot Gibson) defends a European-born Jewish peddler turned successful merchant played by William H. Strauss against a bigoted competitor. The two men place bets on a horse race, with O'Hara riding for the Jewish protagonist. He wins the race and the heart of the Jew's daughter. *Put 'Em Up* (Universal), directed by Edgar Lewis and written by William Lester, includes a thieving gang that intimidates a Jewish merchant who had earlier saved the hero's life. These minor films stand out among action-oriented silent Western dramas, where contemporary social issues, like bigotry and antisemitism, were almost never explored.[19]

The Light of Western Stars (1930)

Jewish ethnic comedy returned in *The Light of Western Stars* (Paramount, 1930). The third of four adaptations of Zane Grey's novel, the film features Harry Green (born Henry Blitzer), a lawyer who became a vaudeville comedian.[20] Green appeared regularly in Jewish roles, including two others from 1930: a cigar store owner in *The Kibitzer* (Paramount), based on a play co-written by Jewish Romanian-born actor Edward G. Robinson, and a boxing manager in *Be Yourself!* (United Artists), starring alongside Jewish dialect comedian Fanny Brice.

In *The Light of Western Stars,* Green plays the supporting role of Plotz the peddler (aka Pie-Pan), a character absent from the novel and the other film adaptations (1918, 1925, 1940). He is the affable, grin-and-bear-it butt of many jokes. His loquacious, heavily accented, eccentrically ethnic portrayal appealed to audiences at the time but soon disappeared with the Production Code. The August 1930 issue of *Screenland* declared, "Harry Green almost runs away with the film. What Harry's doing out on the western Plains is a mystery; but here he is, and very funny, too. You'll have a laugh."[21] Modern viewers are more likely to agree with a review at Pre-Code.com: "Harry Green's Jewish cowboy schtick, which often results in long-winded comedic yarns with a heavily Yiddish accent, [is] especially irksome and dated."[22]

The movie, codirected by Otto Brower and Jewish screenwriter, producer, and director Edwin H. Knopf (with additional uncredited scripting by up-and-comer Joseph L. Mankiewicz) follows a fairly standard ranch plot. A friend of the handsome lead, Dick Bailey (Richard Arlen) is killed by a mysterious assailant, whom Bailey suspects is wealthy landowner H. W. Stack (Fred Kohler), a crony of the town's crooked sheriff (Guy Oliver). Bailey goes on a drunken spree and swears, "I'm going to marry the first white woman I meet!" The comment deliberately forecloses the possibility of miscegenation, one of the main targets of the era's growing censorship movement.[23] The woman is Ruth Hammond (Mary Brian), the sister of Bailey's dead friend, who has arrived in town to take charge of the Hammond ranch. Offended by his rough proposal, she fires Bailey as the ranch foreman. But when Stack tells her he has taken the ranch as payment of back taxes, she rehires Bailey and his friends to fight back.

The film opens on a winter scene. Plotz is driving a covered wagon painted with the words:

> The Pie-Pan Peddler of Hayden
> Pots, Pans, Washtubs, Suits, Socks,
> Sewing Machines, Quinine, Shoes, Shirts,
> Darning Needles, Soap, Hats and Buttons
> And if it's not on here I've still got it

He enters a saloon expecting to make a small fortune during the Christmas season. This may be a nod to Jewish shop and department store owners' role in developing the "Christmas effect." The same customers who did their Christmas shopping at Macy's or Bloomingdale's—both founded by Jews in mid-nineteenth-century New York City—patronized Jewish-owned theaters showing Christmas movies.[24] Out west, Leopold Harris and Charles Jacoby, the Prussian-born Jewish proprietors of Harris & Jacoby, advertised in 1870s Los Angeles, "Santa Claus will hold sway during the season and goods will be offered at excessively low rates!"[25]

We are first introduced to Dick Bailey in the saloon. He is drunk and itching to fight with anything that moves. When Bailey shoots his gun in the air, a frightened Plotz says, "Goodnight" and starts to leave, giving Bailey an excuse to shoot in his direction. Uninterested in confrontation, Plotz—a stereotypically puny and pacifistic Jew with a clever wit—negotiates his way out of the situation. "Can I sell you something? . . . Oh listen, I've got some pillowcases with colored pictures of the Statue of Liberty painted on them. Oh, how you could sleep with liberty underneath your heads." This quip cracks up Bailey and his cowboy buddies. Bailey holsters his gun, puts his arm around Plotz, and the two engage in friendly dialogue. Still drunk but trying to be helpful, Bailey calls the other cowboys over to buy things from Plotz. One of them says he needs a pair of pants—something Plotz isn't selling. "Don't lie to me," says Bailey, "you got a pair on right now. I can see 'em." "But what will I go home in?" Plotz pleads. "I don't care nothin' about your private life, Pie-Pan," remarks Bailey. "What you go home in is none of my business." The scene ends with the men stripping off Plotz's pants, Bailey again shooting in his direction, and Plotz running into the cold in his long johns. When Plotz finally gets his pants back, he says with a shiver in his voice, "Reminds me of the story of Joseph and his brethren. But there they took his coat, not his pants."

Plotz becomes Bailey's sidekick and punctuates the otherwise static film with similar bits of ethnic humor. Yet Plotz departs from the stage Jew in one important way: he has traded in his urban, Hasidic-style garb for dress more associated with the Old West. We first see him in winter gear, then in a typical western shirt and vest, and eventually in a cowboy hat and holster—once even shooting a gun through a window at the approaching bad guys, albeit awkwardly and unsuccessfully. Like most real-life Jews who came west, he is acculturated in appearance, although his comical accent, speech patterns, gestures, and neuroticism are all signatures of theatrical Jewishness.

Cimarron (1931)

A more sentimental Jewish peddler/merchant is found in *Cimarron* (RKO, 1931), the first of just four Westerns to win Academy Awards for best picture, the others being *Dances with Wolves* (Orion, 1990), *Unforgiven* (Warner Bros., 1992), and the Coen brothers' neo-Western crime thriller *No Country for Old Men* (Miramax, 2007). Today, *Cimarron* is among the least revived movies to achieve the award, with critics calling it "a hokey, meandering, and occasionally offensive Western."[26] Audiences in 1931 were understandably wowed by its high production value, beautiful vistas, and massive scope, spanning the forty-year (1889–1929) development of the fictional setting of Osage, Oklahoma. RKO was determined to make a splash with this epic based on the popular 1930 book by Edna Ferber, the first Jewish novelist to win a Pulitzer Prize (*So Big*, 1924). Founded in 1928, just a year before the stock market crash that inaugurated the Great Depression, RKO had struggled to gain its footing. Nevertheless, executives managed to find investors to cover the $125,000 (more than $2 million today) required for the adaptation rights, a record sum at the time.[27]

While no doubt pleased by the financial windfall, Ferber was perturbed that the filmmakers, like the general public, misunderstood the story's satirical intentions: "I am bitterly disappointed. *Cimarron* had been written with a hard and ruthless purpose. It was and is a malevolent picture of what is known as American womanhood and American sentimentality. It contains paragraphs and even chapters of satire, and, I'm afraid, bitterness, but I doubt that more than a dozen people even knew this. All the critics and hundreds of thousands of readers took *Cimarron* as a colorful, romantic Western American novel."[28] However, screenwriter Howard Estabrook, who won an Oscar for the film, amplified Ferber's depiction of pioneer prejudices and critique of westward expansion. Estabrook had read maverick historian William Christie MacLeod's *American Indian Frontier* (1928), which views whites from a Native American perspective and depicts frontiersmen as the "scum of the eastern settlers."[29]

This protorevisionist approach is apparent in the opening scene, which depicts the 1889 rush on land pledged to Native Americans. Reenacting the chaotic descent on two million acres of unassigned lands in central Oklahoma, the sequence was shot near Bakersfield, California, with five thousand extras and an abundance of horses, mules, wagons, carriages, stagecoaches, and even a high-wheel bicycle. Cinematographer Edward Cronjager pulled it off with twenty-eight camera operators, twenty-seven camera assistants, and six still photographers.[30] Equally impressive are crowded shots of Osage's early settlement that capture not only the claustrophobic pandemonium but also the multinational, multiethnic, multiracial, and multigendered makeup of the fledgling town, giving voice to minorities and Native Americans in a way that foreshadowed the New Western History of the late twentieth century.[31] More specifically, the film addresses (albeit with kid gloves on) the mistreatment of the Osage on oil-rich land, a theme revived with brutal realism in Martin Scorsese's *Killers of the Flower Moon* (Paramount, 2023).

Nevertheless, the film contains some unfortunate stereotypes. Isaiah (Eugene Jackson), for example, the Cravat family's Black servant, provides minstrelesque comedy, and the Natives never stray from Hollywood types despite their generally sympathetic portrayal. Critic Paul Miles Schneider chides the depiction of Isaiah in a film that otherwise stands out as an early critique of the standard historiography:

> One of the ironies of this 1931 film is that we watch Yancey and Sabra's son fall in love and marry out of his own race. While presenting a narrative plea for equality, or at least mutual respect as far as the White Man's relationship with Native Americans goes, we also get a cringe-worthy, stereotypical African-American boy (yes, a cartoonish pickaninny) for comic relief. Eugene Jackson, former member of the silent *Our Gang* comedy shorts known as Pineapple, plays Isaiah. I suppose the only saving grace here is that he dies early on, and we are meant to feel sorrow for his sacrifice, or perhaps pity for his loyalty to the family. The laughing stops. The clown is dead. Regardless, over 80 years later, it comes off as clumsy and hypocritical and a definite mixed message as far as the plot's moral compass goes. This film is clearly a product of its time, which reminds me all too well of the complexity of equality and the ongoing struggle (to this day) to achieve it and even depict it in a pure sense.[32]

Cimarron was partly inspired by Thompson Benton Ferguson, publisher of the *Watonga Republican* and governor of the Oklahoma Territory from 1901 to 1905. Ferber spent three weeks at the Ferguson house working on the novel.[33] In the story, Yancey Cravat (Richard Dix) is a restless newspaper editor from Wichita, Kansas, who claims a plot in the Oklahoma boomtown and settles there with his reluctant wife, Sabra (Irene Dunne). Yancey quickly becomes a leading citizen, but as the town becomes established, he loses interest and heads for the Cherokee Strip, leaving behind his growing family. During this and his other absences, Sabra proves to be the responsible one, running the newspaper and eventually getting elected to Congress, concluding the forty-year saga. She also embodies much of the film's undercutting message of xenophobia and anti–Native American bigotry—the latter causing tensions between her and Yancey, a firm advocate for Native rights and perhaps part Native himself. Sabra is initially dismayed by her husband's fascination with other cultures and his defense of nonwhites. But with time and experience, she comes to appreciate diversity, even embracing her son's wife, "a chief's daughter, a full-blooded Osage Indian."

Stricken with chronic wanderlust, Yancey is reduced to a drifter by the end of the film, dying heroically as he protects others from an oilfield explosion. The film concludes with Sabra dedicating a bronze statue of Oklahoma pioneers that depicts a man modeled on Yancey protecting a Native American. The actual Oklahoma pioneer statue, dedicated in 1930 in Ponca City, has a woman leading a child by the hand—an image closer to Ferber's feminist leanings and identification with persevering mothers such as the flawed but ultimately noble Sabra.[34]

Things could have gone south with the film's Jewish character, Sol Levy, played by Polish-born Jewish actor George E. Stone (né Gerschon Lichtenstein). However, he remains dignified, loyal, relatable, and self-aware to the point of knowing that history books would overlook people like him: "Ah, they will always talk about Yancey. He's going to be part of the history of the great Southwest. It's men like him that build the world. The rest of them, like me, we just come along and live in it." In truth, men like Levy—the peddlers, merchants, traders, suppliers, importers, and shopkeepers—were essential to the growth of western towns into major cities, much as Osage develops in the story. Levy's advancement from peddler to modest shop owner to proprietor of a four-story brick mercantile emporium by the time Oklahoma is granted statehood (1907) is a tribute to the unsung multitudes who established the nation's urban centers. Most significantly, Levy, whom Ferber describes as hailing from the German-French region of Alsace, has none of the stage Jew's Eastern European trappings. He is the sort of Jew one might have actually found in the Oklahoma Territory.

There may have been as many as one hundred Jews in the territory in 1889, when the film begins, a number that grew to around twelve hundred when statehood was declared. According to Henry J. Tobias, the earliest of these Jewish settlers were young German-speaking peddlers who arrived in the Northeast, later ventured west, and established themselves economically before getting married or sending for their families to join them. "The tempo and style of their approach to Oklahoma," Tobias writes, "suggests a cautious and undramatic, if steady, advance."[35] Although Levy remains a bachelor, he otherwise follows that trajectory of successfully acculturating frontier Jews, evolving through the film from an immigrant outsider to a confident businessman who wears a three-piece suit, takes his hat off indoors, and advances from selling raw materials to purveying the latest fashions. In

Ferber's novel, Levy sets up a zoo, becomes a real estate holder, and runs unsuccessfully for mayor. Each of these details has parallels in real-life Jewish pioneer stories, thus predating by several decades historians' appreciation of the Jews' participation in settling the West.

In the novel as in the film, anti-Jewish prejudice is baked into Levy's early encounters in the settlement. These episodes, while dramatically and narratively effective, reflect Ferber's experiences with midwestern antisemitism more than historical accounts of such incidents in the Oklahoma Territory. As elsewhere in the nineteenth-century American West, the Jews' European skin tone and Americanizing strategies made them valued players in social and economic development, and their small numbers and mostly dispersed presence largely mitigated any perceived threat of "the Jews" as a controlling or nefarious presence. Of course, personal prejudices did not disappear on the Plains, a point made clear throughout *Cimarron*, but open expressions of antisemitism were rare (or at least rarely reported) and relatively mild.[36] More overt accusations would later surface, most notably with the rumor that Jewish interests lay behind the relocation of the state's capital from its temporary site in Guthrie to Oklahoma City. On November 1, 1912, the *Guthrie Daily Leader* ran a headline, "Shylocks of Oklahoma City Have State By the Throat." The emergence of the Ku Klux Klan in the 1920s, economic discrimination during the Great Depression, and the rise of Nazism in Europe affected Oklahoma's growing Jewish population as it did elsewhere in the country. Even so, writes Tobias, "generous and tolerant feelings, trust, cooperation, and sympathy toward them" mostly prevailed in the western region, even in the darkest times.[37]

In *Cimarron*, Levy's public harassment as well as his steadfast ability to overcome it reflect Ferber's avowed and complicated patriotism: the uphill struggle to become American and the desire to make the United States better through that process. In the novel, she introduces Levy as a vulnerable outsider:

> Sol Levy had come over an immigrant in the noisome bowels of some dreadful ship. His hair was blue-black and very thick, and his face was white in spite of the burning Southwest sun, a black stubble of beard intensified this pallor. He had delicate blue-veined hands and narrow arched feet. His face was delicate, too, and narrow, and his eyes slanted ever so little at the outer

Sol Levy (right), played by George E. Stone, *Cimarron* (RKO, 1931).

> corners, so that he had a faintly Oriental look sometimes seen in the student type of his race. He belonged in crowded places, in populous places, in the color and glow and swift drama of the bazaars. God knows how he found his way to this vast wilderness. Perhaps in Chicago, or in Kansas City, or Omaha he had heard of in this new country and the rush of thousands for its land. And he had bummed his way on foot. He had started to peddle with an oilcloth-covered pack on his back. Through the little hot Western towns in summer. Through the bitter cold Western towns in winter. They turned the dogs on him. The children cried, "Jew! Jew!"[38]

Levy's first appearance in the film is taken directly from the novel. He is a peddler with a mule, marked as a Jew more by his accent and profession than his manner or dress. He chants, "Corset laces, celluloid collars, darning yarns, rug rags, shoe strings, suspenders. . . . Safety pins, collar buttons, needles, thread, thimbles, crochet cotton, celluloid collars." The meek and mild Levy is targeted by rough loafers, similar to Plotz's entrance in *The Light of Western Stars* (minus the comedy). Levy is lassoed by Lon Yountis (Stanley Fields), manages to break free, and has bullets fired in his direction. Exhausted, Levy props himself up on wooden planks, imitating a crucifixion. One of the roughs grabs him and forces him to drink, but Yancey Cravat shows up to rescue the helpless Jewish martyr (just as the cowboy heroes do in the 1928 silent features *The Rawhide Kid* and *Put 'Em Up*).

Yancey, with his natural affection for the marginalized, becomes fast friends with Levy, who in turn helps finance the newspaper. An inaugural church gathering is organized in a large tent, drawing together people of different religious, ethnic, racial, and economic backgrounds. Levy sits up front and asks Yancey, "Is it alright if I'm here?" He gets a warm smile in response. Yancey tells the assemblage, "Fellow citizens, I have been called upon to conduct this opening meeting of the Osage First Methodist, Episcopal, Lutheran, Presbyterian, Congregational, Baptist, Catholic, Unitarian"—he pauses and glances at Levy—"Hebrew Church." This declaration of tolerance on behalf of the "First Osage Church, whose denomination shall be nameless" is pulled directly from Frederick Jackson Turner, who asserted that ethnic, religious, and socioeconomic differences dissolve into a utopian crucible of democracy, cooperation, and settler-colonial exceptionalism. However, this myth is immediately and intentionally upended when Yancey takes a collection and threatens to throw anyone out who does not contribute "two bits," implying that the town's superficial harmony is forced and fragile. (He makes an exception for the Natives: "A Cherokee is too smart to put anything in the contribution box of a race that's robbed him of his birthright.") Yancey's "sermon" is interrupted when Yountis, who had earlier killed the territory's first newspaper editor, fires shots in Yancey's direction. A brief crossfire ensues, with the congregants ducking for cover and Yountis struck and dying in the back of the tent.

Antisemitism never fully disappears from Osage, but Levy learns to brush it off as he ascends the socioeconomic ladder. During the final scene, honoring Sabra's election to Congress, a snooty socialite, Tracy Wyatt (Edna May Oliver), apologizes to Levy for his exclusion from the planning committee, all of whose members are "representatives of principal families": "One of my ancestors was a signer of the Declaration of Independence." Levy, now hatless and fully Americanized, deflates her WASPy arrogance:

"That's all right. A relative of mine, fellow named Moses, wrote the Ten Commandments."

Levy's friendship with the lead protagonists was particularly important to the Jewish author. From age five to twelve, Ferber lived in Ottumwa, Iowa, a coal-mining town so filled with Jew hatred that she blamed it for any hostility she bore toward the world.[39] In her 1939 autobiography, *A Peculiar Treasure*, Ferber describes numerous episodes of antisemitism while growing up in different midwestern states.[40] She mirrored these prejudices in her novels, including *Show Boat* (1926), *Giant* (1956), and *Ice Palace* (1960), all of which were adapted to film. These stories celebrate America's potential while exposing its shortcomings. In the novel *Cimarron*, Levy's violent encounter with Yountis and the taunting Levy receives from prostitutes ("Why don't you smile? Don't you never have no fun? I bet you're rich. Jews is all rich") may not sync with historical accounts of Oklahoma's Jewish settlers, but these incidents reflect Ferber's experiences and the rising antisemitism at the time the book was written.[41]

CHAPTER 3

Code-Era Westerns

During the early years of the Motion Picture Production Code era (1934–68), Jewish characters and themes, both silly and sympathetic, largely disappeared from the screen. In addition to the censorial strictures of the Code, Jewish film executives feared that Jewish themes and characters would exacerbate antisemitism and drive away the public. This trend gradually began to shift during and especially after World War II, with the general decline of antisemitism in the 1940s and '50s. A number of "platoon movies" of the 1940s featured Jewish servicemen, including *Air Force* (Warner Bros., 1943), *The Purple Heart* (Twentieth Century–Fox, 1944), and *Pride of the Marines* (Warner Bros., 1945)—cinematic acknowledgment of the roughly 550,000 American Jews who served in World War II. Perhaps the most notable postwar example is *Gentleman's Agreement* (Twentieth Century–Fox, 1947), about a reporter (Gregory Peck) who pretends to be Jewish to cover a story on antisemitism. Directed by Elia Kazan, a non-Jew, and produced by Darryl F. Zanuck, whose presence at Fox led to it being dubbed "the goy studio," the earnest film framed Jew hatred as a social problem perpetuated by the Christian majority. Jewish communal leaders and studio heads worried that its anti-antisemitism message would once again stir accusations that Hollywood Jews were pushing their own agendas.[1]

Beyond the controversy and acclaim the well-meaning film garnered at the time (including a best picture Oscar), modern viewers note that *Gentleman's Agreement* essentially limits Jewish identity to antisemitism. "Making Jewishness and synagogues a church flavor is in keeping with the universalizing, melting pot model of the post–World War II era," writes Helene Myers in *Movie-Made Jews*. "Yet the film doesn't even sustain this reduction of

Jewishness to religious orientation. There are no synagogues anywhere to be found here, no Torah, no Shabbat, not a rabbi, yarmulke, or tallit in sight."[2] The same can be said for *Crossfire* (RKO), also released in 1947, which centers on an antisemitic murder (and was the first B movie to earn an Academy Award nomination for best picture).

Five years later, U.S. Supreme Court's decision in *Joseph Burstyn, Inc. v. Wilson* gave motion pictures First Amendment protections and significantly chipped away at Hollywood censorship, and the Code was incrementally liberalized through the 1960s. Nevertheless, in Westerns of this period, suggestions of Jewishness were coded, subtextual, and few and far between. These qualities are seen in greater or lesser depth and duration in *The Searchers* (Warner Bros., 1956), *Forty Guns* (Twentieth Century–Fox, 1957), and *For a Few Dollars More* (PEA/United Artists, 1965). A 1960 remake of *Cimarron* (MGM) brought back Sol Levy, whose Jewish identity is more subdued than in the original, largely incidental, and seemingly avoided as much as the story would allow. The result is a somewhere-in-between character, the semicoded Jew.

The Searchers (1956)

John Ford's Technicolor epic *The Searchers*, released by Warner Bros. in 1956, is regularly hailed as one of the greatest Westerns of all time. A self-aware transitional Western, firmly rooted in the genre's ethos but also tentatively seeking to revise it, *The Searchers* is equally notable for perfecting Western conventions—which Ford probably did more than anyone to develop—and challenging some of those conventions by exposing the racism that so often underlies Native American representations, including in Ford's own films. Made at the height of the Cold War, *The Searchers* questions the demonization and Otherization of the enemy, exposing what Richard Slotkin calls "the myth of 'savage war,' and the racism that informs and energizes that myth, at a level of sophistication no previous fiction film had achieved."[3]

At the heart of the film is the Native American hatred of Ethan Edwards (John Wayne), a Confederate veteran who relocates to his brother's Texas ranch to avoid living in the Union-controlled South. Learning that there are Comanche in the area, Ethan looks for them with Martin Pawley (Jeffrey Hunter), a part-Cherokee whom the Edwards clan had adopted after his family was massacred (presumably by Comanche). While they are away,

Comanche attack the ranch and kill all but Ethan's two nieces, who are taken captive. The older girl's body is soon found and buried, and a five-year search for the younger girl, Debbie, ensues. Ethan's hostility toward Natives flares up against Martin, whom Ethan had saved as a child. He even threatens to kill the girl if he finds her because she would have become Nativized and married off as a "squaw." Thus, the "hero" of the story, played by an actor typically identified with heroism, becomes a conflicted and loathsome character, an outdated relic of tropes Wayne himself did much to enshrine. He comes across as a crude, jingoistic, sexist, racist macho man clinging to an untenable ideology in a rapidly changing West. Revisionist Westerns later explored precisely these themes.

Even critics who were unenthusiastic about Ford's oeuvre tended to praise *The Searchers*. David Thomson, who had accused Ford of "invalidat[ing] the Western as a form," gave the movie a pass, calling it "a very moving and mysterious film, that does not cheat on a serious subject, and that beautifully relates the landscape to its theme."[4] Pauline Kael, always the contrarian, derided the film as "peculiarly formal and stilted," with lines that are "awkward and the line readings worse." Yet even she recognized its appeal: "What made this John Ford Western fascinating to the young directors who hailed it in the 70s as a great work and as a key influence on them is the compulsiveness of Ethan's search for his niece (whose mother he loved) and his bitter, vengeful racism."[5]

Although *The Searchers* was lauded as a self-critical Western, Ford biographer Brian Spittles observes ambiguity in the film's attempt to correct the genre's racist legacy, describing the director as "a white anti-racist filmmaker, who was also a product of white supremacist culture."[6] Philosopher Robert B. Pippin goes a step further: "Ford is inviting us at the beginning of the film to take Ethan as *the* John Wayne character, an immensely competent, tough loner of great integrity and heroic capacity. This assumption is so strong that I would venture the guess that many, perhaps most, of the film's viewers simply glide over the fact that Ethan is such a vicious racist and are able to keep ignoring this."[7]

One glaring blind spot in *The Searchers* is Jerem Futterman, an unscrupulous trading post operator with a Jewish surname who offers one of the first clues to Debbie's whereabouts. When the two searchers ask Futterman for information he demands $1,000, but Ethan gives Futterman only a few

"Yankee dollars" for postage on a letter, Debbie's dress, and his time, snarling, "You'll get the reward when I find her and if she's still alive." Futterman, played by a black-haired, olive-skinned Peter Mamakos—a Greek American actor known for playing Greek, Native, Hispanic, French, Italian, and Middle Eastern villains—tells them, "A young buck fetched [the dress] in late last summer. Said it belonged to a captive child of Chief Scar. . . . Scar's band was headed north, to winter in at Fort Wingate eatin' agency beef. That's what this buck said. Maybe he lied." Later that night, when Futterman and two companions try to murder and rob Ethan and Martin, Futterman pays for his treachery with his life. Ethan makes sure to rifle through Futterman's pockets and take back the "Yankee dollars."

Futterman is not called a Jew, but his name, face, slight accent, and stereotypical moneygrubbing point in that direction. Moreover, he is a trader with the Natives, a position held by a number of European-born Jews—although, in real life, Jewish traders were generally favored by the tribes for their honesty, integrity, and avoidance of proselytizing.[8] In addition, many Jewish pioneer merchants provided rudimentary banking services in their stores, making handshake loans and keeping customers' valuables in safes, courtesies that reflected the merchants' dependable and trustworthy reputations.[9] These virtues are a far cry from Futterman, a coded embodiment of the scheming merchant. As Nancy Schoenberger observes, "Though Ford will increasingly question the devaluation of the Native American, one of the minor but important villains in *The Searchers* is Futterman, with the suggestion that he is a Jewish merchant."[10] Pippin sees this as a "dangerous and tricky episode" for Ford, who invites us "to apply the crudest of stereotypes when Ethan must pay for information from Futterman, clearly a Jewish trader who has information about Debbie."[11] Futterman's sneak attack confirms the stereotypes. Yet the act of retrieving the money reveals Ethan to be just as treacherous and avaricious. This detail seems to question the canard of moneygrubbing as a Jewish-specific trait, but the message is muddled by the scene's hero-versus-outlaw framework.

Jerem Futterman may be the closest Ford came to depicting a Jew onscreen. It is hard to say how much of Futterman's characterization was a result of Ford's biases. Screenwriter Frank Nugent, whose mother was Jewish, said that the movies on which he collaborated with Ford were always more the director's.[12] Ford reportedly complimented Nugent on *Wagon*

Master (RKO, 1950), saying, "I like your script. In fact, I actually shot a few pages of it."[13]

The codedness of the portrayal of Futterman contains some (accidental) accuracy in that he fits into the Western setting. Like Plotz in *The Light of Western Stars*, Futterman does not exhibit the external trappings of ethnoreligious garb or accoutrements. Reflecting the real Jewish merchants on whom he is presumably based, Futterman likely left Europe for America and ventured west. He would have negotiated his identity along the way, discarding Old World conventions that were impractical in an environment lacking synagogues and kosher food. As with many Jewish settlers and pioneers, the compromises of mobility meant that his ethnicity was mostly confined to his surname, accent/multilingualism, physical features, and probable business and social ties to other Jews.[14]

Forty Guns (1957)

The character of Barney Cashman, the well-liked bathhouse owner and balladeer in *Forty Guns* (Twentieth Century–Fox, 1957), a B Western written, directed, and produced by Jewish auteur Samuel Fuller, provides an antidote to the callous Futterman type. Although Cashman's surname is perhaps more often Anglo-Saxon than Jewish, the merging of *cash* (alluding to business acumen) and *man* (an ending of many Jewish names) can be taken as an allusion to Jewishness.[15] Neil Simon reused the Barney Cashman name as the lead in his play *Last of the Red Hot Lovers* (1969; filmed 1972), about a middle-aged neurotic nebbish who wants to join the sexual revolution but is too late. Fuller's Cashman is played by singer and nightclub entertainer Jidge Carroll, born Vincenzo Riccio, whose Italian looks passed for Jewish in much the same way as John Turturro's do in *Miller's Crossing* (20th Century Fox, 1990) and *Barton Fink* (20th Century Fox, 1991). Like Futterman, Cashman is a coded Jew who, again appropriately, does not stand out in dress or gestures. But while Futterman retains a subtle accent, Cashman has lost his.

Cashman is a minor but memorable player in Fuller's big-cast noir Western. The film is "undeservedly forgotten today," especially when compared to *The Searchers*, but Fuller aficionados celebrate it for showcasing his signature solutions to scheduling and budgetary constraints: abrupt cutting between long shots and close-ups, fast-paced violence, surprising (and sometimes illogical) plot twists, and plenty of shadows and Dutch angles.[16] Fuller's admirers included French New Wave filmmakers Jean-Luc Godard and François Truffaut, spaghetti Western pioneer Sergio Leone, and Martin Scorsese, who appraised Fuller's "blunt, pulpy, occasionally crude [style], lacking any sense of delicacy or subtlety," as genuine "reflections of his temperament, his journalistic training [as a New York City crime reporter and political cartoonist], and his sense of urgency."[17] Critics see *Forty Guns* and *I Shot Jesse James* (Screen Guild, 1949), Fuller's other key Western, as directly influencing Leone's Dollars Trilogy (United Artists, 1964–66), Sam Peckinpah's *The Wild Bunch* (Warner Bros., 1969), and Quentin Tarantino's *Django Unchained* (Weinstein, 2012).[18] Nicholas Garnham, emeritus media studies professor at the University of Westminster, explains the appeal of *Forty Guns*: "The themes of love and death, marriage and death, sex and violence, are given their most original and powerful treatment in *Forty Guns*. This is the Fuller movie about which it is hardest to write because more than any other it is pure experience, pure movie. . . . Out of this violent clash comes the intimate connection in Fuller's work, as in American society, between sex and violence, and in particular between sex and guns, the ultimate expression of frontier virility."[19]

Made in just ten days on a tight budget and filmed in black-and-white CinemaScope (a format mostly reserved for color productions at the time), the expressionistic film is set in 1880s Tombstone, where former gunslinger turned lawman Griff Bonnell (Barry Sullivan) and his brothers Wes (Gene Barry) and Chico (Robert Dix)—stand-ins for the Earp brothers—arrest Howard Swain (Chuck Roberson) for mail robbery. Swain is one of the forty guns hired by ironfisted land baroness Jessica Drummond (Barbara Stanwyck), "a woman who wears the pants"—a "high ridin' woman with a whip," as Cashman sings in the film.[20] Her brother, Brockie Drummond (John Ericson), leads the guns in terrorizing the town with drunken abandonment. Meanwhile, Wes Bonnell falls in love with local gunsmith Louvenia Spanger (Eve Brent), another gender role reversal. Their mutual passion is consummated in a euphemistic down-the-rifle-barrel point-of-view shot, which Godard recycled in *Breathless* (Société nouvelle de cinématographie, 1960).[21] Griff becomes romantically involved with the villainess Jessica after saving her from a raging tornado, leading to what Garnham calls their "mutual rape."[22] Scenes of sexual tension and rampant violence build to the movie's

Forty Guns, poster (Twentieth Century–Fox, 1957).

surprising climax. Griff has a standoff with Brockie, who is holding Jessica hostage. Griff shoots Jessica first, dropping her to the ground and leaving her brother open to be killed. "Get a doctor. She'll live," Griff says as he coolly walks away. Fuller originally intended Griff to kill them both, but the studio nixed the idea, leading Fuller to comment, "For Chrissakes, my gunman had to think about box-office receipts before he decided to pull the trigger!"[23] As Griff rides away, Jessica runs after him, calling out, "Griff! Mr. Bonnell!" They presumably ride off together for California.

The portrayal of Cashman as a coded Jewish bathhouse operator is consistent with the American Jewish immigrant experience. At the turn of the twentieth century, only 8 percent of Jewish families on Manhattan's Lower East Side had bathtubs, and they typically had no hot water. As a result, by 1897 more than half of New York's sixty bathhouses—including swimming, vapor, medicated, Russian, and Turkish bathhouses—were run by and catered to Jews.[24] Cashman had conceivably begun in one of these urban bathhouses before heading West and opening his own. A historical parallel might be Emanuel Linoberg, who settled in the California Gold Rush town of Sonora in 1849. He operated a mine, a large general store (Tiende Mexicano), and an entertainment hall; served on the town council; and ran a Russian bath. In *Forty Guns*, Cashman is a modest version of the industrious Linoberg.[25] A multitalented pillar of the community, Cashman's outdoor baths are a regular meeting place for Tombstone's men, who soak together under the hot sun, sharing dialogue peppered with sexual innuendo.[26]

One of the film's more drastic mood shifts comes at the wedding of Wes and Louvenia, when the groom is abruptly shot in a surprise attack by one of Jessica's gunmen. The bright and smiley scene, with bouncy scoring by Jewish composer Harry Sukman, quickly cuts to an angled shot of the bride, now in a black dress and black veil, standing beside two black horses attached to a black funeral carriage. Cashman, acting as "cowboy cantor," sings a dirge written by Jewish songwriter Victor Young and lyricist Harold Adamson. The song includes the verse, "God has his hands around me, I am not afraid," echoing the final words of the Hebrew prayer Adon Olam, "God is with me, I will not fear." In some Jewish traditions, these words make the prayer suitable for the deathbed and thus a fitting liturgical reference in a vaguely Jewish funeral scene.[27]

Cimarron (1960)

MGM remade *Cimarron* in 1960. Like the original, the updated version features a spectacular run on Oklahoma's unassigned lands. Now in color CinemaScope, it is even more daring and impressive than the original—apparently the only justification for the remake. Bosley Crowther's review in the *New York Times* commended the "dynamic and illustrative" land-rush sequence but complained that once it was over, "in this almost two-and-one-half-hour-long film—and we have to tell you it is assembled and completed within the first half-hour—the remaining dramatization of Miss Ferber's bursting 'Cimarron' simmers down to a stereotyped and sentimental cinema saga of the taming of the frontier."[28] A *Time* reviewer quipped that *Cimarron* "might more suitably have been called Cimarron-and-on-and-on-and-on. It lasts 2 hours and 27 minutes, and for at least half of that time most spectators will probably be Oklacomatose."[29]

A product of the Production Code era, the film eliminates Isaiah and his minstrelsy, makes the Cravats' servants white, and tones down frontier bigotry as much as possible without losing sight of Ferber's novel. Sol Levy is still in the story, now played by David Opatoshu, an actor best remembered as Akiva Ben Canaan in the founding-of-Israel epic *Exodus* (United Artists), also from 1960. Yet there is little to identify Levy as a Jew other than the harassment he receives from the local troublemakers. He occupies something of a liminal category, the named-yet-coded Jew.

Despite having a Jewish director, Anthony Mann; a Jewish screenwriter, Arnold Schulman; and a Coplandesque score supplied by a veteran Jewish film composer, Franz Waxman, 1960's *Cimarron* downplays Levy's Jewish traits. He is introduced not as a struggling peddler but as a newspaper-reading, already acculturated bystander with an accent—an "American with a difference."[30] He happens upon a group of rowdy men placing bets on whether one of them can shoot a bottle from another's hand. "I don't see any point in killing a white man," says a gruff man who doubts the shooter's aim. "Hey Moses," he points at Levy, "or is it Izzy?" Before Levy can reply, the man strikes him in the face. Levy tries to fight back, breaking the passive Jew mold, but is forced to hold up two bottles in a cross-like pose recalling the 1931 original. (The *Time* review scoffed, "There is the theme of race prejudice, but that continually dissolves in sanctimonious absurdity—as when a Jew, forced by a target-happy gunman to hold two whisky bottles with outstretched arms, lifts his eyes to heaven in a shockingly tasteless travesty of the Crucifixion.")[31] Sabra (Maria Schell), now with a French accent and a softer heart, comes to Levy's aid before Yancey (Glenn Ford) intervenes.

Outside this scene of overripe and unprovoked antisemitism, Levy's Jewishness is basically confined to his accent and sweet demeanor. He even becomes romantically attracted to Sabra, departing not only from Ferber's novel and the 1931 adaptation but also from the long-established convention of effeminate/asexual Jewish male caricatures. (Ferber wrote Levy as a disinterested bachelor.) Other relationships and events are also changed in the movie, apparently just to do so. Through it all, Opatoshu gives a delightful performance but cannot salvage this "indifferent sprawling soap opera."[32]

The subdued 1960 characterization of Levy reflects long-standing trepidations. As the first overtly Jewish character in a Western since the 1931 original, his portrayal embodies lingering fears of resurrecting old stereotypes. Yet even with his toned-down traits and identities, Levy—and the coded Jews in *The Searchers* and *Forty Guns*—continued a cinematic trope Patricia Erens traces back to silent one-reelers: "In those films where Jews are tangential to the plot, without exception they are represented as businessmen—merchants, peddlers, or pawnbrokers," types she sees as "synonymous with Jewishness, a sign like the ten-gallon hat that signifies cowboy."[33]

Released the same year as *Exodus*, *Cimarron* portrays an updated Levy who can be seen as a mild projection of Israel's assertive, self-confident, anti-passive "new Jew" onto the Wild West. The name *Sabra*, especially when spoken by Opatoshu, might even take on another, unintended meaning—a native-born Jewish Israeli. *Exodus* itself has been compared to a good-versus-evil Western, with some suggesting that Leon Uris's 1958 novel on which the film is based grew from his screenplay for *Gunfight at the O.K. Corral* (Paramount, 1957).[34] A *Time* reviewer opined, "Leon Uris writes Jewish westerns. In *Exodus*, the good guys were Zionists, the homesteaders who fought for and founded the new state of Israel. The British and the Arabs were the bad guys, and no cattle rustler could be as sordid as the Arabs."[35] Whether or not these points are overstated, American Westerns were popular in Israel during the late 1950s. Rachel Leket-Mor describes how

Israelis made comparisons between the "mythological West and the Zionist Project": "Both settlement projects were programmatically carried out by European pioneers who settled in what they described as 'empty' regions, and through much physical hardship and violent clashes with indigenous populations created a new culture."[36]

Years later, Jewish director Ted Kotcheff made a Western in Israel, *Billy Two Hats* (United Artists, 1974), using Jewish actors as Natives and receiving subsidies from the Israeli government.[37] (The movie was produced by Norman Jewison, who was also planning to direct the rock opera *Jesus Christ Superstar* in Israel.) Kotcheff was criticized for failing to hire a Native American consultant for the revisionist-era film. He brushed off the criticism, claiming that "there are, in actuality, no ethnic differences in people, there is only the shared human experience" and that there is thus no need to portray Indigenous cultures with anything more than generic Hollywood features.[38] This defense rang hollow. Kotcheff's ancestors had been targeted for ethnoreligious genocide in ways similar to Native Americans, and the film was shot in a country that many believed was colonized in ways analogous to the United States. Kotcheff's apparent obliviousness suggests a continued conflation of triumphalist Zionism and Westerns, as Leket-Mor describes it, well into the 1970s. Driving home the point, Rita Keshena, the late chief justice of the Menominee Nation court, pointed out that Kotcheff made another film in 1974, *The Apprenticeship of Duddy Kravitz* (Astral), about a Jewish hustler from a working-class Montreal family: "One can only wonder at the response had someone suggested that an American Indian make the Montreal film—with or without a Jewish advisor."[39]

For a Few Dollars More (1965)

A thinly coded Jew reappears in Leone's Italian Western *For a Few Dollars More*, released in the United States by United Artists in 1965. Bounty hunter Douglas Mortimer (Lee Van Cleef), a former army colonel in pursuit of a ruthless bank robber, boards a train and sits across from a man resembling the bearded, black-coated, derby-hat-wearing Jew of the silent film era. In a slightly Yiddish-tinged accent (in the English dub), the peddler tells Mortimer, who is reading a large Bible, "Excuse me, but you've made a mistake, Reverend. I couldn't help hearing you're going to Tucumcari. I peddle goods around here and I better tell you, you're on the wrong train." Mortimer gives the peddler an intimidating stare, tells him the train will stop at Tucumcari, pulls the emergency cord, and gets off the train with his horse. While he does not say or do anything explicitly Jewish, the peddler, played by veteran actor Jesús Guzmán—who returns as Pardue the hotel owner in Leone's *The Good, the Bad, and the Ugly* (United Artists, 1966)—appears as a brief homage to an earlier type.

CHAPTER 4

Television Westerns

A 1961 television report includes a small section on Jewish representation. Noting the effectiveness of the 1952 television code of the National Association of Broadcasters, which, like its earlier film equivalent, decreed that "racial or nationality types shall not be shown . . . in such a manner as to ridicule," the report states that while Americans of Italian descent at times vocally opposed the identification of Italians as gangsters, Blacks and Jews—"the two most sensitive minorities"—had successfully eliminated old, offensive stereotypes.[1] To be sure, there were exceptions to Jewish invisibility. "Yiddish-spiced variety shows" hosted by Sid Caesar, Milton Berle, and Jerry Lewis persisted through the late 1950s, along with *The Goldbergs* (CBS, 1949–56), a Jewish family comedy centered on matriarchal yenta Molly Goldberg, played by pathbreaking actor/writer/producer Gertrude Berg.[2] *The Goldbergs*, which began as a radio show (1929–46), was remarkable for depicting a Jewish family as "typical Americans" (with a difference) and engaging with big issues of the day, including antisemitism.[3] Yet for the most part, concerns over negative portrayals resulted in a baby-with-the-bathwater approach. "The caricature of the derbied Jewish peddler or of Little Farina blanching with fear is never seen on television," the report notes. "In fact the Jew as a character has all but disappeared from the performing arts and it is said that the new generation of television viewers is being raised with a brand new stereotype—the nonexistent Jew—that might prove as unwelcome as the exaggerations of the past."[4]

At the time the 1961 report was being prepared, Jewish characters were slowly reappearing on television in unlikely places: Western drama series. Donning the discarded guise of the "derbied Jewish peddler"—and related

Jewish merchant and craftsman—they were precisely the types reviled in the report. Unlike Sol Levy in the 1960 *Cimarron* remake, these peddlers looked, acted, and talked the part. Arriving on the prairies and frontier towns of TV Westerns, they were throwbacks to the comedic Cohens and Levys of the silent shorts but with the farce and frivolity replaced by seriousness and sentimentality. Presented as sages of the sagebrush, they would teach tolerance and understanding to frontier folks. It was inconsequential to the directors and writers, usually Jews themselves, that these shtetl-style peddlers were anachronistic, emulating the Jews who had immigrated to America at the turn of the twentieth century, not the predominantly Central European Jews of the mid-nineteenth-century West. What mattered was that audiences would immediately recognize them as Jews. Jewish viewers eagerly received them as positive representations at a time of heightened ethnic pride. Like characters from the 1964 musical *Fiddler on the Roof*, which became a film in 1971, they were reclaimed, romanticized tokens of a European past.

Forgotten Pioneer, a 1963 book of vignettes of peddlers in America, offers insights into the substance and impetus of these Western TV episodes. Written by Harry Golden, a journalist and social critic born in Galicia and raised on Manhattan's Lower East Side, the book opens with clarifying personal anecdotes. Growing up in a crowded immigrant neighborhood, Golden had many encounters with Jewish peddlers between 1905 and 1920. "Our family doctor on the Lower East Side of New York had been a peddler; he said that for an immigrant, peddling was the 'preparatory school' of America." Golden writes that "at least a quarter of a million Jewish men alone had been peddlers of one sort or another" in the United States between 1850 and 1920 and suggests that "maybe because so many of the peddlers in the last hundred years have been Jews is the reason no one pays much attention to their role." The book periodizes the peddler's presence in America from the colonial era through the early twentieth century, with others preceding Jews in that trade. But Golden's affection was for the Eastern European Jewish peddlers of his youth, whom he saw brutalized and arrested by police officers on charges of obstructing streets, peddling without a license, and creating a public nuisance.[5]

Like Golden, many of the writers and directors of the Western episodes were New Yorkers familiar with the pushcart peddlers of their childhoods.

Following the adage to "write what you know," they transplanted these types onto the Western frontier, where Eastern European Jews replaced more historically accurate Central European peddlers who were generally viewed as "another kind of German," and had these Eastern Europeans suffer the same victimization as they did in New York, projecting the actions and attitudes of urban policemen onto ignorant ranchers and townsfolk.[6]

This is not to say that Jewish peddlers in the West were immune to the oldest hatred. Memoirs and life stories of former Jewish peddlers across U.S. regions describe incidents of hearing anti-Jewish slurs, being spat upon, having rocks thrown at them, getting barked at by dogs, or being challenged by local clergy and elites.[7] Suspicions that Jewish peddlers were black-market war profiteers informed General Ulysses S. Grant's infamous General Order No. 11 (1862) expelling all Jews "as a class" from his military district (Tennessee, Mississippi, and Kentucky). In the late 1880s, North Carolina passed a law requiring peddlers to show proof of citizenship to obtain licenses. In 1891, the city council of Key West, Florida, legislated that foreign peddlers be taxed at $1,000 a head. Yet at the same time, Jews occasionally spent nights in Christian homes or at inns run by Christians, some of whom had never before met (or never knew they had met) a Jew.[8] The severity and regularity of such harassment was not uniform, and the further west one traveled, the more minimal or even aberrational antisemitism was perceived to be. A report published in San Francisco's *Jewish Progress* in 1896 boasted, "There is very little *rishus* [antisemitic prejudice] on this Coast . . . and it is pleasing to note the genuine fellow feeling that exists between Jew and Gentile. . . . [T]here is more freedom from bigotry and fanaticism on this Coast than anywhere in the world."[9]

This statement was truer for San Francisco, home to some twenty thousand Jews at the time, than it was for Los Angeles, whose Jewish population of around two thousand was similarly well entrenched and largely prosperous but by the 1890s had entered a period of social exclusion owing to the arrival of Midwest Protestants. Writing in the 1970s, Norton B. Stern and William M. Kramer framed the scarcity of newspaper reports on anti-Jewish incidents in Turneresque terms: "The essential democratic motif of the frontier, the fellowship among whites that it called forth, the fact that almost everyone started near the bottom of the ladder were some of the elements which made a difference even in the ages-old phenomenon of anti-Semitism"; the individual could "rise above" antagonisms that periodically emerged between white groups and sometimes took the form of antisemitism.[10]

Frontier peddlers, particularly on the rural outskirts, took advantage of their European extraction, interacted mostly with non-Jews, and generally sidestepped social tensions by providing much-needed goods to farms, mining camps, towns, outposts, and city fringes, selling to rich and poor, white and nonwhite and catering primarily to a customer base of women who made purchases outside of the presence of their husbands.[11] This mobility, inherited from generations of Jewish peddlers—a near-ubiquitous Jewish trade in many parts of Europe and beyond—likewise instilled a knack for adaptation wherein outward ethnoreligious trappings could be modified to fit the majority culture and dietary and ritual strictures could be loosened and replaced by "intent."[12] In fact, peddlers in America tended to prefer less-developed rural areas where underdeveloped transportation, a shortage of settled merchants, and the distance between one settlement and the next made the peddlers' services essential.[13] The biggest danger these peddlers faced was not anti-immigrant or anti-Jewish hatred but the perils of lightly traveled roads, where thieves and bandits awaited easy targets.[14]

Most important for Golden and the television writers was restoring the peddler to the narrative of American expansion:

> We should not neglect anyone who took part in the building of America, certainly not the peddler. After all, he was as adventurous as the fellow riding shotgun on the stagecoach, or the cowboy, the homesteader, the miner, and the dance-hall girl, but he did not breathe fire nor brashly look for fights. He had fight enough with the wind and dust storms, the heavy blizzards and floods. The peddler with the pack on his back was a hard-working, practical fellow, and after the 1840s, almost always a foreigner, who looked "different" and who had difficulty with the language. The nature of his work gave him little time for play, so he rarely went to the Last Chance Saloon around which most of our Western literature depends. Instead, the peddler made certain that at sundown he was not too far from a farmhouse where he nearly always found it possible to barter some of his goods for a night's lodging and early morning breakfast. The pioneering idea of the wagon train has been immortalized in our drama, song, motion pictures, and television, and yet I have

> the evidence spread on my desk that on some occasions the peddler was there before the wagon train. Always he followed the Western movement and was often its co-traveler.[15]

In addition to educating viewers regarding the Jewish peddler's vital role in the Wild West, the TV episodes used Jewish characters to act out intergenerational struggles, engage issues of intermarriage and assimilation, and teach lessons about bigotry. More than mere correctives of representation, these revisionist episodes addressed contemporary concerns.

Have Gun—Will Travel (1960, 1961)

In December 1960, CBS aired "The Fatalist," an episode of the adult Western series *Have Gun—Will Travel* featuring a Russian Jewish immigrant family. Set in the 1870s, the series starred Richard Boone as Paladin, a hired gentleman investigator/gunfighter who traveled the Old West from his home base in San Francisco. Boone, whose mother was Jewish and father was a descendant of Daniel Boone, made trips to Israel in the 1960s to assist its nascent film industry. He had the title role in the 1970 Western *Madron* (G.B.C.-Edric-Isracine), the first feature film made in Israel that was set in a non-Israeli location (and the first in which Israelis played Native Americans).[16] "The Fatalist" was helmed by Jewish director Buzz Kulik and written by prolific German-born Jewish TV scripter Shimon Wincelberg, an influential advocate for accurate and positive portrayals of Jews on the small screen and a longtime mentor to Orthodox Jews in the arts.[17] Peeved at the opposition to Jewish subjects on TV, Wincelberg quipped that networks "rationed you: one Jewish character a year."[18] Nathan Shotness from the "Fatalist," played by Jewish actor Martin Gabel, and his daughter Rivka (Roxanne Berard) were his "one" character in 1960. They returned the following year for another *Have Gun—Will Travel* episode, "A Drop of Blood."

"The Fatalist" begins with Rivka Shotness delivering an urgent message to Paladin. She explains that in Hebrew his name, which she found on a business card, means "wonder" (*pala*) and "judge" (*din*). Nathan, a tough-as-nails mail carrier, had reported a murder, but the culprit, Billy Buckstone (Noah Keen), intimidated the jury into letting him off, and now she fears for her father's life. Nathan, however, refuses to leave town or back away from the murderer's gang. One of the ruffians pulls out his gun, expecting to strike fear in the old Jew. But in a reversal of type, Nathan grabs the gun, takes it apart, points out its defects, and insults the "boychik": "About the only thing it's still good for is driving nails. This boy wants to be a gunman. He doesn't even know how to buy himself a working piece of equipment." Nathan later divulges that he had served in the Russian czar's army and received a marksmanship medal, giving his surname, *Shotness*, something of a literal meaning. Military service was made compulsory for Jews in Russia in 1827, with draft ages between twelve and twenty-five years.[19]

Nathan is upset to learn that Rivka has hired Paladin, believing it made them no better than "a little Cossack": "For that we came to Columbus's country? To hire killers, and be as bad as they are?" However, when he hears Paladin inexplicitly quoting Mishnah, first in Hebrew and then in English—"Where there is no law, there is no bread" (Avot 3:17)—Nathan softens and lets Paladin ride along on the mail wagon.

Meanwhile, Rivka is kidnapped by the gang and held at knifepoint. "I seen your daddy butcher a cow once," her captor remarks. "You people got some special way of doing that, ain't ya?" Paladin intervenes and rescues Rivka, taking a bullet in the shoulder in the process. Later, during Shabbat dinner at the Shotness home, Nathan asks Paladin, "In what other country could you find a hired killer who would quote you the words of the holy so high?" "Nathan Shotness," replies Paladin, "I am not a hired killer."

"The Fatalist" was the first of many Western series episodes to feature Jewish characters, and Wincelberg deserves credit for establishing many of the stock features of these episodes: the Jew or Jewish family is the only one in the frontier town, they teach about Jewish thought and practice, and they praise the virtues of America, which despite their present conflicts far outweigh the flaws of the Old Country. To be sure, Wincelberg's insistence on cultural accuracy had its limits. Rivka sings a familiar setting of Adon Olam (Sovereign of the Universe) that was composed by Eliezer Gerovitch in 1904, some thirty years after the episode takes place.[20] Nathan and Rivka are stand-ins for Eastern European Jewish immigrants, who began crowding New York City neighborhoods several years after the episode's time frame (and mostly stayed there). Jewish settlers and pioneers usually relied on Jewish family and business networks rather than being true loners. In rural economies, Jewish denizens acted as intermediaries, freely interacting with non-Jews of all walks of life instead of being Otherized outsiders, as they invariably appear on screen.[21] Thus, despite Wincelberg's best efforts and positive Jewish messaging, "The Fatalist" set a template for the tokenism and anachronism that pervades these portrayals.

That said, the episode stands out in its depiction of Nathan as a self-reliant, battle-worn Jew, going further than 1960's *Cimarron* in presenting the Jewish pioneer as what media scholar Vincent Brook calls "the Zionist image of the Muscle Jew, a counter to the belittling, anti-Semitic constructions of the past." In this sense, Wincelberg's muscular response to the timid, meek, painfully out-of-place peddler—actualized in Gabel's convincing performance—predated the ethnic pride that made American Jews "stand a little taller" after the Six-Day War (1967).[22]

A follow-up episode, "A Drop of Blood" (1961), has a glamorous Rivka Shotness engaged to Faivel Melamed, who at first appears as a typical big-brained, physically weak yeshiva bocher. Melamed is played by Mike Kellin, who, like Gabel, was born to Jewish immigrant parents and whose character's surname similarly fits: *melamed* means "religious teacher." Written by Wincelberg and directed by up-and-coming young Jewish director Richard Donner, the episode opens with Paladin receiving a wedding invitation dated the twelfth of the Hebrew month Tammuz 5639 (1879). Nathan greets Paladin with a rifle in his hands and asks the gentleman gunfighter to serve as best man since the Shotnesses have no family in America. Nathan explains that Buckstone is seeking revenge and intends to crash the wedding with his "Cossacks." "When an outlaw goes free," Nathan tells Paladin, "neighbors do not want to help. 'It isn't my cow that's stolen.' 'It isn't my brother that was killed.'" Faivel, sporting a black coat, black hat, and *peyes* (pious sideburns), is roughed up in front of Rivka. Paladin comes to his aid and later that evening joins Nathan, Rivka, and Faivel for a home-cooked dinner, wearing a kippah on his head. Inverting expectations, the bookish Faivel asks to examine Paladin's gun and then demonstrates a sharp aim and technical knowledge of firearms. Again, Wincelberg is suggesting that whatever appearance or reputation shtetl Jews might have, they are tougher—and more modern—than people think.

Paladin recites a few more rabbinic quotes, prompting the officiating rabbi (Milton Selzer, who lip-synchs to Wincelberg's ceremonial chants) to remark, "If you gave up your unfortunate profession and grew a beard, who knows what great things you might achieve." As predicted, the wedding is crashed by the Buckstone gang. The breaking of dishes, throwing of rocks, and hurling of torches prompts the patient rabbi to pronounce, "He who shames the neighbor in public, it is as though he has shed his blood," at which point Nathan, Faivel, and Paladin commence beating up the thugs. The scene plays out like a revenge fantasy: a successful shtetl defense carried out by New Jews in old clothes (and their honorary Jewish companion). The wedding concludes with a fiddler playing "Khosn, Kale Mazel Tov" (Congratulations, Bride and Groom), another assumed traditional melody that was actually composed in the United States by Yiddish theater songwriter Sigmund Mogulesko for the 1909 operetta *Blimele* (Flowers).[23]

Rawhide (1962)

"The Peddler," a 1962 episode of *Rawhide* (CBS), reintroduced the bumbling comic peddler with comedian Shelley Berman as Mendel Sorkin, a down-on-his-luck Jewish immigrant from Holland. Sorkin, in Old World garb, tries to push cattle from his cart carrying "buttons, lace, thread, garters, peppermint, candles, plates, pots," and, most prominently, "firearms." When the dust settles, the cows have run off, the wagon has lost a wheel, and the goods have been strewn all around. Taking pity on the foreigner, trail boss Gil Favor (Eric Fleming) and a few of his men help Sorkin fix his wagon and take him back to their camp. All the while, Sorkin tries to sell them tchotchkes with a Borscht Belt delivery.

The episode's teachable moments are done through Berman's delightful comedy. He mishears the cook's assistant, Mushy, introduce himself. "Moishe? Are you Jewish?" "Well, I don't think—," Mushy replies. "Be proud of your heritage, Moishe. You come from a proud people." When he calls himself a schlimazel, Rowdy Yates (Clint Eastwood) asks what that means: "If a schlimazel kills a chicken, it walks. If he winds a clock, it stops." The cowboys are captivated by the smell of schmaltz and onions from Sorkin's Shabbat dinner. Perturbed by their preference for Sorkin's delicacies, the camp cook, Wishbone (Paul Brinegar), prepares a new dish: helzel (stuffed chicken neck) and knishes. Sorkin also teaches the cowboys to say "Mazel tov." More stereotypically, he guilts the entire camp into buying knickknacks to send home to their mothers.

There are serious themes as well. Sorkin, who has spent ten unsuccessful years in America, talks of returning to Holland: "I'm a stranger here—an outsider. My ways are different, my prayers are different. What I'm trying to say is I've got nobody to belong to, nobody who belongs to me, no roots." While acclimation and adjustment were hallmarks of Jewish pioneers and made their outsider status less pronounced, not every pioneer was successful financially or socially. In a pivotal scene, Sorkin sidetracks the cattle run without disclosing his motives. As it turns out, he is intent on visiting the grave of his recently deceased friend Samuel Friedman, with whom he had planned to return to Holland: "He was a stranger in this country too." Initially upset about the lost time, the cowboys learn that the alternate route had sent them around a skirmish between some farmers and Native Americans. "Why, that little son-of-a-gun," Yates chuckles. "He probably figured if we knew there was a war, we'd want to get right in the fight. Bet that's why he didn't say anything."

Meanwhile, Sorkin has become friendly with a beautiful Indigenous woman who works for and is brutally mistreated by a store owner who had been married to the woman's mother before her death. While visiting the store to collect money he is owed, Sorkin hears the man beating the woman, rescues her, and takes her to the camp. At the end of the episode, the two decide to get married. Sorkin finally feels at home in America. "Home is where your love is," he smiles. "It doesn't matter if it's Amsterdam or Laredo or a wigwam." As the couple rides off to an Eastern Europe–infused score, Yates tells Favor, "One of these days we're gonna run across an Indian, and he's gonna raise his hand and say 'Mazel tov,' and we're gonna know it's one of the Mendel Sorkin tribe."

The episode's treatment of intermarriage as an uncomplicated solution to the characters' outsider status is intriguing. Sorkin the Jew is self-consciously unacclimated to the Plains, and his bride is an Indigenous woman who lives away from her tribe. Marriages between Jewish men and Native women were not wholly uncommon, and Jews could usually remain Jewish in Indian Country. Yet those who made this choice tended to be less traditionally observant and more flexible in their Jewish identities.[24] In "The Peddler," Sorkin remains an Old World Jew after a decade in America and shows signs of strict observance. According to Jonathan and Judith Pearl, this depiction strains believability: "Mendel the immigrant is portrayed as a proud practicing Jew, yet he expresses no difficulty with the idea of intermarrying. Although he may have been compelled to intermarry due to the paucity of Jewish women in the Old West, the absence of any hint of reluctance to do so adds a sense that their match is ideal. Any differences between them are projected as superficial, insignificant, and easily bridgeable, paling in comparison to those that divide them from the outside world. They are perfect mates, scorning a fate of second-class status to find solace with each other in their commonality."[25]

The Pearls cite another simplified endorsement of intermarriage in a *Philco TV Playhouse* segment, "And Crown Thy Good" (NBC, 1954), about the travails of nineteenth-century Dakota settlers and a love story between a daughter of Jewish immigrants and a non-Jewish man from Norway. The story details hardship and loss in the harsh terrain but sweeps aside religious differences and potential controversy. "Their union is presented as a harmonious and hopeful vision, the very essence of a new America to come."[26] *Rawhide* adds the fulfillment of the immigrant wish that by marrying a Native American and being accepted by a tribe, a Jew would be fast-tracked into becoming a *real* American—a more immediate variation of what David Koffman calls "becoming American by imagining the Indian within."[27] The promotion of these "only in America" love stories bespeaks a patriotic romanticism that soon became eclipsed by fears that Jewish intermarriage, which began rising in the mid-1960s, threatened the existence of American Jewry.[28] The countermessage of Jewish endogamy later surfaced in an episode of *Here Come the Brides.*

Wagon Train (1962)

"The Levy-McGowan Story," an episode of *Wagon Train* (NBC, 1962) written by Jewish screenwriter Bob Barbash, deals with ethnic tensions on the trail. After Jewish merchant Simon Levy (Leo Fuchs, a native of what is today Lviv, Ukraine) beats Irish merchant Patrick McGowan (Liam Redmond) at checkers three times in a row, the two develop a not-so-friendly rivalry. Both men are headed with their families to Sacramento, where they will be competitors: Levy intends to open a general store, and McGowan plans to open a livery and harness shop. McGowan is suspicious of the Jew's "cunningness," while Levy dismisses McGowan's lack of education. When Levy finally loses to McGowan at checkers, the Irishman wonders how "an educated scholar" could lose to a "clumsy dumb ox." McGowan also mocks Levy's inexperience with physical labor: "Here I am, a humble, simple-minded soul, trying to tell an educated man of learning" what to do. The men's young sons engage in perpetual wrestling matches, while their older children, Rachel Levy (Lory Patrick) and Sean McGowan (Gary Vinson), fall in love. This is a reversal of the Jewish-Irish romance found in several early films, capped by *Abie's Irish Rose* (Paramount, 1928), in which Jewish men fall for Irish women. Simon Levy, a widower who is not outwardly observant, encourages his daughter to dance with Sean and even joins her for a "country dance" performed to an impromptu klezmer ditty played on banjo, accordion, and violin.

The humorous mood, centered on clashes between Irish working-class values and Jewish smarts, turns dark when villain Frank Lassiter (Paul Birch) blocks the trail, demands a large fee to allow the travelers to pass, and sets a wagon on fire. McGowan, the typical fighting Irishman, wants to press through, but Levy deliberates. "My father's not a coward," Rachel insists. She alludes to pogroms when she says, "You don't know what he's been through." Levy ultimately agrees that they must stand up to Lassiter and his henchmen. In an emotional speech directed at both the onscreen actors and civil-rights-era viewers, Levy convinces the wagon train to join his side:

> I am a Jew and I am proud to be a Jew. But back in the Old Country, there are not too many places where a Jew has the same right as the next man. . . . Don't you know the blessings you have here? All my life, I only had to look for a way to escape, as my father did before me, and his father before him. A place to escape from men who feed on the misery and weakness of others. Men without souls, without human dignity. Terrorists, like this Lassiter. But, no, not here. Here in America you can say a man has the same right as the next man. So here I will not teach my children to look for back doors. And if I have to fight for this, I will fight. With my bare hands if I have to! What this Lassiter did to us tonight, this terrible intimidation, I have lived through before. This, I know about, and I beg you: Please, listen to me. If you pay now, you will be paying men like Lassiter for the rest of your lives! Hear me. I know about these things. I told my children, America means freedom. America means justice, human dignity. . . . How can we show them we were wrong?

McGowan thanks Levy and hands him a rifle. "I've never fired one of these," Levy confesses, "but maybe you can teach me how to load one." The wagon train men chase away the baddies. In gratitude, the two ex-rivals are presented with a sign, "Levy & McGowan, Co. General Store & Livery," enshrining their newfound interethnic harmony and destiny as business partners.

Although the episode's Turneresque image of frontier cooperation is at times overstated, it was used to inspire present-day viewers. A tender scene with Levy and his son drives home the point. When the boy asks if these dangers had followed them across the Atlantic and into the American West, Levy responds, "We said we wouldn't think about what happened back there. It's all in the past. Like another world. Here in America things are different. Here a man works, makes friends, and builds a future. This is a new land, a land where everybody is the same."

Bonanza (1963)

"The Way of Aaron," a 1963 episode of *Bonanza* (NBC), opens with Aaron Kaufman's general merchandise wagon making a sales call to the Cartwright family's Ponderosa Ranch. Kaufman, a pious peddler played by seasoned Austrian Jewish actor Ludwig Donath, is accompanied by his fully Americanized daughter Rebecca (Aneta Corsaut). Adam Cartwright (Pernell Roberts) is immediately attracted to Rebecca, who returns his affection. Like Mendel Sorkin in *Rawhide*, Aaron Kaufman is a strictly observant Jew who permits his daughter to develop a relationship with a non-Jewish man, raising no religious objections. Aaron's only concern is that Adam is not a *lamden* (scholar). Rebecca protests that this classically Jewish ideal gives no thought to "the ruggedness of jaw, stone hardness of his muscle, or strength of his hands. All those things that suddenly seem very attractive to me."

On the Friday ride back to Carson City, the Kaufmans stop their wagon to welcome Shabbat "under the canopy of heaven." Adam, who is also riding to Carson City to invite the Kaufmans to a party at the family ranch, happens upon their makeshift ritual. Watching from a distance, he sees Rebecca pour water on her father's hands and light the candles on a table adorned with challah, wine, fresh fruit, and a fine tablecloth. He hears Rebecca recite the candle blessing and Aaron chant Shabbat prayers with native fluency, although his rendition of a 1918 melody for Shalom Aleichem

("Peace unto You") by Israel Goldfarb, another tune thought to be "eternal folk," is anachronistic in the 1860s setting. Rebecca spots Adam, who appraises the ceremony as "lovely." Unfortunately, two thieves are also watching the rituals. One of the thieves pistol-whips Adam and robs Aaron at gunpoint. The following morning, we see Adam bound and gagged and Aaron shirtless, bloodied, and roped to his wagon in a crucifixion pose reminiscent of Sol Levy in *Cimarron*. The crooks are still there, demanding that Aaron show them where he has hidden the rest of his money. When they untie Aaron, he reaches into a secret compartment, produces a six-shooter, and kills the two men. Aaron is distraught, but Rebecca is proud of her father's sudden machismo. Aaron recovers with the Cartwrights but wishes to return home: "I am a man of strict Orthodox faith. I would be a most difficult guest in your house." Yet in the same soliloquy, he acknowledges what Rebecca has taught him: "This was a new land that welcomes all people and all cultures." He invites Adam to dinner, and Adam responds with a wink, "On one condition. It has to be strictly kosher."

"The Way of Aaron" has several standard Jewish peddler tropes: Old World father, modernizing daughter, Judaism 101, interreligious relationship, and a celebration of American tolerance. Ben Cartwright—the family patriarch played by Jewish actor Lorne Greene and loosely based on Bonanza creator David Dortort's Jewish immigrant father—is especially respectful of Aaron's folkways.[29] Where the episode departs is in making the Kaufmans residents of a modest population center, Carson City (founded in 1858) rather than frontier wanderers. Carson City had enough observant Jews to hold High Holiday services in 1862, and a Hebrew Benevolent Society—typically the first sign of an established Jewish community—was formed there the following year. By the late 1870s, the city's population had grown to around four thousand, including roughly ninety Jews, mostly merchants and their families.[30] Carson City thus constitutes a realistic setting for Aaron Kaufman, who required the amenities of at least a tiny Jewish community as a home base from which to travel his peddling circuit.

The Loner (1965)

The Loner, Rod Serling's ill-fated, single-season follow-up to *The Twilight Zone*, introduced a Jewish merchant in "Westward the Shoemaker" (CBS, 1965). David Opatoshu of 1960's *Cimarron* reprises the role of sweet and good-natured Jewish merchant. This time, he is Hyman Rabinovitch, a late-nineteenth-century Eastern European immigrant who is out of chronology in the mid-nineteenth-century American frontier.

Originally airing late on Saturday nights, *The Loner* is a dialogue-heavy, introspective show intended for older viewers. The titular loner is William Colton (Lloyd Bridges), an ex-captain in the Union cavalry who is wandering the West and who, like Serling, a World War II combat veteran, is haunted by war. The weighty tone and themes generated poor ratings. *TV Guide* critic Cleveland Amory speculated that the show was "either too real for a public grown used to the unreal Western or too adult for juvenile Easterners."[31] As with *The Twilight Zone*, action sequences are used sparingly and the plots mainly deal with moral dilemmas.

Serling was raised in a Jewish family in Syracuse, New York, and was later involved in the Unitarian Community Church of Santa Monica, California, led by Ernest Pipes, a humanist minister whose outlook on politics and humanity resonated with Serling's.[32] As a boy, Serling was "always playing cowboys," and as a young writer he worked on *Have Gun—Will Travel* and other Westerns.[33] *The Twilight Zone* featured a handful of Western- and Civil War–themed episodes, including two peddler-centric stories: "Mr. Denton on Doomsday" (1959), about Al Denton, a guilt-filled former quick-draw who turns to alcohol after killing a teenage challenger, and a mysterious peddler, Henry J. Fate (Malcolm Atterbury), who restores Denton's expert shooting touch; and "Dust" (1961), about Sykes, a verbose peddler (Thomas Gomez) who tricks a distraught and desperate old man, played by Jewish Russian-born actor Vladimir Sokoloff, into buying "magic dust" that "turns hate into love" to save his son from a hanging—and somehow it actually works. Fate is a candidate for coded Jew, described in Serling's introduction as "a peddler, a rather fanciful-looking little man in a black frock coat." However, outside of two episodes dealing with the Holocaust, "Deaths-Head Revisited" (1961) and "He's Alive" (1963), *The Twilight Zone*, as bold as it was—and as much freedom as Serling had to tackle social issues through science-fiction/fantasy conceits—did not feature expressly Jewish characters or themes. It is unclear whether Serling ever intended to do so, but his 1956 *United States Steel Hour* script for "Noon at Doomsday," concerning a "neurotic malcontent" who kills an elderly Jewish pawnshop owner and is acquitted by a small-town jury, was censored. The script was intended as an allegory for the Emmett Till case, but U.S. Steel demanded numerous changes, including the whitewashing of the victim.[34] "The script was gone over with a fine-toothed comb by thirty different people, and I attended at least two meetings a day for over a week, taking down notes as to what had to be changed," Serling explained. "My victim could no longer be anyone as specific as an old Jew. He was to be called an unnamed foreigner, and even this was a concession to me, since the agency felt that there should not really be a suggestion of a minority at all; this was too close to the Till case. Further, it was suggested that the killer in the case was not a psychopathic malcontent—just a good, decent, American boy momentarily gone wrong."[35]

Serling occasionally featured Jewish protagonists in his post–*Twilight Zone* projects. In addition to "Westward the Shoemaker," the *Night Gallery* story "The Messiah on Mott Street" (NBC, 1971) is notable for Edward G. Robinson's performance as a dying, bedridden Jewish man in a snowy New York slum. His grandson believes he has found the healing messiah, played by Black actor Yaphet Kotto. The grandfather miraculously recovers, capping off an uplifting holiday-season tale that mixes Christianity and Judaism, Blacks and Jews, and Christmas and Hanukkah.

In "Westward the Shoemaker," Hyman Rabinovitch is introduced as a frightened foreigner clutching a small bag containing his life's savings. In broken English, he explains that he had been a shoemaker in Latvia before arriving in America a year earlier. He mistakes a group of passing cavalry riders as Cossacks: "Back in Latvia, Cossacks come, burn houses, kill people, kill my grandfather, kill my father. Every time I see uniform, I think Cossacks after Hyman. But I am wrong? Not in America? Not in Wild West? No Cossacks here?" The presence of a Jew from Latvia, then part of the Russian Empire, in the mid-1860s American West is unlikely but not impossible. Historian Oscar Handlin, writing in a 1948 issue of *Commentary*, noted that the 1820–80 period, generally recognized as an era of German Jewish immigration to America, also saw the founding of a Polish synagogue in Boston in the 1840s; in addition, nearly half of New York's synagogues attracted Eastern European Jews in the early 1860s, and many of the "German Jews" were actually Czech or Hungarian.[36] Still, Rabinovitch's *Fiddler on the Roof*–inspired appearance and affectations are a historical stretch.

Back in New York, a man had convinced Rabinowitz to head to the West, where "everybody needs shoes." Rabinowitz sold the man a family ring for $400, planning to use the money to start a shoe business. When Rabinowitz reaches the frontier town, he is waiting outside an empty store for the owner to return when a gambler invites him for a beer in a saloon across the street. Rabinowitz becomes drunk and is coaxed into betting and losing his entire fortune. Colton enters the game and wins the money back, only to discover that the money is worthless Confederate bills. Feeling sorry for the devastated immigrant, the store owner lowers the price of the property and the men standing around the card table contribute coins.

The episode does more than recycle the old trope of the cowboy hero rescuing the helpless Jew: Rabinowitz's good nature and naive optimism are his salvation. His despair brings out the best in the rugged townsmen and sprinkles a bit of hope into Serling's generally dark view of the world. Rabinowitz opens his shoe store as cavalrymen ride by, with Colton offering a reminder: "Not Cossacks; not any more." "Not any more," agrees Rabinowitz; "not in America."

The Wild Wild West (1966)

An unusual example of Jews in Western TV comes from the science-fiction espionage series *The Wild Wild West* (CBS). "The Night of the Druid's Blood" (1966) guest stars Jewish insult comic Don Rickles as Asmodeus (Hebrew: Ashmedai), the king of demons in Jewish lore who, like Puck in Shakespeare's *A Midsummer Night's Dream*, acts as a mischievous prankster.[37] In the episode, directed by veteran Jewish television director Ralph Senensky, Jim West (Robert Conrad) is called on by his old archaeology professor (Don Beddoe), who relates an encounter with the beautiful Lilith (Ann Elder) during an excavation at a Sumerian site. She turns out to be the evil Lilith of Mesopotamian and Jewish mythology, depicted variously as a primordial demon, as the evil reflection of God's feminine aspect, and as Adam's rebellious first wife.[38] The scene ends with her photograph bursting into flames and the professor combusting along with it. Senator Waterford (Bartlett Robinson), who had recently married Lilith—now calling herself Astarte (a Canaanite goddess of sex and war)—bars West from investigating the case.[39] As the plot thickens, we discover that Asmodeus, Lilith, and the sinister Dr. Tristam (Rhys Williams) are harnessing the collective power of brains harvested from distinguished scientists. Rickles's Asmodeus, appearing as a New York magician, performs a number of tricks in the episode, which was the first in the series to deal with the occult.[40] His usual wisecracking persona is restrained, but there is enough Catskills bite to turn the ancient Jewish demon into a modern Jew.[41]

West's series sidekick, Artemus Gordon, a master of gadgets and disguises played by Jewish actor Ross Martin, can be seen as a hip, updated, thinly coded "clever Jew." His adeptness at theatrical role-playing in particular was a staple of Jewish comedy and an essential real-life skill for Jews adapting to new and often-hostile times and places.[42]

The Big Valley (1967)

Legendary comedian Milton Berle guest stars in "A Flock of Trouble," a 1967 episode of *The Big Valley*—one of two ABC Westerns (the other was *The Rifleman*) from the Jewish production company founded by Jules V. Levy, Arthur Gardner, and Arnold Laven, who met in the Air Force's First Motion Picture Unit during World War II. Without a hint of comedy, Berle plays Josiah Freeman, who intentionally loses a game of cards to Nick Barkley (Peter Breck) and pays up with some sheep. Freeman has a plan to combine their flocks, share Barkley's sheepdog, and let him and his niece, whose parents died in a barn fire, join Freeman on his ranch. The episode highlights feuds between shepherds and cattlemen, with cowboys attacking Freeman and ridiculing tough-guy Barkley. Barkley eventually teams up with Freeman against the bad guys who want to rid the valley of sheep.

Freeman's Jewishness is both present and absent in the episode. On the one hand, he is played by a well-known Jew, Milton Berle; wears glasses; hatches a clever scheme; spends his spare time reading; sells goods from a wagon ("Josiah Freeman's Mobile Emporium"); puts on perfume and carries a purse (signaling effeminateness); and quotes from the Bible: "He that is slow to anger is better than the mighty" (Prov. 16:2). On the other hand, he is a shepherd (only rarely a Jewish pioneer trade), has a very blond niece, is handy with a rifle, lacks an accent and distinguishing attire, and has a surname that may or may not be an Anglicization of Friedman(n).[43] The downplaying of one's Jewishness was common in the real Wild West, making this depiction somewhat more accurate than others. But vagueness and subtlety were not hallmarks of Western series, and it is possible that Freeman's original Jewishness was minimized or negotiated out in the writers' room.

Here Come the Brides (1968)

Here Come the Brides (ABC, 1968–70) was loosely based on Asa Mercer's 1860s effort to bring marriageable women from the East Coast to Seattle. A first-season episode, "A Jew Named Sullivan" (1968), centers on a frustrated young woman, Rachel Miller (Linda Marsh), who resolves to return east because there are "no Jews here in Seattle." The matter is discussed over cards by some of the townsmen, one of whom quips, "I worked for a Jew once in California. Kominsky, his name was. He was just like they all are. Stingiest man I ever met." William Sullivan (Daniel J. Travanti) elbows the man in the ribs and leaves with a bottle of sweet Concord grape wine he had ordered for Passover. (Manischewitz is not named, but this seems like an anachronistic nod to the kosher brand, which did not enter the wine business until 1947, when it began lending its name to syrupy wine produced by the Monarch company.)[44] Sullivan later shares that his Jewish mother had married an Irishman—an anomalous Irish-Jewish coupling in that the woman is Jewish. Meanwhile, other aspirational brides make Jew-phobic remarks to and about Rachel. The episode ends with Sullivan and Rachel marrying after a rocky courtship. Prior to the wedding, Rachel bathes in a makeshift mikvah barrel (which may or may not be connected to the requisite running spring or well). The wedding has the customary chuppah, ring ceremony, and breaking of glass, with Captain Clancy (Henry Beckman) presiding from a book emblazoned with the Hebrew word *siddur*—a prayer book of daily liturgical services that rarely if ever contains the wedding ceremony.

Throughout the episode, there are moments when non-Jewish characters are introduced to Jewish customs, learn the basics of keeping kosher, discover that Hebrew is read right to left, and realize the wrongness of their inherited bigotry. But the real message seems to be aimed at Jewish viewers. Directed by Jerrold Bernstein, the episode addresses growing concerns about Jewish intermarriage rates, which Jewish commentators and community leaders began calling a crisis in the mid-1960s.[45] Jewish viewers, who were no doubt pleased by the positive representation, also heard Rachel confess, "When I came out here . . . I knew that I wouldn't meet any Jewish men. But I said, 'Well, I won't be Jewish anymore.' And I thought I could do it, too. I was never the most Jewish girl in my family. But it meant more to me than I knew. It's a history. It's where I come from. And my mother. And her mother before her, and on back thousands and thousands of years. I'm proud of that. I can't turn my back on it."

In 1968, the same year "A Jew Named Sullivan" aired, psychologist Louis Berman's book *Jews and Intermarriage: A Study in Personality and Culture* joined a chorus of writings pathologizing intermarried Jews as status-seeking assimilators who despised their parents.[46] Marshall Sklare, a prominent Jewish sociologist and Conservative movement loyalist, painted intermarried Jews as selfish rebels who called "into question the very basis on which American Jewish life has proceeded—that Jewish survival is possible in an open society."[47] Some Jewish observers went so far as to call intermarriage a "silent Holocaust."[48] In the episode, Rachel confesses and overcomes these alleged personality flaws, an implicit nudge to young Jewish viewers to discover Rachel's renewed sense of pride, which invariably leads to endogamy.

In reality, throughout the nineteenth century, marriage between Jews and non-Jews was fairly common in sparsely populated areas of the West, especially when compared to urban centers where prospective Jewish partners were more numerous.[49] Seattle had a total population of just 188 in 1860 and 1,151 in 1870, roughly when *Here Come the Brides* is set, furthering the impression that the episode's intermarriage stance reflected contemporary concerns more than historical facts.[50]

Gunsmoke (1973)

Jews appear in "This Golden Land," a 1973 episode of *Gunsmoke* (CBS) written by Jewish writer, producer, and director Hal Sitowitz. The episode earned a National Media Award from the National Conference of Christians and Jews for its exploration of religious tensions. Sitowitz specialized in topical and socially relevant television. He produced "Cliffy," a 1975 episode of the police procedural series *The Rookies* (ABC) about a mentally challenged man who witnesses a murder, dreams of being a policeman, and is harassed by his prejudiced neighbors. Sitowitz also wrote the 1977 television movie *In the Matter of Karen Ann Quinlan* (NBC), based on the true story of New Jersey parents who must decide whether to keep their comatose daughter on life support or let her die with dignity; directed the 1979 television movie *A Cry for Help* (ABC), about a suicidal seventeen-year-old teenage girl; and cowrote the 1983 made-for-TV movie *The Face of Rage* (ABC), a documentary-style drama set in a rehabilitation facility where rapists are confronted face-to-face by their victims.

The *Gunsmoke* episode centers on a Russian Jewish farmer, Moshe Gorofsky (Paul Stevens), who has purchased a Kansas farm. The Gorofsky family wagon breaks a wheel on the ride to the farm, and the two older sons, Laibel (Joseph Hindy) and Gearshon (a young Richard Dreyfuss), go off to find materials to fix the wheel. Meanwhile, three drunken brothers interrupt Moshe and his youngest son, Semel (Scott Selles), as they are praying next to the broken wagon. "What kind of praying you call that?" mocks one of the hooligans. "Why they have them little boxes on their heads for?" The scene escalates with the boy being lassoed and dragged off. The Gorofskys retrieve the badly injured Semel, who later dies in the town hospital. His parents and two brothers tear pieces of their clothes; the father recites in Hebrew, "Blessed is the true judge"; and they bury Semel with the Mourner's Kaddish—all according to Jewish custom.

Moshe, who saw his son being roughed up but nothing lethal, hesitates to cooperate with the investigation, citing the Talmud's requirement that one who testifies must be an eyewitness. The strictness of this ruling is expressed in Sanhedrin 37b: "If you saw the accused pursuing the victim into a ruin (where no other person is likely to be lurking), and you ran after them, and you found the accused holding a sword dripping blood and the victim in the throes of death—know that you have witnessed nothing." Gearshon, who disagrees with his father's pacifism and old-fashioned stance, buys a shotgun and attempts to take matters into his own hands. "A gun," Moshe fuses, "like a Cossack?" Tensions rise between the Gorofskys and the xenophobic hoodlums, who tell Moshe to "get out of Kansas." Marshal Matt Dillon (James Arness) tries and fails to convince Moshe to identify the killer. The perpetrator ultimately confesses to Moshe that Semel broke away, tripped on the rope, and cracked his skull on a rock. Moshe reports the confession to Dillon, who agrees to charge the brothers with assault. Moshe says he will testify if needed.

"The Golden Land" is an effective exploration of frontier justice and differing cultural conceptions of law and order. Departing from the knee-jerk capital punishment typically carried out in Old West tales, the episode offers a Talmud-based revisionist critique of virtuous violence. Through his reliance on age-old wisdom, Moshe teaches Gearshon—and the viewers at home—that true justice requires thoughtful deliberation and is often more nuanced and complex than a bullet or noose.

Little House on the Prairie (1979, 1981)

In "The Craftsman," a 1979 episode of *Little House on the Prairie*, young Albert Ingalls (Matthew Labyorteaux) becomes an apprentice to Jewish immigrant craftsman Isaac Singerman, portrayed by Polish-born Jewish actor John Bleifer. Singerman requires an apprentice after his adult son, Aaron (Alvin Kupperman), reluctantly leaves his father for New York, where he has an arranged marriage. Singerman teaches Albert to take pride in his work, and the boy becomes Singerman's defender against the prairie's many bigots.

The episode was directed by the show's Jewish star, Michael Landon, and scripted by Paul Wolff, who went on to teach screenwriting at the University of Southern California, become a certified maggid (Jewish storyteller), and work with Jewish seniors and Jews in recovery in Los Angeles.[51] Wolff recalls that when "The Craftsman" was in production, Landon's "Jewish *neshamah*" (soul) was pining for expression, and he jumped at the opportunity to direct the episode. In *Over the Top Judaism*, an exploration of TV depictions of Jews and Jewish practice, Rabbi Elliot B. Gertel calls "The Craftsman" "the best television episode ever with a Jewish theme" and "a masterpiece of insight into the Jewish soul." Gertel's appraisal itself might be over the top, but his point is that the episode's sincerity and attention to detail outshine the usual tokenism. He is especially moved by how the story builds scenes around Jewish concepts: "Singerman teaches the boy the meaning of the Jewish concept of compassion or '*rachmones*.' . . . The word is actually used and the concept nicely explained on the show. He illustrates this Jewish value-concept by taking the little boy to visit an elderly Gentile neighbor whose walking cane was broken by some rowdy children. Singerman brings the man a new cane. Since the neighbor is too poor to buy it, the old Jew 'trades' the cane for some worthless article, thus carrying out the Rabbinic teaching that the best way to give charity is to make the poor person feel that he is somehow giving something in return. The boy is most impressed by this object lesson in *rachmones*."[52]

Singerman also plants an oak tree in return for using wood, knowing that he will not be around to see the tree grow to maturity. This is an allusion to the Talmudic tale of Choni (Taanit 23a), who witnesses a man planting a carob tree. Choni asks, "This tree, after how many years will it bear fruit?" The man replies, "It will not have fruit until seventy years have passed." Choni is puzzled: "Is it obvious to you that you will live seventy years, that you expect to benefit from this tree?" The man says, "Just as my ancestors planted for me, I too am planting for my descendants." When Singerman dies at the end of the story, Albert plants an acorn, in keeping with his mentor's teaching. Less genuine is the score's use and Singerman's singing of "Oyfn Pripetshik," yet another thought-to-be folk song that was actually written by Yiddish poet and composer Mark Warshavsky in 1899, long after the episode's 1870s setting.[53]

"The Craftsman" also exposes antisemitism as small-minded ignorance. When gruff farmer Jud Larrabee (Don "Red" Barry) sees Singerman and his son arrive at the general store, he scoffs, "Here come the Heebs. Hold your nose and hold onto your wallets." Harriet Oleson (Katherine MacGregor), whose antisemitism resurfaces two seasons later when her daughter, Nellie (Alison Arngrim), marries a Jewish man, laughs approvingly at these remarks. Albert is taunted by his classmates, including Nellie, for spending so much time with Singerman. Their bigoted barbs are consistently disproved by Singerman's kindness and humanity. Whereas Singerman teaches compassion through his actions, Landon, playing Albert's father, Charles, delivers the compulsory moralizing, telling Albert, "If you don't speak up to people—bigots—then you're no better than they are. Worse, in fact, because you know that it's wrong and you allow them to think that you feel the same way they do."

"Come, Let Us Reason Together" (1981), another *Little House* episode directed by Landon, has none of the gentle subtleties of "The Craftsman." Lacking Wolff's light touch, the writers (Carole and Michael Raschella) go broad, making the main bigot, Harriet Oleson, loud and proud in her Jew hatred and the Jewish visitors, Benjamin Cohen (E. M. Margolese) and his wife Edna (Bea Silvern), rigidly tied to the "old ways."

The theme of intermarriage again takes central stage, now set against an early 1980s backdrop. The decade was predicted (and proved to be) one of accelerated Jewish intermarriage, with "continuity" advocates demanding that non-Jewish spouses convert. A 1979 national study concluded that "most non-Jewish spouses do not convert to Judaism; the level of Jewish content and practice in mixed marriages is low; only about one-third of the Jewish partners in such marriages view their children as Jewish; and most such children are exposed to little by way of Jewish culture or religion."[54] These contemporary intermarriage concerns are projected onto the prairie. The Cohens arrive from New York, accompanied by the familiar strains of "Oyfn Pripetshik," to ensure that their son's soon-to-be-born child is raised Jewish even though the baby's mother is not of the faith. (According to strict Jewish law, only children born to Jewish mothers are considered Jewish, but that fact goes unmentioned in the episode.) Harriet Oleson is equally determined to preserve the child's Christian identity. Her son-in-law, Percival (Steve Tracey), has changed his surname to Dalton, making his Jewishness "the best kept secret in town," but the presence of his extroverted, Old World parents threatens to reveal that secret. Harriet is in a tizzy: "Cohen, Cohen. . . . I wonder if they look different. . . . Those hook noses and those beady eyes." Her husband, Nels (Richard Bull), remains a levelheaded voice of reason and tolerance, which only exacerbates Harriet's hysterics. When Harriet fumes and complains that she is "sick and tired of him trying to shove his religion down my throat" because Benjamin has affixed a mezuzah (which Harriet calls a "medusa") to a doorway, Nels calmly explains the custom. Benjamin Cohen, who has anger-management issues and a bad heart, is similarly upset by his son's decision to submerge his Jewish roots: "Understand, my son: We Jews must survive. Since the beginning of time, other men have tried to destroy us." Percival responds, "Papa, people are enlightened now. That kind of craziness won't happen again. It's almost the twentieth century." These words, however, are undermined by Percival's earlier admission that locals would not hire him if they knew he was Jewish as well as by what viewers know about the twentieth century's genocidal antisemitism.

Other inconsistencies plague the episode. When the Cohens first greet the Olesons, Benjamin gives Harriet an emphatic hug and kiss on the cheek. Narratively, this physical contact heightens Harriet's discomfort, but it goes against the Jewish law of *negiah*, which forbids such contact with a member of the opposite sex aside from one's spouse or close relative. When the traditionally observant Cohens have dinner at the Olesons' home—an unlikely occurrence—Benjamin is dumfounded to learn that they mix milk with meat but has no trouble drinking their nonkosher wine or eating vegetables from a nonkoshered plate. Edna Cohen later eats nonkosher cake with Harriet. On Shabbat morning, Benjamin secures the local church for a private service for him and Percival—an act that is both unrealistic (an Orthodox Jew would not likely pray in a church) and unnecessary (the two men are well short of a minyan and do not require a public prayer space). Moreover, they sing the Shema, an affirmation of God's oneness, to a melody that is commonly thought to be European (often attributed to nineteenth-century Viennese cantor Salomon Sulzer) but was first published in the American Reform movement's *Union Hymnal* in 1932.[55]

"Come, Let Us Reason Together" does have a few amusing moments that lampoon bigotry. Harriet complains to Nels, "Could you imagine my daughter giving birth to a Jew? Could you imagine what that child would be like? Nervy and greedy and pushy. Always after food and cheap, cheap, cheap!" "If what you say about the way they act is true," Nels says glibly, "then you must be Jewish." But the solution to the child-of-intermarriage problem is so absurd that not even the most desperate 1980s alarmist would entertain it. The grandparents agree that if the baby is a boy, he will be raised Jewish, but if it is a girl, she will be raised Christian. Everyone is delighted when the baby turns out to be twins: a girl and a boy. Imagining the messiness of how these children would be reared flies in the face of Benjamin's warning to Percival: "Your child must not be confused."

I Married Wyatt Earp (1983)

In 1983, NBC aired a television movie adaptation of *I Married Wyatt Earp*, starring Marie Osmond as Josephine Marcus Earp, the Jewish common-law wife of the famed lawman and gambler. The best-selling 1976 book on which it is based, *I Married Wyatt Earp: The Recollections of Josephine Sarah Marcus*, initially gained acceptance as a genuine memoir and a faithful portrayal of Josie's life with Earp, whom she met in Tombstone, Arizona, in 1881.[56] Its editor, amateur history buff Glenn G. Boyer, quickly rose in the ranks of Earp scholars. But in 1994 the book was revealed as a fraud, or what Boyer later admitted was "100 percent Boyer." "This is an artistic effort," he said defensively. "I don't have to adhere to the kind of jacket that these people are putting on me. I am not a historian. I'm a storyteller." Boyer refused to let others access source documentation and could not prove the existence of the so-called Clum manuscript that detailed the Earps' life in Tombstone. In addition, the publisher, University of Arizona Press, apparently was aware of Boyer's embellishments of the account.[57]

Boyer's creative liberties were in keeping with Josie's tendency to invent and embroider. For example, she claimed that her father was a successful German Jewish businessman in New York City when in fact he was a modest Prussian baker. She said she was raised in a prosperous Jewish community when she actually lived in a crowded, multiethnic, working-class neighborhood polluted by factory smoke.[58] Her family relocated to San Francisco in 1868, when she was seven years old. She ran off to Arizona at age thirteen or fourteen, joining a theatrical troupe, becoming a prostitute, or both. Josie was evasive about her life in Tombstone from around 1874 to 1882, preventing novelists, historians, and screenwriters from attempting reconstructions.[59] As a result, Boyer, writing three decades after her death, had an opening in which to invent gap-filling details. This hazy period, based on Boyer's largely fictitious account, forms the basis of the made-for-TV movie.

When the movie version of *I Married Wyatt Earp* aired, it was thought to be a corrective in ongoing debates about whether Earp was a hero or a gangster. After Wyatt's death, Josie defended her husband's reputation against the unflattering accounts of various biographers. *I Married Wyatt Earp* is very much in that apologetic vein. What attracted and continues to attract Jews to Josie's story is the fact that she and Wyatt are buried side by side in a Jewish cemetery. As Harriet and Fred Rochlin write in *Pioneer Jews*, "Told and retold, stories of the legendary couple continue to draw devotees and detractors. Wyatt died in 1929, Josie fifteen years later. Both are buried in the Marcus family plot in the Hills of Eternity Memorial Park, in Colma, near San Francisco. Theirs is the most visited gravesite in the Jewish cemetery."[60]

The movie begins with Josie visiting Earp's tombstone and narrating her intention of "setting the record straight"—specifically about events leading up to the fabled gunfight at the O.K. Corral. In the movie as in real life, Josie's Jewish identity is mostly hidden. This seems to be a by-product of her penchant for reinvention rather than internalized Jew hatred (she was, after all, buried in a Jewish cemetery). The only exceptions are scenes involving Jacob Spiegler, played by Ross Martin of *The Wild Wild West* fame, a Jewish hardware store proprietor who had known Josie's father in New York and came from the same German town. Wearing a skullcap and speaking through a thick accent, Spiegler hands Josie a letter from her father and invites her to live with Spiegler and his wife. Later, Josie asks Wyatt to dinner at the Spiegler residence, but he politely declines. These brief scenes, along with an opening scene in the cemetery, serve as sentimental reminders of the home and heritage Josie had left behind.

Dr. Quinn, Medicine Woman (1994)

In 1994, *Dr. Quinn, Medicine Woman* (CBS) added "The First Christmas" to televised Western Jewish lore. Airing more than thirty years after the frontier Jew had first graced TV screens and more than ten years after his last appearance, the episode keeps alive a number of tropes: an out-of-place Eastern European Hasidic Jewish family, lessons about Jewish customs, America as a land of opportunity, and antisemitism dissolving into loving acceptance. However, with this chronological distance came depleted authenticity in the acting and script. Unlike previous peddlers, Bruce Nozick, who plays Itzhak Frankel, is not himself an immigrant, and his unconvincing accent and imitative mannerisms suggest little or no direct exposure to Yiddish or Jewish religious culture. In one scene, he mispronounces the blessing for the Hanukkah menorah, saying "elocheinu" instead of "eloheinu" ("our God"). The episode's scripter, William Schmidt, is similarly disconnected from the type's source material. When Frankel sells wares from his overstuffed wagon, he simply repeats "Customers come here" rather than the detailed litany of items chanted by his predecessors, notably George E. Stone's Sol Levy.

Anachronisms are also present. *Dr. Quinn* begins in 1867, when Colorado Springs's miniscule Jewish population was predominantly of Central European background.[61] Eastern European Orthodox Jews did not arrive there until several decades later. Frankel sells "very sturdy" denim pants from "a man in San Francisco," though Levi Strauss and Jacob Davis did not patent their blue jeans until 1873. The story, which takes place during the Christmas season, suggests that Eastern European Jews were completely unaware of Christmas. A town boy, Brian Cooper (Shawn Toovey), explains to Frankel's son Aaron (J. D. Daniels) what a manger is and who Jesus was, even though Hasidic Jews in Europe had long engaged in superstitious Christmas Eve (Nittel Nacht) customs intended to ward off evil spirits and ensure that the Christian messiah was not glorified.[62] More believable is the Jewish boy explaining to the town boy what a kippah is—one of the episode's many forays into Judaism 101.

The drama of "The First Christmas" concerns prejudiced shopkeeper Loren Bray (Orson Bean) and Mayor Jake Slicker (Jim Knobeloch) conspiring to ban peddling with the not-so-hidden agenda of driving out the Jewish family. Frankel presents his case to the town council: "We came here because we are looking for a home. We will work hard, we will help others. We will live with you in peace, if you let us. That is all we are asking. Please." When the town council votes against the ban, the mayor asks the reverend how he could support the peddler since "these people killed Jesus." Dr. Quinn, played by Jewish actor Jane Seymour, is a steadfast supporter of the new arrivals. "It's one of the great things about our country," she explains; "we get to meet people of all nations and we learn from each other." She later nurses the Frankels' sick baby back to health and attends a Hanukkah dinner where Frankel recounts the story of the Maccabees. Meanwhile, shopkeeper Bray, who insists that Jews drove his father out of business, organizes a mob to ransack Frankel's wagon, which ends up crashing on top of the peddler. Quinn bandages Frankel, who sighs that his family is leaving town after Hanukkah. The townspeople, under the direction of the benevolent reverend, gather outside the Frankel family dwelling in a show of support. They offer to fix the wagon, promise to buy goods from Itzhak, invite the family to dinner, give them a free subscription to the paper, extend complimentary haircuts, and inform them about a farm that is for sale. Itzhak even gets a business proposition from the all-of-a-sudden unprejudiced Bray. "Why are you doing all this?" Itzhak asks the crowd. The answer: "It's Christmas."

This saccharine message of tolerance revives Frederick Jackson Turner's frontier thesis, reminding viewers that America was built and strengthened on acceptance and cooperation across differences. However, this message is undercut by its presentation as the "Christmas spirit," implying that America's embrace of the Other, real or imagined, is rooted in the benevolence of its Christian hegemony.

Deadwood (2004–2006)

Created by Jewish writer and producer David Milch, *Deadwood* (HBO, 2004–6) is a gritty, profanity-laced, critically acclaimed, multiple-award-winning Western drama set in 1870s Deadwood prior to its annexation by the Dakota Territory. Milch used diaries and local newspapers as reference points for plots and characters. These sources provided information about Jewish merchant Sol Star (John Hawkes), who appears in all thirty-six episodes of the three-season series and its long-awaited conclusion, *Deadwood: The Movie* (HBO Films, 2019). He thus became the first Jewish main cast member in a Western series. Sol's narrative arc mostly follows that of his real-life inspiration. He settles in Deadwood with his Protestant business partner Seth Bullock (Timothy Olyphant) in 1876, becomes a successful businessman, and is elected mayor of the mining town.

The show of course takes some creative liberties—most strikingly Sol Star's romance with brothel girl Trixie (Paula Malcomson) and their eventual

Sol Star, played by John Hawkes, *Deadwood* (HBO, 2004–6).

marriage (in the movie). The real Sol was a lifelong bachelor who died alone on his ranch in 1917. His birthplace of Bavaria is also changed to Vienna in the series, and while census records indicate he spoke both Yiddish and German, his television version has no detectable accent.[63]

In real life, ten-year-old Sol, one of ten children, was sent to live with his mother's brother, a clothing merchant, in Ohio in 1850. At age twenty-five, he left Ohio for Virginia City, Montana, where he ran a clothing store and bank until 1872. In the series, Sol often quotes business maxims from his Viennese father. However, his actual father was a merchant in Bavaria. The historical Sol spent his formative years with his uncle, initially taking up his uncle's clothing trade and making the uncle a more likely business mentor.

Other aspects of Sol's remarkable life are likewise changed or left out of *Deadwood*. For example, in 1872, President Ulysses S. Grant appointed Sol as receiver of the Land Office in Helena, Montana. He then served as Montana's territorial auditor from 1874 to 1875 before forming a hardware and mining supply business with Helena's sheriff, Seth Bullock, and relocating to Deadwood in July 1876. Within a year, Star and Bullock Hardware was fully established, and Sol was named Deadwood's postmaster. By 1879, the partners had extended their business into mining as well as agriculture and raising livestock, then the fastest-growing sector of the local economy. Other business ventures followed. Sol also served as Deadwood's mayor for fourteen years, was twice elected to the South Dakota House of Representatives (1889 and 1892), served a term as a state senator (1893–94), and was elected as Lawrence County clerk of courts in 1889.[64]

Following other Western series, *Deadwood* portrays Sol Star as the only Jew in Deadwood. While this works for dramatic purposes, at least two other European-born Jewish merchants, Jack Goldberg and Sam Schwarzwald, also arrived in Deadwood from Montana in 1876, and three Jews were buried in town's Mount Moriah Cemetery within six months of its establishment in 1878.[65] As many as one-third of Deadwood's businesses were Jewish-run during Sol's time there.[66] During Deadwood's pioneer period, historian Ann Haber Stanton has identified more than three hundred Jewish names in cemetery, business, and social association records; newspapers; and announcements for weddings, funerals, and holidays. In the series, Al Swearengen (Ian McShane), the ruthless proprietor of the Gem Saloon, Deadwood's notorious brothel, incessantly mocks Sol's Jewishness, but he remains calm and levelheaded. While Sol's peacemaking reflects what is known about his real-life personality and participation in civil service, Stanton notes, "In looking for overt antisemitism in newspaper accounts of early Deadwood, with few striking exceptions, one is hard-pressed to find any serious instances of this blight." This absence does not mean that antisemitism did not exist or that there were no vicious individuals; however, according to Stanton, "not only were Jews considered a valued segment of the establishment," but "the community relied on them for fairness, regardless of the nationality of the person with whom they were dealing." And she cites Sol as a prime example of this phenomenon.[67] According to a 1901 biographical sketch of Sol, "Although his interest in public affairs has been so conspicuous, his activity in fraternal affairs has been scarcely less marked. He is a member of the popular Olympic club of Deadwood. He is a member of the Masonic order in which he has reached the thirty-second degree. He is also a Knight of Pythias and a member of the order of Red Men, as well as a member of the Ancient Order of United Workmen. . . . He is just in the prime of life, and whatever good fortune the future has in store for him, there are but few, if any, of whatever social or political position, high or low degree, but will rejoice in his success."[68]

Deadwood's Sol effectively conveys this comfortable acculturation. As *Tablet* magazine's arts and letters columnist Steven Vider notes, "What separates Sol from his on-screen forebears is his ordinariness—the utter lack of comedy or sentiment in Hawkes' portrayal. Played with natural conviction and no accent, Sol might make reference to his German background and his father's favorite maxims, but he never mentions his religion, let alone practices it."[69] Yet even here, the degree of cultural assimilation appears to be a stretch. According to Stanton, the real Sol Star was a Yiddish speaker, likely observed Shabbat in some fashion, was a member of Deadwood's Hebrew congregation, may have had a bar mitzvah or been confirmed, was "most comfortable with the more liberal Reform Judaism," and knew enough Hebrew to read scripture at the funeral of Anna Franklin, the mother of another Jewish Deadwood mayor, Nathan Franklin, who served from 1914 to 1918.[70] Thus, while Sol's television portrayal is dramatically rich, sympathetic, and a welcome departure from earlier caricatures, he is also a Jewishly watered-down departure from the historical record.

CHAPTER 5

Post-Code Westerns

By the 1960s, the Motion Picture Production Code had grown outdated and ineffective. In 1968, after years of gradual liberalization, the Motion Picture Association of America instituted an age-based rating system. This shift coincided with the emergence of ethnic pride movements of the late 1960s and 1970s, which challenged the assimilationist model and brought renewed popular and academic attention to nonwhite groups, including Blacks, Latino/as, Asian Americans, and Native Americans. Celebrations of Jewish distinctiveness joined these precursors of today's multiculturalism, inspired in part by romanticized accounts of Israel's victory in the Six-Day War (1967) but even more so by a general sense that the acculturation of previous generations had gone too far. American Jews could—and should—be proud of their hyphenated identities.[1]

In cinema, the Jewish ethnic revival found "unselfconscious representation" as part of the broader multiethnic and multiracial social landscape, projecting a "post–melting pot and post-assimilatory" message that Jews, as Jews, were "at home" in America.[2] In addition to Jewish jokes and references in the films of Mel Brooks and Woody Allen, *Fiddler on the Roof* (United Artists, 1971) offered a musical wellspring of "ethnic *pride* and cultural heritage." A handful of other movies explored "assimilation and its discontents," including Jewish director Sydney Pollack's *The Way We Were* (Columbia, 1973), a McCarthy-era romantic drama centered on Katie Morosky (Barbra Streisand), a vocal Marxist Jew with antiwar opinions, and her apolitical WASP boyfriend, Hubbell Gardiner (Robert Redford); and Jewish director Paul Mazursky's *Next Stop, Greenwich Village* (Twentieth Century–Fox,

1976), a comedy-drama set in 1953 about Larry Lipinsky (Lenny Baker), a young Jewish man from Brooklyn who dreams of movie stardom.[3]

Still, a general avoidance of Jewish topics and characters persisted in the film industry, outliving the studio system's gradual decline (which began with the 1948 antitrust decision in *United States v. Paramount Pictures, Inc.*, and culminated in the 1960s with the end of huge production facilities and long-term contract personnel). *Crossing Delancey* (Warner Bros., 1988), a romantic comedy about a single woman in Manhattan who meets a man through her grandmother's matchmaker, was rejected by three major studios and fifteen distribution companies.[4] The Isaac Bashevis Singer story *Enemies, a Love Story* (20th Century Fox, 1989), concerning the tangled lives of Holocaust survivors in New York City, received a cold reception, with one executive asking, "Isn't there another Holocaust this film could be about?"[5] *School Ties* (Paramount, 1992), about a closeted Jewish football star at a prep school where antisemitic views are rampant, was turned down by "every studio" and took nine years to reach the screen.[6]

The 1970s also witnessed the rapid decline of Western productions, with their successors, revisionist Westerns, following precipitously into the 1980s. Older tropes were kept alive on long-running small-screen series such as *Bonanza*, *Gunsmoke*, and *Little House on the Prairie*, but theatergoers had largely moved on. Not only did market-driven producers and distributors resist opportunities for Jewish Westerns, but they were unlikely to manifest in a dying genre that had never had more than a little room for Jewish themes or characters.

This chapter examines three Jewish Westerns released between 1979 and 2019. All of them depart from general Western conventions and Jewish Western types in significant ways. *The Frisco Kid* (Warner Bros., 1979) follows the overland trek of a Polish-born rabbi from the East Coast to San Francisco, where he is called to serve as spiritual leader. While the main characters, wide-eyed Rabbi Avram Belinski (Gene Wilder) and good-hearted outlaw Tommy Lillard (Harrison Ford), are purely fictional, the screenwriters, Michael Elias and Frank Shaw, subscribed to the *Western States Jewish Historical Quarterly* and drew inspiration from its articles on Jewish pioneer farmers, merchants, and traders and on the San Francisco community. Pulling from that research, they used comical vignettes to present a historically grounded tale about little-known aspects of the American

Jewish experience with the goal of engendering Jewish American pride and raising awareness of the Jews' role in developing the country. In Elias's words, Jews "had never seen ourselves on screen as participants and contributors to American culture," let alone the formation of the American West.[7] These aims were better achieved in the original screenplay, which, in addition to unfilmed scenes involving Rabbi Belinski's encounters with Jewish settlers and more realistic interactions with Native Americans, is more tonally consistent and thematically clear than the notoriously all-over-the-place film.

The Steven Spielberg–produced animated adventure *Fievel Goes West* (Universal, 1991), a sequel to *An American Tail* (Universal, 1986), is about a boy mouse, Fievel Mousekewitz, his family, and other immigrant mice. The mice relocate from New York tenements to the Wild West in hopes of a better life. Less effective than its predecessor, the movie offers little more than a change of scenery: despite promises to the contrary, the cats on the frontier are just as terrifying and mouse-hungry as those in the crowded cities, an allegory for the virulent and ever-lurking specter of antisemitism. The film, which is almost all action, misses an opportunity to explore how the West actually was different for pioneer Jews, who faced less antisemitism and were much better integrated into frontier towns and fledgling cities than Jews in most parts of Europe or the East Coast. In the *Fievel* film, this important difference is replaced by what some see as a foreshadowing of *Schindler's List* (Universal, 1993) with trains that transport hopeful mice to desert "death camps."[8] On the positive side, the movie gives a glimpse at Jewish family and group migration, which is rarely seen or acknowledged in film or television depictions of Jewish settlers and pioneers.

Finally, filmmaker Kelly Reichardt's 2019 film, *First Cow* (A24), is a decidedly antimacho Western set in the Oregon Territory during the 1820s. Reichardt is known for her sensitive, low-key depictions of working-class characters in rural settings, and in *First Cow*, Cookie Figowitz, a mild-mannered Jewish cook, has traveled West with a band of fur trappers and befriends a Chinese immigrant. In addition to shifting attention to ethnic characters who are at best bit players in standard cowboy shoot-'em-ups, the film uses these unconventional men to show the daily hardships and unsettling tranquility of the undeveloped Pacific Northwest, revealing personal tragedies papered over by the American dream mythology.

The Frisco Kid (1979)

By a strict definition, *The Frisco Kid* (Warner Bros., 1979) is the only truly Jewish Western movie and thus warrants more space than the other examples in this book.[9] Not only does it include "significant content and characters related to Jewish life," but it also discusses "what it means to be Jewish."[10] With veteran Western director Robert Aldrich at the helm, the movie follows young Polish rabbi Avram Belinski (Gene Wilder), who arrives in Philadelphia, travels through a number of loosely connected Western vignettes, and arrives in San Francisco, where he is hired to lead a new congregation. Along the way, he befriends a compassionate outlaw, Tommy Lillard (Harrison Ford), setting up an odd-couple buddy comedy that upends clichés associated with Old West Jews. Belinski's odyssey is one of inward transformation, a spiritual quest, whereas Lillard, the Gentile cowboy, is on a financial quest, thereby challenging the notion that Jews ventured to the Far West solely to exploit the Gold Rush: as co-screenwriter Michael Elias puts it, "Miners mined the mines, but Jews mined the miners."[11] Elias sought to show how Jewish settlers—even those with more observant backgrounds—adjusted their beliefs and practices as they traversed a vast landscape that lacked a Jewish infrastructure (ready access to kosher food, mikvahs, synagogues, and so forth). Rabbi Belinski's experience affirms the thesis, articulated most recently by Shari Rabin in *Jews on the Frontier*, that migration

Harrison Ford and Gene Wilder in *The Frisco Kid* (Warner Bros., 1979).

and opportunity in the American West resulted in practical and organic changes to Jewish religious identity: "Their religious lives—and those they encountered—were not cases of secularization, assimilation, or Protestantization, but rather were reactions to the profound effects of their unfettered mobility."[12] In Elias's vision, this phenomenon provided a powerful metaphor for American Jewish identity writ large.[13]

The Frisco Kid opens with Belinski leaving Poland and arriving in Philadelphia, small Torah in tow, expecting to board another ship to California. In addition to the rabbinic position, he is promised marriage to Sarah Mindl (Beege Barkette), the elder daughter of Samuel Bender (Jack Somack), leader of San Francisco's Jewish community. Unfortunately, all the ships have already sailed off with gold rushers. Naive and inexperienced, Belinski is taken in by three con artists, brothers Matt and Darryl Diggs (William Smith and George DiCenzo) and their partner Mr. Jones (Ramon Bieri), who trick him into paying for a wagon going west. The wagon veers from the convoy and Belinski is beaten, robbed, and left stranded. After gathering his clothing and precious Torah scroll, he finds a group of Amish men, mistaking them for his Hasidic kinsmen. He recuperates among the Amish, who respect him as a holy man and buy him a train ticket.

Belinski is oblivious when Lillard holds up the train. We next find the rabbi toiling alongside multiethnic railroad workers. Unaccustomed to physical labor, he accidently bludgeons an imposing Italian worker. In spite of this ineptitude, the affable Belinski wins over his victim and his Chinese sidekick, who see Belinski off on a horse purchased with his earnings.

A short while later, raccoons plunder Belinski's makeshift campsite. Lillard spots the rabbi in a creek, struggling to stab fish with a stick. Lillard shoots two fish, and the two men bond over a campfire and roasted trout.

The rabbi and cowboy ride off together, establishing the familiar road-movie pair of an innocent protagonist and hardened companion. Their conflicting outlooks and behaviors make for humorous and dramatic moments, and the pair ultimately humanize each other. For example, after Lillard robs a bank on a Friday, he learns that Jewish law prohibits riding a horse on Shabbat, so Belinski, an Orthodox Jew, will not ride the following day, even with a hanging posse pursuing them. Belinski finally compromises, agreeing to ride after the sun dips below an adjacent mountaintop instead of waiting for the official end of Shabbat when three stars appear in the sky, a key moment in Belinski's negotiation of identity.[14] Later, when the duo is caught in a snowstorm, the macho Lillard invites Belinski to snuggle up to generate warmth. Following an encounter with Native Americans and an overdosing of a hallucinogenic plant, the rabbi recovers at a Trappist monastery.[15] Tommy accompanies him there, sighing maternally, "You had me really worried."

Stopping in a town near San Francisco (San Jose in the original screenplay), Belinski finds a Wells Fargo office and returns his half of the money Lillard stole from the bank.[16] Lillard storms off into a nearby saloon. When Belinski enters hours later he sees the Diggs brothers and Jones and demands that they return his money. He again takes a beating but is rescued by a half-dressed Lillard, who emerges from the upstairs brothel, gun in hand, and forces the con artists to give back the money.

With San Francisco now in sight, Belinski and Lillard declare their friendship on a sandy beach. Their joyous mood is interrupted by the revenge-seeking Diggs brothers and Jones. A shootout ensues, and Belinski rushes to save the Torah, which is nearly consumed by a smoldering campfire. After Lillard has killed Jones and is himself wounded, Belinski reluctantly picks up a gun and shoots Darryl Diggs in self-defense. The rabbi descends into a crisis of faith, believing he cannot be a rabbi after killing someone. Moreover, he is wracked with guilt for having cared more about protecting the Torah than his best friend.

When they reach San Francisco, Belinski dresses in Lillard's clothes and delivers the Torah to the Bender home on the "rabbi's behalf," trying to pull off a Texas accent. There, he meets Rosalie Bender, the younger sister of the woman he is supposed to marry.

Lillard convinces Belinski to stick to his rabbinic calling, reminding him that his actions had saved their lives. Belinski is welcomed by the San Francisco congregation and everything seems to be going well. Then, however, Matt Diggs suddenly challenges Belinski to a duel. The Jewish crowd is shocked to learn that their rabbi has killed a man. Lillard defends him, explaining the heroic circumstances. Belinski refuses to partake in the duel and, with the help of Lillard's pointed gun, exiles Diggs: "I'll take San Francisco. You take the rest of America." The movie ends with Belinski marrying Rosalie, whose sister has fallen for another man.

Originally titled *No-Knife*—a name Belinski receives from Native Americans in the original script because he lacks that weapon—the screenplay was passed around for years before Warner Bros. produced it. (Warner Bros. made an unrelated 1935 film also titled *The Frisco Kid* that starred James Cagney.) As choppily edited and narratively inconsistent as it is, *The Frisco Kid* stands out for its sensitive treatment of Jewish identity. According to Patricia Erens, it is "one of the few films to seriously question the difference between Jewish and American values, finding neither inherently superior. In the end, Avram has to come to terms with a composite system which takes into account both traditions." She further notes that, outside of *Hester Street* (Midwest, 1975), an independent movie, and Yiddish words sprinkled into a few Hollywood films—*Bye Bye Braverman* (Warner Bros., 1968), *Portnoy's Complaint* (Warner Bros., 1972), and *Just Tell Me What You Want* (Warner Bros., 1980)—*The Frisco Kid* was one of the few films of the era to "appreciably use Yiddish."[17]

This nuance is largely lost on non-Jewish critics and Western film buffs, who generally dismiss the movie as a "lame, overlong genre comedy."[18] Roger Ebert thought it was a poorly executed "good idea." "'The Frisco Kid' tries for almost every possible tone," Ebert observed; "it has slapstick (Wilder, on a railroad work gang, consistently slamming his sledgehammer down on the toes of the biggest member of the gang). It has poignancy (Wilder and Ford get to like and respect one another, and it's a shame when they have to part). It has dialect jokes and costume jokes, puns and double entendres, romance (a bride awaits Wilder in San Francisco) and action (Wilder is taken captive by Indians). But what it doesn't have is a consistent comic logic to lead us through its Western smorgasbord."[19]

In *What Ever Happened to Robert Aldrich?*, Alain Silver and James Ursini deride the film as "disconnected," lacking "a dramatic underpinning," and even having an "ironic sub-text" of antisemitism. To them, Belinski, the yeshiva rabbis he leaves behind in Poland, and the San Francisco congregation are little more than "cigar store Jews."[20] In much the same way, Shaina Hammerman's study of Hasidic representations in cinema frames *The Frisco Kid* as a modern take on vaudeville's stage Jew, who played up Yiddish dialects, stereotypical physiognomies, and other ethnic peculiarities for laughs, including through the cowboy Jew.[21]

John Wayne was initially slated to play Tommy the cowboy, a decision that left Wilder "relieved" because, he remembered, "in spite of the presence of the rabbi, with John Wayne starring, *The Frisco Kid* would be perceived as a Western, not a Jewish film."[22] Wilder, an atheist and cultural Jew (he was born Jerome Silberman), convincingly delivers Hebrew prayers in the film, relying on recordings from a cantor he hired.[23] However, his parents were not observant, and he was apparently uncomfortable playing a Jewish character on screen. He maintained that Belinski was the only Jewish role he ever played, characterizing Leo Bloom in *The Producers* (Embassy, 1967), directed by legendary cultural Jew Mel Brooks, as not a Jewish character per se but an extension of the director's trademark New York Jewish sensibility.[24] *Blazing Saddles* (Warner Bros., 1974), Brooks's Western comedy starring Wilder as a gunslinger, also weds what Brooks termed a Jewish "je ne sais quoi" with this American movie genre.[25] But while *Blazing Saddles* is a classic comedy, it does not significantly comment on Jewish identity, thus making (inevitable) comparisons with *The Frisco Kid* off target. Perhaps adding to the confusion, *The Frisco Kid*'s screenwriters Elias and Shaw also wrote the pilot for *Black Bart* (CBS, 1975), an unproduced television series based on *Blazing Saddles* starring Louis Gossett Jr. as a Black sheriff fighting bigotry and corruption in the Old West.

Wilder was himself unclear about the film and his character. He lobbied to reprise his gunfighting role from *Blazing Saddles* despite being cast as a pacifistic frontier rabbi.[26] As a Hollywood star, Wilder had a lot of say in the final product, and his rewrites, which Elias believed were "not always smart," reveal tensions between his hesitancy to make a "Jewish" movie and the intended story of a foreign-born rabbi who becomes Americanized through his westward trek.[27] "I wrote a lot of that movie," Wilder stated, and "when I was writing I was thinking, 'What would be funny for a rabbi to do?'"[28] This grasping for low-hanging laughs at times overwhelmed the movie's sincere and earnest premise and resulted in the excision of some of the more moving and historically interesting scenes, including a few involving meaningful encounters with a Jewish emporium proprietor and a Jewish farmer who model ways of being acclimated American frontier Jews.[29]

In the film, Belinski appears as a classic schlemiel who, despite or because of his childlike perspective, is able to navigate the harsh surroundings, turn enemies into friends, and reach his destination (relatively) unscathed.[30] The schlemiel character was a fixture of folklore in persecuted diaspora communities, personifying the crucial survival strategy of "laughter and trembling" (to use Saul Bellow's phrase).[31] Belinski's "nature as a *tam*" (simpleton), writes Wendy Zierler, a professor of Jewish literature, "his gullibility, his susceptibility to misunderstandings, his simple faith in people and his naïve generosity of spirit, make him a target for hardship but also allow him to be open to the wonders and possibilities of the American road."[32]

This characterization is more pronounced in the film than in the original screenplay, where Belinski, while often out of his depth, is not necessarily a fool. Throughout the original script, he is haunted by nightmares of Cossack raids, suggesting that an urgency to leave Poland has motivated him to learn English and thus made him a candidate for the San Francisco position. In a scene absent from the film, Belinski is shown aboard ship with other Jews heading to America, dispensing rabbinic advice and earning their respect.[33] In the movie, his suitability for the San Francisco post is never made clear; viewers are left wondering why any synagogue would hire this nincompoop. Wilder's comedic caricature was presumably easier for the studio and general public to swallow than allusions to pogroms or a multidimensional dispenser of folksy wisdom would have been. The decision to make Belinski an utter schlemiel has garnered mixed reviews, with some concluding that Wilder's appearance, accent, and mannerisms "more often reinforce rather than question stereotypes," and others calling the movie "light on plot development and heavy on gimmicky ethnic stereotypes."[34]

Yet even with the movie's confused tone and muddled message, many Jewish viewers are fond of the film. One appreciation cites it as a rare opportunity to "see Wilder at his most endearing, sweet, soulful, resilient schlemiel-esque self."[35] According to culture writer B. C. Wallin, who was raised as an Orthodox Jew, "The 1979 comedy western starring Gene Wilder as a fish-out-of-water Orthodox Jew made me feel like less of an outsider."[36] Over the years, Elias has received many heartfelt comments from Jewish fans echoing these remarks.[37] Lawrence J. Epstein, writing in the aptly titled *American Jewish Films: The Search for Identity*, calls the movie an "incredibly interesting and entertaining example of how to blend Jewish and American values."[38]

Elias, who was born in 1940 in "a little Catskills town with an Orthodox synagogue" in Upstate New York, saw himself as part of the "Exodus generation," a reference to Leon Uris's 1958 novel and the Jewish-centric Israeli identity it encapsulated.[39] Another model was the shtetl nostalgia of *Fiddler on the Roof*, the hit Broadway show (1964) and film adaptation (1971) that reinvented lost Eastern European roots for second- and third-generation American Jews (and had more to say about 1960s America than 1880s "Anatevka").[40] With *The Frisco Kid*, Elias sought to elevate a third source of Jewish self-esteem: the Jews' long and productive history on American soil. Consciously or not, this message was an outgrowth of the civil rights movement and the various ethnic pride movements (Italian, Polish, Native American, Asian American, Latin American, Jewish) that stemmed from it. Indeed, the film presents the Wild West as a multiethnic landscape populated by Mexicans, Chinese, Blacks, and Europeans of different backgrounds, shaking up the Western genre's Anglo-Saxon Protestant mythology.[41] As Zierler points out, the movie "exudes cultural confidence born out of the discovery and celebration in the late 1970s and 1980s of ethnicity and hyphenated identities."[42]

Being "ignorant about Jewish pioneers in the Old West," Elias read all he could on the subject, which in those days basically meant articles published in *Western States Jewish Historical Quarterly* and a few items at the Jewish Community Library in Los Angeles. It was a high-stakes, personal project, aspiring to show the transformation of an Old World dogmatist into an American rabbi as a metaphor for negotiations and evolving identities of American Jews as a whole.[43]

The story is set in 1850, the year California achieved statehood, propelled by Mexico's defeat in the Mexican-American War (1846–48) and the consequent U.S. confiscation of nearly half of Mexico's territory as well as the sudden population growth and land development brought on by the Gold Rush (1848–55), particularly in San Francisco.[44] The Americanization of the state coincides with Rabbi Belinski's process of Americanization, which fittingly concludes with his marriage into San Francisco's Jewish community. In a voice-over in the original screenplay, Belinski says he left the village of his birth on March 16, 1850. He arrives in America in May (sixty-three days later), and takes several months to reach San Francisco, a time frame that would have put him in the city shortly after California Admission Day on September 9.[45] With 1850 serving as a symbolic year, the film takes some liberties in presenting 1880s-style frontier towns on the way to San Francisco and Wells Fargo, an express and banking company that formed in 1852 and opened its San Francisco office in July of that year.[46] The inclusion of Wells Fargo could be a subtle nod to Isaias W. Hellman, a Bavarian-born Jewish banker and real estate developer who settled in Los Angeles in 1859 and in 1880 cofounded the University of Southern California (with Protestant Ozro Childs and Catholic John Downey). Hellman later moved to San Francisco, where he acquired the banking division of Wells Fargo in 1905 and merged it with his Nevada Bank, thus organizing the forerunner of today's Wells Fargo Bank.[47] On the surface, placing these and other details in 1850 supports the contention that the Western genre exists in an "imaginary West" and inhabits an "imprecise time and place."[48] *The Frisco Kid* more properly features a compressed timeline, with vignettes inspired by several decades of actual history but depicted in the space of several months. Notwithstanding this sometimes-fuzzy chronology, telling an accurate history was the screenwriters' prime concern.[49]

The formation of a fictional Jewish congregation in San Francisco in 1850 is similarly rooted in the historical record. Evidence indicates that a congregation assembled for the High Holidays in 1849 and that the city had about three thousand Jews by the 1850s. Two key elements likely informed the screenwriters: the 1849 worshipers considered building their own synagogue but had no Torah scroll, so they read from a printed Pentateuch. This congregation did not grow into the film's Beth Israel (a suitably generic name meaning "House of Israel"). However, in the What if? scenario of the film, such a synagogue would have been under construction at the time of Rabbi Belinski's journey and would have welcomed the arrival of a rabbi and his Torah, both of which were in short supply in the American West. Indeed, another temporary congregation formed in San Francisco for the 1850 High Holidays, and a Torah scroll likely arrived prior to those services.[50] Together, these facts form a solid historical basis for the film's fictionalized account.

These events preceded the April 1851 founding of the city's first permanent synagogues, Congregation Emanu-El (German rite) and Congregation Sherith Israel (Polish rite). Both congregations began as Orthodox and hired their first rabbis during the 1850s. That these rabbis were of Polish descent adds to the plausibility that someone like Belinski could be a candidate.[51] Yet as Rabin points out, both men had previously served other congregations in the United States, and as a rule, Western Jews were not inclined to hire greenhorns regardless of their English skills. Further, while Orthodox Jews often founded synagogues in the American West, their traditionalism usually subsided as the congregations gained membership from the broader, more eclectic Jewish community. Such was certainly the case in San Francisco. That Belinski needed to loosen his religious strictures to become a San Francisco rabbi is a point well made in the film and especially in the original script.

The film captures the diversity among San Francisco's Jewish immigrants. A group of men gather to hear Samuel Bender read a letter (written in Yiddish) announcing that the rabbi and Torah are coming to town. The men have beards of varying lengths (and some are clean-shaven) and are wearing clothes indicative of diverse European regions: stovetop and bowler hats from London; a shtetl-style tweed cap and coat; large black kippahs; neckties of various styles; and so on. In the original script, the men converse in "a variety of languages: Yiddish, Polish, Russian, German, English" before order is called by Isaac Bialik, who states in Yiddish that the meeting will take place in English.[52] All of these well-dressed and well-heeled men are Americanized in their own way, representing types of Jews who would occupy the elite category of "German Jew." Whether such men would want a Hasid like Belinski to lead them is another question. Most of the Polish Jews who came to America, particularly after the failed revolutions in 1848, were from the Prussian province of Posen, and the majority spoke German.[53] This aided their reinvention as "Germans" on American soil even as they maintained the Polish prayer rite (frequently conducted in German).[54] Nevertheless, for the purposes of the film, it was important to show Belinski—a character who fits more with the third wave of Jewish immigrants from the Russian Empire (1880–1924)—as an Old Country counterpoint to the acclimated San Francisco Jews. (The novelization of the movie, written by Robert Grossbach, names the Galician town of Kołomyja [now Kolomyia in western Ukraine] as Belinski's place of origin.)[55]

Not every critic caught on to Elias's aim, largely as a result of the film's execution, which even fans and academic appreciators admit "falls well short of being a masterpiece."[56] According to Elias, Aldrich, a non-Jew, was a poor choice to direct the movie although he had previously directed several Westerns, including *Apache* (United Artists, 1954), *Vera Cruz* (United Artists,

1954), *The Last Sunset* (Universal, 1961), *4 for Texas* (Warner Bros., 1963), and *Ulzana's Raid* (Universal, 1974). (Mike Nichols, born Mikhail Igor Peschkowsky and a Jew, was originally slated to direct.) Visiting the set one day, Elias observed a scene involving the San Francisco Jews. During filming, a kippah fell off the head of one of the actors. Aldrich called out, "Can someone pick up that Torah?" That an actual Torah is central to the film made his ignorance of basic Jewish terms all the less excusable and signaled to Elias, who had great affection for Aldrich, that the movie was in trouble. In addition, Elias contends, "Aldrich didn't know if it was a comedy or a Western, or what kind of comedy."[57]

Fievel Goes West (1991)

The precursor to *Fievel Goes West* (Universal, 1991) was *An American Tail* (Universal, 1986), directed by devout Mormon Don Bluth, derived from a story by Jewish writer David Kirschner, written by the Jewish team of Judy Freudberg and Tony Geiss, and produced by hands-on Jewish executive producer Steven Spielberg. *An American Tail* follows young Fievel Mousekewitz (Phillip Glasser) and his family, who leave oppressive conditions in 1885 Russia and sail to America. While at sea, a storm throws Fievel from the ship, and he loses contact with his family. He floats in a bottle to New York's Lower East Side, where an Irish mouse, an Italian mouse, and kindly cat, Tiger (Dom DeLuise), help the boy search for his loved ones.

In an effort to universalize the immigration story, *An American Tail* intentionally whitewashes anti-Jewish hatred: except for Tiger, all cats, whether in Russia or America, are "Cossacks" who attack mice indiscriminately, regardless of ethnicity, nationality, or place of origin. Distinctions are replaced by cartoon animal jingoism between cats and mice. In their book *Jewish American Filmmakers*, David Desser and Lester D. Friedman link this narrative choice to Spielberg's melting-pot vision of American equality: the film "uses the historical specificity of Russian anti-Semitism and the mass migration of Russian Jews to America [even] as it denies the uniqueness of the Jewish experience in favor of universalizing it. It does so by using mice to displace the ethnic and historical realities behind anti-Semitism and the mass immigration of Eastern European Jews. Spielberg's seeming reproduction of the strategy of displacement by the European émigrés of the first generation of Jewish directors in America is actually the Jewish assimilation into the American melting pot. All ethnic groups—Jews, Irish, and Italian alike—are now one and the same."[58] Film scholar Joshua Louis Moss likewise observes that "Fievel's textual Jewish absence but thematic Jewish presence give the film a universal appeal in keeping with other Jewish metamorphs of the 1980s."[59]

Spielberg's simplified and family-friendly angle contrasted sharply with Art Spiegelman's unvarnished illustrated Holocaust family memoir *Maus*, which also features Jewish mice and consequently drew comparisons with *An American Tail*—including by a perturbed Spiegelman, who rushed his work into publication in response to what he saw as a "pandering-to-the-mob" co-opting of key elements from *Maus*.[60] (Spiegelman's work, the first graphic novel to win a Pulitzer Prize, is much more complex and symbolically rich, with Jews depicted as mice, Germans as predatory cats, Poles as pigs, Swedes as deer, Americans as dogs, Roma as butterflies, and French people as frogs.)

Other analysts are more charitable, arguing that *An American Tail* was more personal than Spielberg's *Schindler's List*, which itself might have grown from his Mousekewitz-driven "Jewish turn."[61] Spielberg, a lifelong animation lover and owner of an impressive collection of original animation art, named the rodent protagonist after his maternal grandfather, Philip Posner, an impoverished Russian immigrant whose Yiddish name was Fievel.[62] A more recent reappraisal by Abigail Weil, a scholar of Slavic languages and literature, points out that although *An American Tail* is a cultural touchstone for a generation of Jews who saw it as kids, the film is "too rough, too real, too truthful" to achieve "classic kid's movie" status. According to Weil, the story reveals "the inevitable disillusionment that comes from holding up the United States as the promised land. . . . Those global refugees who pin their hopes on the United States, do they find it better or worse than their native countries? Better or worse than refugees did 150 years ago? Maybe better *and* worse, both in different ways."[63] Some of the film's perceived authenticity can be attributed to Papa Mousekewitz, voiced by Nehemiah Persoff, who had played Barbra Streisand's rabbi father in *Yentl* (MGM, 1983).

An American Tail overcame a host of production problems (a slower-than-expected animation process, larger-than-expected costs, and the deletion of a number of songs and scenes that left holes in the story), to more than double the gross receipts of Disney's release that year, *The Great Mouse*

Detective (another mouse movie). The success of *An American Tail* led to the 1991 Western sequel, *An American Tail: Fievel Goes West.* The original's enduring appeal has largely evaded the sequel, although it spun off into a Saturday morning cartoon series, *Fievel's American Tails* (CBS, 1992). Taking place five years after the original, *Fievel Goes West* finds the impoverished Mousekewitz family disappointed by their unimproved lives in New York. They join a group of mice lured West by villainous feline British aristocrat Cat R. Waul (John Cleese), who proclaims that cats and mice coexist peacefully on the frontier but secretly plans to turn the rodents into "mouse burgers." The Mousekewitz children are especially excited about the new locale. Fievel, who spends his days reading cowboy pulps and fantasizing about bloodhound sheriff Wylie Burp (James Stewart, in his final role), gets to meet him in real life, while Fievel's sister Tanya (Cathy Cavadini) becomes a variety show singer. Ultimately, Fievel teams up with the now over-the-hill Wylie to rid the settler town of vicious cats, and the desolate landscape blooms with flowers and the American dream.

Fievel Mousekewitz in *An American Tail: Fievel Goes West* (Universal, 1991).

Bluth and the original writers were not involved with *Fievel Goes West*, which lacks the original film's heart and sincerity. Reviews were mostly dismissive, commending the movie's visual attractiveness and flowing animation but noting that these technical achievements were "sabotaged by the fast timing and overall speedy pace of the film. The movie feels like someone in the projection booth had a finger on the fast-forward button throughout the picture."[64] The overdone action and long chase scenes were perhaps meant to compensate for the genre's diminished appeal. Westerns were not at all popular at the time, and Spielberg's nostalgia for the genre—now immortalized in the semiautobiographical *The Fablemans* (Universal, 2022) when his younger self meets a grizzled John Ford—may have sparked the idea. (Spielberg also later produced the 2005 miniseries *Into the West* for TNT.)

Fievel Goes West leaves much to be desired from a historical standpoint. Accounts of frontier Jews indicate that for the most part, the West offered them substantially improved social and economic conditions rather than repeating the same old troubles with the same old cats in a new land. Papa's promise to Fievel—"You will see that out West, the cats are good"—is closer to the historical truth of decreased antisemitism.

Furthermore, many Eastern European Jewish immigrants were in fact sent West to agricultural settlements beginning in the late nineteenth century, backed by the Hebrew Emigrant Aid Society and Baron Maurice de Hirsch, founder of the Jewish Colonization Association, and other well-meaning philanthropists. Presented as utopian alternatives to crowded tenements, Jewish agricultural collectives were established in Kansas, Louisiana, Utah, New York, California, Oregon, North and South Dakota, Florida, Michigan, Arkansas, and New Jersey, but almost all of them failed in short order.[65]

Most egregious is the movie's offensively stereotypical, 1930s-style cartoon depiction of Native American mice, which was already long out-of-date in 1992. A third direct-to-video *American Tail* film, *The Treasure of Manhattan Island* (Universal Family, 1998), attempts to correct the error, with Fievel learning of the atrocities committed against Native Americans by European colonizers. However, no link is made between the suffering of European Jews and that of Indigenous Americans.

Fievel Goes West does have a few nice moments. After the final shootout (with slingshots instead of guns) comes to a predictably happy end, in which

Papa Mousekewitz, a violin maker, plays a victory tune on his fiddle that begins with an Eastern European strain and continues into a country hoedown, symbolizing his transition to a new Western persona. In contrast, Fievel flips his cowboy hat back into his familiar immigrant hat. Unlike the picture slides for 1907's "Yonkle the Cow-Boy Jew," which downgrade Yonkle's hat from a Stetson to a bowler to illustrate his ill-suitedness as a cowboy, Fievel's hat change conveys his desire to stay connected to the past even as he and his family chart an optimistic course into the future. More than anywhere else in the movie, these symbolic acts of father and son capture the challenges, opportunities, and bittersweetness of transforming identities.

First Cow (2019)

The most recent cinematic portrayal of a Jew on the frontier is also the subtlest. *First Cow,* directed, edited, and cowritten by slow cinema auteur Kelly Reichardt and based on *The Half-Life*, a novel by co-screenwriter Jonathan Raymond, is set in Oregon Country in the 1820s.[66] The story centers on an unlikely friendship between Otis "Cookie" Figowitz and King-Lu. A sensitive and deliberately slow-paced film with sparse dialogue and lingering shots of natural landscapes, *First Cow* flows with the rhythms of everyday life. A 2018 script for the two-hour film is just seventy-four pages long and includes more scenes and spoken lines than appear in the film.[67] *First Cow* is similar to Reichardt's other Western, *Meek's Cutoff* (Oscilloscope, 2010), also written by Raymond and loosely based on an ill-fated 1845 journey through the Oregon desert, a story of survival on the unforgiving frontier that moves "at a contemplative speed unseen in most Westerns."[68]

First Cow pushes aside Old West myths and archetypes, making room for mundane toils, multiethnic representations, "masculine tenderness," and unresolved tensions around commerce, capitalism, colonialism, and human ambition.[69] As critic Karen Gordon writes, the film is miles away from conventional Western fare: "Minus winners and losers, villains and heroes, this is a sparsely settled, muddy world where some people seek fortunes, and others do what they need day-to-day to survive."[70] K. Austin Collins concurs in his *Vanity Fair* review: "If Reichardt's covert domain is history, one of her more obvious subjects is the everyday. . . . In place of the vast and symbolic possibilities of Monument Valley, per Western masters like

John Ford, we get tight, local depths: forest scenes and local life shot in a tight, old-school Academy aspect ratio that, in other hands, would make a movie feel constricted."[71] Notably, the film has no gun violence, although the story's tragic end comes with implied rifle shots. Instead, the primary genre signature is mud, a "shorthand for authenticity" in a number of latter-day Westerns.[72]

Consistent with this quiet, understated approach, Cookie Figowitz—played by John Magaro, whose mother is Jewish and father is of Italian descent—is never called a Jew in the movie (or in the novel), and his place of origin is not stated. Rather, he is Jewish by surname and profession. He is first introduced as a hired cook for fur trappers and later starts a baking business with King-Lu (Orion Lee), a Chinese immigrant whom Figowitz finds in the woods hiding from a group of Russians who believe King-Lu has murdered their companion. The two men meet again in a rugged settlement built around a trading post, and King-Lu invites Figowitz to stay in his makeshift cabin. King-Lu's entrepreneurial spirit is sparked by the arrival of the area's first dairy cow, belonging to Chief Factor (Toby Jones),

King-Lu (Orion Lee, left) and Cookie Figowitz (John Magaro) in *First Cow* (A24, 2019).

a rich British landowner. Figowitz and King-Lu sneak out each night to milk the cow, and Cookie uses the milk to make "oily cakes." They set up a blanket and sell the "fried, sugared, puffy dough," which is an instant hit. When asked what the cakes are made of, King-Lu replies, "Ancient Chinese secret." Even Chief Factor, who is unaware that his cow is being milked, enthusiastically tells the men, "I taste London in this cake." The scheme is eventually exposed, and the two men are tracked down by Factor's men and killed by one of his guards as they sleep in the woods.

To enhance the movie's genuine feel, Lee and Margaro spent preparation time in the Oregon woods, Magaro studied Lewis and Clark's cookbooks, and the Grande Ronde, a confederation of Oregon tribes, provided assistance, leading to a refreshingly "quotidian and unexotic" representation of the Native Americans in the film.[73] Less authentic are the absence of accents or dialects (both Figowitz and King-Lu speak perfect American English) and the references to San Francisco as the location where the men hope to build their business. At the time, San Francisco was still known as Yerba Buena and was a small town under Mexican rule.[74] Both are choices of convenience. The avoidance of accents bypasses potentially insensitive caricaturizing, puts the ethnic partners on equal footing, and gives a once-upon-a-time universality to a story of hope, struggle, and friendship. San Francisco—which may be intended as a colloquial rather than official name for the town (Mission San Francisco de Asís was founded there in 1776)—is a metaphor for capitalist aspirations and big-city dreams, even though Yerba Buena was just a tiny glimmer of the cosmopolitan center San Francisco became during the Gold Rush era.

Most poignantly, the friends' quick success and quicker end effectively deny Frederick Jackson Turner's economic myth that nationality, previous social status, and ethnic or religious background mattered little on the Western frontier, where anyone with the needed skills and fortitude could succeed. On the one hand, the downplaying of Figowitz's Jewishness is believable in this early nineteenth-century Western setting: a traditionally observant Jew would not have ventured so far from the requisite trappings of Jewish ritual life. On the other hand, Figowitz's ultimate and tragic failure contrasts with the usual telling of pioneer Jewish history, as summed up by David Epstein, founding director of the Jewish Museum of the American West: "This is the story of what happened when a group of people, persecuted for 2,000 years, was let loose in a vast new area—the American Wild West—where virtually no one cared about their religion, and where they were free to explore seemingly endless avenues to make a living and raise their families."[75] This rags-to-riches narrative applied to some Jews but not to all (or even most). Figowitz and King-Lu remain outsiders to wealth and power, and Chief Factor, a WASP with old money, is both the unwitting source of their success and the direct cause of their demise. The partnership of the two men seems less about the possibility of turning a humble baking business into an American success story and more about the natural instinct for perennial outsiders to stick together to survive.[76]

CHAPTER 6

Comedic Sensibility

Jewish identity begins with sensibility: a certain way of thinking, expressing, and responding to things.[1] A "classical" Jewish sensibility might look at values-driven actions or behaviors, such as making distinctions, honoring others, repenting/returning, preserving life, striving for peace, healing the world, maintaining hope, remembering ancestors, or being an upstanding person.[2] A Jewish comedic sensibility has its own set of values: a critical edge, antiauthoritarian bite, and a mocking tone (including self-mocking).[3] The seriousness assumed of a classical Jewish sensibility does not melt away with the laughter. Jewish comedy, while often satirical, irreverent, and vulgar, has shaped the course of Jewish history in ways rivaling—or even exceeding—that of theology or ritual practice.[4] If the Pew Research Center's findings are any indication of the forces driving contemporary American Jewish life, it is telling that when asked "What does it mean to be Jewish?" 42 percent of those who responded said, "Having a good sense of humor," while just 19 percent said, "Observing Jewish law."[5]

Highlighting the overlapping importance of humor and religiosity, *MAD* magazine, founded in 1952 by two New York Jews, Harvey Kurtzman and William Gaines, has been called a "secular Talmud": a self-referential, intertextual mélange of parodic commentaries filled with Yiddish words and Jewish references that unabashedly critiqued the era's social issues and intellectual concerns, which ranged from suburbia and disarmament to bohemianism and psychoanalysis.[6] Jewish humor was not comedy for its own sake but a disarmingly raucous means of deconstructing existing power structures. A distillation of Mel Brooks's comedy (often misattributed to him) posits that a survival instinct motivates these impulses: "Feeling different, feeling alienated, feeling persecuted, feeling that the only way to deal with the world is to laugh—because if you don't laugh you're going to cry and never stop crying—that's probably what's responsible for the Jews having developed such a great sense of humor. The people who had the greatest reason to weep, learned more than anyone else how to laugh."[7]

Of course, social commentary, the outsider's perspective, and ridiculing those in power are not exclusive to Jewish humor. Minority groups of all kinds use laughter as a survival strategy in navigating sociopolitical and economic realities and managing interactions with majority group members.[8] Historically unable to gain autonomy or forge new political systems (modern efforts in socialism, communism, anarchism, and Zionism notwithstanding), Jews have turned to humor as an avenue of empowerment—a tendency often traced back to the Book of Esther, written in the Persian diaspora (between 400 and 300 BCE), which tells a Jewish survival story satirizing Persian celebrations, literary forms, royal extravagances, government edicts, and pretensions of the ruling class.[9] When Eastern European Jews began arriving in America in the late nineteenth century, they continued a self- and social-critical style of humor that enabled them to respond to cognitive dissonances, endure disappointments, negotiate their marginal status, and find new avenues of success. Whether in ancient Persia or modern-day America, these comedic strategies simultaneously punch at and into the mainstream, giving Jews their own adaptive niche in a strange land.

During a 2022 interview on NPR's *Fresh Air*, Brooks told host Terry Gross, "I'm tribal. I love being a Jew, and I love Jewish humor, and I loved the—I don't know, the *je ne sais quoi* that the Jews [have]." This certain something—an indescribable yet apparent feature—is embedded in Jewish-made Western parodies, where obvious Jewishness takes a back seat to what Brooks calls a Jewish "attitude" involving the subversion of well-worn formulas through biting critiques and reversals of expectations.[10] Brooks brought this attitude to the Old West with *Blazing Saddles* (Warner Bros., 1974), a stew of outlandish twists on almost every conceivable genre marker.

At the time, *Blazing Saddles* was accused of killing the Western.[11] Yet this accusation was not only misleading—Western productions were already in steep decline—but also premature: Westerns have persisted in "afterlife" incarnations and minirevivals, losing their former grip on the popular imagination but appealing to specialized tastes and occasional interests.[12] More generally, blaming parodies for a genre's decline is misguided. Takeoffs depend on popular awareness of the genres they lampoon. As John Shelton Lawrence notes in his filmography of Hollywood Westerns, spoofs and parodies "appeared steadily in every decade, with notable comedians such as Bob Hope, W. C. Fields, Mae West, the Stooges, Laurel and Hardy, and Abbot and Costello. If the Western was killed by *Blazing Saddles* (1974), it had certainly already been weakened by generations of laughter about its plot and character conventions."[13] The earliest such parody, Fatty Arbuckle's 1918 short *Out West* (Paramount), is almost as old as the Western itself.

Jewish Western Comedy Schtick

Recognizably Jewish elements, such as Hebrew phrases or Yiddish-speaking Native Americans, are occasionally tossed into Western scenes. *Shanghai Noon* (Buena Vista, 2000), a martial arts Western comedy starring Jackie Chan and Owen Wilson that self-reflexively mashes Far Eastern and Western clichés, has a scene in which a dumbfounded settler family stares at Chinese imperial guards practicing their sword techniques. "They don't look like any Injuns I ever seen, Jedidiah." "That's because they aren't Injuns, woman, they're Jews!" The guards later step off the settlers' wagon and Jedidiah says goodbye with a hearty "Shalom." These brief exchanges play on tendencies to lump together "exotic" foreigners, Hollywood's history of casting Jews as Native Americans, and long-standing confusions between Native Americans and the biblical Lost Tribes, commonly (and inaccurately) called Jews in literature dating back to Europe's "discovery" of the New World.

Cat Ballou (Columbia, 1965), a comic inversion of a serious novel by Roy Chanslor, concerns the murder of a ranch owner who refuses to sell his land to the railroad and how his daughter, Cat Ballou (Jane Fonda), forms a gang to exact revenge. Themes of women's liberation (Ballou starts off as an uptight schoolmarm and becomes a proactive outlaw) and antiauthoritarianism (the sheriff is on the villain's side) are punctuated by antics that turn Western clichés upside-down, as when a barn dance dissolves into an all-ages, intergender melee or when the train-riding priest is shown to be first a drunk and then not really a priest. Directed by Elliot Silverstein and produced by Harold Hecht, with onscreen narration by banjo-playing songsters Nat King Cole and Stubby Kaye, whose musical partnership hints at an urban Black-Jewish alliance (the songs were written by the Jewish team of Mack David and Jerry Livingston), the film is tinged with a socially conscious, 1960s-era Jewish sensibility. Politics and Jewish humor converge in a scene critiquing whites' insistence on defining Native Americans and stripping them of self-determination. In perhaps cinema's clearest poke at the Hebraic Indian theory, Cat Ballou's father, Frankie (John Marley), is convinced that his Indigenous ranch hand, Jackson Two-Bears (Tom Nardini), is a transplant from ancient Israel. Frankie tells Cat, "Injuns is the lost tribe of Israel, but he won't admit it." "Just ain't true," Jackson protests. Calling Jackson stubborn, Frankie explains that when he "brought Mr. Bernstein, the telegraph operator, out here last month," Bernstein "stood right here and spoke Hebrew at Jackson for ten minutes. And Jackson pretended he didn't understand a word." Here and elsewhere, the film's heavier messages are lightened by humor, making it tame enough to win at the box office and earn Lee Marvin an Academy Award for his dual roles as Kid Shelleen and Tim Strawn.[14]

In 1962, Moe Howard of the Three Stooges made a rare comedy standup (really sit-down) television appearance on an unsold pilot for *Strictly for Laffs*. Hosted by Dave Barry, the pilot was filmed in a living room set with the audience casually lounging around on sofas and Barry and his guests sitting at a cluttered coffee table and trying to act natural. The roster of guests included Jewish entertainers Sid Melton, Buddy Lester, and Mel Blanc, recently recovered from a near-fatal car accident that had left him bedridden for a year.[15] Playing on the Jewish Indian lark, Moe recounted a Canadian hunting trip where his Native guide was named Lipschitz.

An episode of *The Simpsons*, "Dude, Where's My Ranch?" (Fox, 2003), upends identity expectations in another direction. The Simpson family vacations on a ranch run by what seem to be stereotypical ranchers. In one scene, Cookie, the rifle-carrying old-codger cook, ridicules a chicken he tied to a stump: "Free range my ass. Tonight, you're gonna be swimming next to a matzo ball." At the end of the episode, Luke, a sensitive young environmentalist ranch hand for whom Lisa Simpson has fallen, learns that she had tried to foil what she thought was a romance between Luke and a pretty girl who turned out to be his sister. "That's despicable," Luke fumes. "You're the kind of city slicker my family left Central Park West to avoid. You've got a lot of chutzpah, missy!" The suggestion that the episode's ranchers are in fact East Coast Jews reverses the comic formula of urban Jews coming West and clashing with the rugged cowboy lifestyle. Here, the decidedly Gentile Simpsons find themselves out of place among Jewish ranchers.

An earlier episode of the series, "Lisa's Substitute" (Fox, 1991), has Lisa Simpson becoming infatuated with her substitute teacher Mr. Bergstrom, voiced by Dustin Hoffman. Like many early *Simpsons* guest stars, Hoffman was uneasy about being identified with a cartoon and, on the whim of series producer James L. Brooks, took the pseudonym Sam Etic—a play on "Semitic," alluding to the character's (and Hoffman's) Jewish identity.[16] When Mr. Bergstrom, whose likeness is based on Jewish *Simpsons* writer/producer Mike Reiss, introduces himself to Lisa's class, he is dressed as a guitar-slinging cowboy. Lisa tells him, "You seem to be of the Jewish faith. . . . There weren't any Jewish cowboys." "Very good, that's excellent," he replies, impressed by Lisa's knowledge of his deliberate anachronisms. "And I'm also wearing a digital watch, but I'll accept that." He puts his hat on Lisa's head: "Here you go, little lady. And for the record, there were a few Jewish cowboys—big guys who were great shots and spent money freely."

Jewish comedic sensibility is also expressed through coded or semicoded behaviors and character types, such as out-of-depth entertainers and nebbishy cowboy wannabees. On *Your Show of Shows* (NBC, 1953), Sid Caesar assumed the cowboy persona in "Strange," a parody of the Western *Shane*. Trying to look heroic on horseback, Caesar, an obvious outsider, winces and struggles to find a comfortable saddle position. When he arrives at a saloon, the barkeeper inquires, "You seem to be mighty thirsty. Have a long, dry ride?" Caesar responds, "No, I had herring for breakfast." Caesar returned as a bookish cowboy in the *Caesar's Hour* sketch "Vacant Holsters" (NBC, 1955), where the opening minutes follow his slow-walking legs and empty holsters and warn of his "heart full of hate." The camera finally pans up to show a very nearsighted bumbling tough-guy nerd with thick glasses.

In the musical comedy *Cowboy from Brooklyn* (Warner Bros., 1938), with songs by British-born Jewish composer Adolph Deutsch, a New York entertainer with a debilitating fear of animals ends up on a Wyoming dude ranch, where a slick promoter tries to reinvent him as a singing cowboy. A 1948 remake, *Two Guys from Texas* (Warner Bros.), scripted by Jewish screenwriters Allen Boretz and I. A. L. Diamond with music by Jewish composer Leo F. Forbstein, has two vaudeville entertainers stranded on a Texas ranch. One of them is cripplingly afraid of animals, leading to an animated dream sequence starring the ultimate (and possibly Jewish) vaudevillian, Bugs Bunny.

With *Annie Get Your Gun* (MGM, 1950), Broadway reinvents the West in its own images. Written by Jewish playwright Sidney Sheldon and derived from the stage musical by Jewish siblings Dorothy and Herbert Fields with music by the incomparable Irving Berlin, whose father was a cantor, the story centers on the presumed irregularity of a woman gunslinger and is loosely based on the exploits of Annie Oakley. When asked to write novelty numbers for the show, Berlin famously replied, "What do I know about hillbilly music?"[17] The resulting songs, oozing with an urban Jewish sensibility, appealed to city audiences familiar with the Tin Pan Alley/Broadway aesthetic and charmed by the supposedly outlandish gender-bending notion of a sharpshooting cowgirl. In the show/film, Annie sings the Broadway anthem "There's No Business Like Show Business" alongside the Native-stereotype-infused "I'm an Indian Too."

In Jewish-sensibility Western comedies, outsiders imitate and often mangle existing genre signifiers: shootouts, western wear, singing cowboys, saloon brawls, riding into the sunset, and so on. In the process, these outsiders carve a place in the supposedly incongruous setting. Following Jewish bandleader and comedian Mickey Katz, who recorded cowboy parody songs in the 1950s like "Roiselle from Texas" (sung to "The Yellow Rose of Texas"), "Borscht Riders in the Sky" (sung to "Ghost Riders in the Sky"), and "Duvid Crockett" (sung to the "Ballad of Davy Crockett"), these cinematic send-ups to a greater or lesser degree turn the Wild West into "a great big Bar Mitzvah Ranch."[18]

Whoopee! (1930)

Whoopee! (United Artists, 1930) began as a 1928 Ziegfeld Broadway musical based on Owen Davis's play *Nervous Wreck*, which was itself made into a silent comedy in 1926 and drew from E. J. Rath's novel *The Wreck* (1923). The durable story involves an eastern hypochondriac, Henry Williams (Eddie Cantor), who winds up on a California ranch for his health. The local sheriff, Bob Wells (Jack Rutherford), and the rancher's daughter, Sally Morgan (Eleanor Hunt), are set to be married, but she is in love with Wanenis (Paul

Whoopee!, poster (United Artists, 1930).

Gregory), whose part-Native heritage makes their coupling taboo. Sally leaves Wells stranded at their wedding, hitching a ride with an unsuspecting Henry, who takes her to the ranch of Jerome Underwood (Spencer Charters). Sally had left a note explaining that she and Henry had eloped, setting off a chase led by the jilted sheriff. Following a series of escapades and show tunes, the movie ends with Wanenis learning that he is a full-blooded white man who was adopted and raised by Natives, making his relationship with Sally kosher.

Actor/singer/comedian Cantor toured with the show before taking it to Hollywood, where a large budget awaited the lavish production shot in innovative two-color (red and green) Technicolor. A pre-Code production, *Whoopee!* is held together by Cantor's out-in-the-open ethnic humor and Jewish sensibility. Born to Russian Jewish immigrants and orphaned at age three, Cantor used show business as a vehicle for social mobility, beginning on stage in the 1910s and continuing through the 1950s in theater, film, radio, and television. Rising in the ranks of celebrity, Cantor never hid his Jewish roots, and oscillating between his Jewish and American personas was his comedy's most defining trait. Even his shapeshifting from one character type to another—blackface minstrel to Greek cook to Native chief to female, often within a single scene—symbolized the liminal space occupied by Jewish immigrants, who picked up on social cues, modified their language and demeanor, and navigated the margins in their quest for the American dream. Cantor biographer David Weinstein notes that in *Whoopee!* and a string of other 1931–37 films, Cantor finds himself in a strange new locale with little money or social standing but survives through his quick wit, fast talking, and chameleon-like adaptation. "In these metaphors for the immigrant experience," Weinstein writes, "Cantor's naïve character learns to master new and dangerous situations, despite his initial confusion and weakness, through a combination of astonishing luck, savvy wisecracks, a strong sense of moral decency, and a propensity for leading lavish song-and-dance routines when all else fails."[19]

Some of the more outwardly Jewish moments in *Whoopee!* include an exchange between Henry and Wanenis. "For this girl that I love," Wanenis tells Henry, "I've studied the ways of your race. Why, I've even gone to your schools." Surprised, Henry replies, "An Indian in a Hebrew school?" Henry is later stopped by Native Americans on the road, who say something close to "Oy, oy." "Look," he quips, "Jewish traffic cops." Mr. Underwood, owner of the Bar M Ranch, wears a vest adorned with six-pointed stars, perhaps suggesting that the *M* stands for mitzvah, as in *Bar Mitzvah Ranch*. At one point, Henry assumes the guise of a Jewish street merchant, insisting that his customer haggle over goods and peppering in Yiddish expressions. Taking on the appearance of a Native American, Henry says, "Me Big Chief Izzy Horowitz" and dances an "Indian dance" to "Tanz, Tanz Yidelekh," the quintessential 1917 klezmer tune from the Abe Schwartz Orchestra.[20]

Cantor's schtick was also grounded in stereotypes of Jewish male effeminateness, nebbishness, and lack of physicality. He perpetuated and transcended these expectations, often playing "hapless, simple, clumsy, inept victims" whose masculinity is "thoroughly extinct" and whose "traditional male virtues such as strength, courage, pride, fortitude, are prominent only in their absence" but who is also the object of attraction for a lovely lady.[21] In *Whoopee!*, that role is played by the attending nurse, Mary Custer (Ethel Shutta), who goes from being glamorous in her big number to being the tough-girl butch to Henry's femme in their many interactions.[22] Henry's illness, while left undefined and carrying a host of symptoms hyperbolizing the Jew's "born to kvetch" reputation, includes an unspecified operation that is implied to be his circumcision.[23] Beyond placing the "operation" at the psychosomatic root of Henry's illness, the story spoofs antisemitic views of Jewish males as helplessly feminized and disproportionately homosexual, in large part because of the procedure.[24] Nevertheless, Mary lusts after feeble Henry, whose disinterest (hinting at homosexuality) only inflames her desire.

Cantor's combination of ethnic humor, social nimbleness, and quirky charm was a winning formula in New York and other cities with large immigrant audiences but mostly failed in the South and Midwest, where the "Broadway style" rubbed against xenophobic nativism.[25] Producer Samuel Goldwyn and United Artists folded this reaction into a "de-Semitization" campaign that was further influenced by rising antisemitism in the United States, epitomized by Father Charles Coughlin, the Reverend Gerald L. K. Smith, and aviator Charles Lindbergh. Cantor was forced to purge "all overt acknowledgment of his ethnic identity" from his post-*Whoopee!* films. Not only did the studio face Depression-era pressures to reach the widest audiences possible, including in the "hinterlands," but it also relied on distribution in rapidly Nazifying Europe.[26] The suppression of Cantor's Jewish heritage was amplified by the Motion Picture Code Administration and by calls from the Anti-Defamation League, leaving his subsequent films more coded though still recognizably Jewish to those in the know. (The same concerns led to the downplaying of a similar character, taxi driver Gieber Goldberg, in the 1932 RKO film version of the easterners-out-west musical *Girl Crazy*, where he is de-ethnicized and renamed Jimmy. The character is erased completely from the 1943 remake.)[27]

While the humor in *Whoopee!* is at times particularistic and even disruptive, the story pulls from and coincides with Western themes, repeating rather than challenging them. *Whoopee!* is a classic Western love story filtered through a Jewish sensibility, presenting an idiosyncratic nebbish who, at least in large and medium-sized cities, appealed to audiences beyond those who got the inside jokes. For Jewish performers, Cantor set a model for infusing Jewishness into their acts: Yiddish words, jokes about delis, references to rituals, hammed-up stereotypes, and allusions to the Lower East Side.

The Terror of Tiny Town (1938) and *Harlem on the Prairie* (1937)

In both the all-little-people Western *The Terror of Tiny Town* (Columbia, 1938) and the all-Black Western *Harlem on the Prairie* (Sack Amusement, 1937), director Sam Newfield's Jewish sensibility upends the sameness of the genre. Through parody, gimmicks, and unlikely characters, both films make outsiders the insiders of their own stories, eliminating the standard, white, normal-sized genre types along the way. Indeed, without this implicit commentary, there would be nothing remarkable about these quickly made B Westerns.

The Terror of Tiny Town, produced by Jed Buell and directed by Newfield, who made 250 feature films from the silent era to 1958, is a conventional low-budget musical comedy about two warring families fighting over cattle, an evil gunslinger terrorizing the townspeople, and a cowboy hero saving the day, with singing and dancing interspersed throughout.[28] Where it differs is in its all-little-people cast. Called Buell's Midgets in the opening credits, many of the actors came from Austrian manager Leo Singer's vaudeville troupe, Singer's Midgets, and had strong Austrian accents. When filming ended, much of the cast went to the Munchkinland set of *The Wizard of Oz* (MGM, 1939). This unusual casting, which has been called deplorable exploitation, cutting-edge satire, desperate cash grabbing, and a host of other things, makes *The Terror of Tiny Town* one of Hollywood's oddest novelty Westerns.

Whether *The Terror of Tiny Town* is even a comedy is up for debate. The gags, puns, and antics are done at the cast's expense: characters walking under hitching posts, roping calves, and making short jokes ("I never thought she could be so small," "You'll get smallpox from him," "That's a big order for me"). The movie opens with an average-height announcer saying that the story has everything one would expect from a Western but with an "all-midget cast—the first of its kind ever to be produced" and cautioning the audience not to take it too seriously. He is then corrected by the hero, Buck Lawson (Billy Curtis), who assures the announcer that the movie is in fact serious. Curtis was apparently just as convinced of the film's seriousness as the character he played, later airing his frustrations: "Small, in the minds of stupid people, is kiddie stuff. So first they try to exploit little people. Then they patronize you. And when the picture comes out, then the audience laughs at you. Why? Not because we were low budget, because most Westerns then were B's. Because we rode ponies. What would a person my size ride—a stallion? I played the good guy who put the bad guy behind bars at the end—just like John Wayne. And I kissed the pretty girl—just like he did. So what the hell's so funny?"[29]

The Terror of Tiny Town has been dubbed a "mutant Western": an intentional perversion of the genre that both uses and obliterates its established icons.[30] A financial success at the time, the film is now a divisive cult classic, with some critics finding it irredeemably offensive and others, like Richard Crouse, calling it "the *height* of exploitation filmmaking" yet still including it in his book, *The 100 Best Movies You've Never Seen.*[31]

Another Buell and Newfield Western, *Harlem on the Prairie*, was billed as the first all-Black Western musical. Made for the era's African American theaters and distributed by Sack Amusement Enterprises, headed by Alfred N. Sack, a Mississippi-born Jew who specialized in race films, *Harlem on the Prairie* stars Herb Jeffries as the singing cowboy hero who helps a young woman find her dead father's lost gold. Like *The Terror of Tiny Town*, it is more novelty than comedy. A review in the NAACP magazine *The Crisis* noted, "'Harlem on the Prairie' is a western with transplanted Harlem

Negroes on the hunt for buried treasure, it is labeled comedy and is not quite complete."[32]

Jeffries wanted the film and other all-Black Westerns in which he starred—*Bronze Buckaroo* (Sack Amusement, 1938), *Harlem Rides the Range* (Sack Amusement, 1939), and *Two-Gun Man from Harlem* (Sack Amusement, 1939)—to give Black youth a positive role model.[33] Filmed at N. B. Murray's Black dude ranch near Victorville, California, *Harlem on the Prairie* was sold primarily to small segregated theaters in the South and West, but it also played in a few prestigious movie houses in Los Angeles and New York. While the "Harlem" in the title implies an easterner-goes-west comic conceit, the movie directly questioned Western cinema's whitewashed mythology, restoring Blacks to the multifaceted roles they played on the real American frontier: foremen, drovers, cowpunchers, cattle rustlers, cooks, wranglers, musicians, performers, riders, ropers, bulldoggers, bronco busters, and more. As Jeffries explained,

> I had studied about black cowboys at my school in Detroit and knew that the black cowboy was very instrumental in pioneering our country. One out of every three cowboys who helped to set the state boundary lines during Westward-Ho were black. These black cowboys came about back during the slavery period. Some slaves escaped and were taken in by the Indian tribes. The Indians were great riders of horses. They also rode bareback, without saddles. When these blacks reentered the social structure after the Civil War, they had become great riders. In many instances, the ranchers who were transporting cattle back and forth from Kansas to California preferred the black cowboys, because they could powwow with the Indians and get the cattle through when many of the white drovers couldn't.[34]

Rather than interrogating racism or white supremacist violence, Black-audience Westerns were entertainment films that modified a popular genre by replacing familiar white faces with Black ones, approximating standard conventions without directly commenting on the Black experience in America. But this ostensibly apolitical approach was itself a response to racial politics. Most Black people could not see a first-run Hollywood film without sitting in balcony seats or viewing "midnight rambles." With these Black-audience movies, writes film scholar Julia Leyda, viewers saw "an on-screen

America in which African Americans had access to all locations in life, both high and low and even tall in the saddle."[35]

Go West (1940)

The Marx Brothers' parody *Go West* (MGM, 1940) begins with a foreword: "In 1851, Horace Greeley uttered a phrase that did much to change the history of these United States. He said: 'Go West, young man, go West.' This is a story of three men who made Horace Greeley sorry he said that." Conman S. Quentin Quale (Groucho) heads west to seek his fortune but is short ten dollars for a train ticket. At the railroad station, he attempts to swindle the money from two brothers, Joe (Chico) and Rusty (Harpo) Panello, who are themselves con artists and instead swindle Quale. The Panello brothers are also going west to meet an old prospector friend whose near-worthless property, Dead Man's Gulch, has no gold. In return for loaning him their last ten dollars, the prospector gives them the deed as collateral. Terry Turner (John Carroll), beau to the prospector's granddaughter, Eve Wilson (Diana Lewis), arrives from New York to persuade the railroad to buy the gulch, convincing company officials that it is the only reasonable route through the mountains. Quale attempts to swindle the Panellos out of the deed, but a crooked railroad executive and shady saloon owner steal the deed from Quale. In the end, Quale and the Panello brothers help Terry and Eve retrieve the deed and deliver it to the railroad office in New York.

The film received a lukewarm reception. The *New York Times* called it "an unevenly paced show" with "only one really funny sequence," the train-dismantling climax. *Film Daily* appraised it as "wildly funny in places, amusing for the most part and dead in one or two spots that a little editing could improve."[36] Contemporary Western movie buff Michael Pitts deems *Go West* a "none-too-good Marx Brothers vehicle, only a fair satire and certainly not much of a Western."[37] These reviews point to the tameness—even blandness—of the film compared to earlier Marx Brothers efforts and a general trend among 1940s comedies to be more constructive than destructive.[38] For the Marx Brothers, the tonal shift occurred when they left Paramount, where their stage and radio schtick was adapted to screen and they "showed no mercy in the quest for laughs," and went to MGM, which expected a tamer, more polished product. Jewish aspects were specifically deemphasized, following the pattern of Cantor's films.[39]

Go West's pedestrian railroad plot contains two distinct layers. One is a Depression-era rags-to-riches story of a young couple who sell their land to the railroad. Their rapid financial turnaround resonated with audiences who dreamed of the same good fortune and reflected MGM producer Irving Thalberg's insistence that the Marx Brothers dampen their chaotic/anarchistic energy as epitomized in *Duck Soup* (Paramount, 1933).[40] Thalberg was diagnosed with pneumonia while on the set of *A Day at the Races* (MGM, 1937) and died a short while later, leaving the Marx Brothers without clear direction. Nat Perrin, who contributed gags and storylines to several Marx Brothers films, attributed the disappointment of *Go West* to an attempt to replicate Thalberg's winning formula—used in their two most profitable films, *A Night at the Opera* (MGM, 1935) and *A Day at the Races*—after the producer's death. "Without [Thalberg's] strong hand, you had three comedians who paid very little attention to the story line," Perrin explained. The script itself was much more story-driven than the brothers' earlier free-flowing fare, where "a good bit of business or a funny line" got in "no matter what damage it did to the rest of the scene."[41] Without a competent producer to balance the story and schtick, the result falls flat.

The second, more interesting layer involves urban easterners going west. Novels like Owen Wister's *The Virginian* (1902) had built up contrasting images of the West as a symbol of freedom and unregulated opportunity and the East as a bastion of regulation and tradition. With help from a cowboy hero, the easterner, whose beliefs and attitudes initially clash with the new setting, eventually acclimates to the code of the West.[42] The Marx Brothers reverse the formula, presenting the East as an anything-goes environment and showing no interest in adjusting to the comparatively stodgy West. In one of the film's better lines, Chico admits, "I'd like the West better if it were in the East." Groucho later remarks, "There's only one law in the West: the law of blood and bullets. It's either shoot or get shot. What are we gonna do?" Chico responds, "Sue 'em."

An earlier, somewhat related reversal of the easterner goes West conceit comes from 1932's *Tenderfoot* (Warner Bros.), a pre-Code comedy Western starring Joe E. Brown as a Texas cowboy who travels to New York City to invest in a Broadway show. In a memorable New York street scene, the cowboy hitches a horse-drawn wagon ride with a Jewish peddler (Joe Barton), whose fast-paced Yiddish dialogue causes the befuddled cowboy to remark, "Guess you're a native, alright. Can't understand a word you said."

For the Marx Brothers, the Old West was just another New York. Their vaudeville careers had begun in the days of racial humor, with Harpo starting off as a stage Irish caricature, Chico as a stage Italian, and Groucho as a stage Dutch/German. In *Go West*, these eastern, urban types descend on the dusty environment, reenacting and satirizing Western conventions. Although the film's humor is more subdued than that found in their earlier romps, the Marx Brothers brand is on display: their presence turns the West into a multiethnic, immigrant, polyglot neighborhood. There were, in fact, important historical parallels between the West of the nineteenth century and the East of the early twentieth century. As historian Daniel J. Boorstin observes, each was a tumultuous and disordered setting, with "its own special vagueness, its own mysteries, its own false promises and booster hopes."[43] These similarities do not exist in the mythic West, freeing the Marx Brothers to exploit and exaggerate the presumed discordance.

The Three Stooges

The Three Stooges comedy team was active from 1922 to 1970, a nearly fifty-year span that began in vaudeville and is best remembered for 190 Columbia shorts. The original three Stooges were Moe Howard, his brother Curly Howard, and Larry Fine. Curly retired in 1946 following a massive stroke, and the Stooges were subsequently joined by Shemp Howard (Moe and Curly's older brother), then Joe Besser, and finally Curly Joe DeRita. All of the Stooges aside from DeRita were born to Jewish immigrant parents. Their humor and personas were decidedly working class, portraying blue-collar laborers, relying on physical comedy, wearing ill-fitting baggy clothes, and appearing exceptionally dumpy next to the tall and slender actors with whom they were cast (Moe was five foot three; Larry, Besser, and DeRita were five foot four; Curly was five foot five; and Shemp was five foot seven). A common complaint about the Stooges, articulated in a February 1940 issue of *Variety* (and repeated to this day), is that their humor is "informal, inane and uninhibited. It's a series of eye-jabbing, head-thumping, nose-tweaking antics threaded on a string of rapid-fire chatter and embellished by double and triple takes."[44]

Even DeRita, who joined the trio in 1958, was not a fan of their comedy: "I don't think the Stooges were funny. I'm not putting you on, I'm telling the truth—they were physical, but they just didn't have any humor about them. Take, for instance, Laurel and Hardy. I can watch their films and I still laugh at them and maybe I've seen them four or five times before. But when I see that pie or seltzer bottle, I know that it's not just lying around for no reason. It's going to be used for something. I was with the Stooges for 12 years and it was a very pleasant association but I just don't think they were funny."[45] It could be that DeRita, a non-Jew, was culturally distant from the Stooges' idiosyncratic Jewishness, rooted in the broad mockery of Purim spiels and the mainstay folklore characters of the schlemiel (an inept, clumsy person) and schlimazel (an unlucky person). Thirty-eight Stooges shorts contain Yiddish phrases, including *Mutts to You* (1938), where Larry, impersonating a Chinese laundryman, tells a policeman, "*Hak mir nisht keyn tshaynik*, and I don't mean *efsher*" (Stop bugging me, and I don't mean maybe).[46] Moe, also in yellowface, adds, "He from China. East Side."

In *You Nazty Spy* (Columbia, 1940), Moe was the first American actor to portray Hitler onscreen, preceding Charlie Chaplain's more refined performance in *The Great Dictator* (United Artists, 1940) and Tom Dugan in *To Be or Not to Be* (United Artists, 1942). Curly also played a knuckleheaded Mussolini in the film. Yet because the Stooges are decried as "sadistically physical comedians," this important piece of political satire is habitually dismissed or forgotten.[47] In addition to its sheer brazenness, what makes *You Nazty Spy* unique is its foregrounding of the Stooges' Jewishness. Made with frequent Stooge collaborators, Jewish director Jules White and Jewish writer Felix Adler, the film lampoons the Morons of Moronika—stand-ins for the Germans of Germany—who are easily swayed by the lies and promises of fascist propaganda. The trio, who start out as menial laborers, are recruited by three munitions manufacturing magnates to turn the peaceful Moronika into a war-driven dictatorship. They exclaim "Beblach!" (beans) and salute with "Shalom aleichem!," making clear that these are Jewish comedians spitting at the Nazis. During Moe's mostly gibberish Hitlerian speech, he slips in the phrase, "In pupik gehabt haben" (I've had it in the bellybutton). Reflecting on the Stooges' Jewish identity, journalist Benjamin Ivry highlights their relevance both at the time and subsequently: "The Stooges' sheer outlandish violence suited a moment of impending horror, just as Larry Fine's expectation and acceptance of physical torment appeared to match a tradition of scapegoating Jews from the old country. The occasion was ripe for the Stooges, and recent historical events have not shown humanity in any more refined light."[48]

Biting criticism is mostly lacking in the Stooges' Westerns, where low-hanging laughs and genre takeoffs prevail. More spoof than satire, these films have fun with the genre but do not seek to attack anyone or anything in particular, going for pure and unpretentious humor that rings louder with those familiar with the tropes.[49] Jules White summed up the horseplay and roughhousing, drawing comparisons between the essential slapstick of the Stooges and the necessity of gunfights in Westerns, and alluding to how the trio brought together these elements: "If we removed the knockabout aspect from these comedies it would have taken away their appeal. Their flavor would be gone. . . . It's like with westerns: take away the cowboy's six-shooter and there's no gunplay; without gunplay, it's a lousy western. The same applies to slapstick comedy: no slapstick, no laughs."[50] These Westerns are Jewish more as a consequence of subtext or sensibility than of any overtly Jewish words or references: the Stooges are East Coast urban outsiders, physically and temperamentally out of place in the rugged, stoic, Anglo Wild West.

In *Horses' Collars* (Columbia, 1935), the first of the Stooges' seventeen Westerns, Larry, Moe, and Curly are city detectives sent west to recover an IOU from an outlaw played by veteran Western villain Fred Kohler, who plans to steal a ranch owned by a young woman.[51] The short film introduces a saloon gag in which the Stooges try to fit in by ordering strong drinks, only to react with wild gestures and winces. *Goofs and Saddles* (Columbia, 1937) has the Stooges as cavalry scouts Buffalo Billius (Curly), Wild Bill Hiccup (Moe), and Just Plain Bill (Larry)—references, respectively, to Buffalo Bill, Wild Bill Hickok, and a popular radio soap opera, *Just Plain Bill*. In *Yes, We Have No Bonanza* (Columbia, 1939), a title parodying the 1923 song "Yes, We Have No Bananas," Larry, Moe, and Curly are incompetent, unmacho prospectors who lose their clothes, have no idea how to use their tools, and happen upon a bundle of coins and bills buried by bank robbers. In *Phony Express* (Columbia, 1943), Curly is called "tall, dark, and handsome"—a phrase associated with Rudolph Valentino—by a saloon woman who is much taller, darker, and handsomer than he is. *The Three*

Troubledoers (Columbia, 1946) takes place in Dead Man's Gulch, a name recycled from the Marx Brothers' *Go West* and the title of a 1943 Republic picture. After Coney Island Curly's gun belt fires by accident, scaring off the villain, the townsfolk make him the next in a long line of sheriffs with tragically short careers, with Moe and Larry as his deputies. *Out West* (Columbia, 1947), featuring Larry, Moe, and Shemp, follows the Stooges' westward migration in hopes of healing Shemp's enlarged leg vein. Upon arriving, Moe tells his partners, "We're out west, boys, so we gotta be tough. . . . Okay, boys, get western." They order strong drinks at a saloon, again prompting over-the-top reactions. Local crooks overhear them mentioning Shemp's vein and think they are talking about a gold vein. Their assumption is "confirmed" when they see a doctor's drawing of the leg, which looks oddly like a map. The short features a great fourth-wall-breaking cavalry joke. The Arizona Kid (Jock Mahoney), an ally of the Stooges, informs the colonel of trouble at Coyote Pass, adding, "I hope you're not too late." "Son," the colonel responds proudly, "never in the history of motion pictures has the United States Cavalry been too late." Of course, they do arrive late. Jock Mahoney returns in *Punchy Cowpunchers* (Columbia, 1950) as a handsome, dumb "six-gun schlemiel" who fumbles around, forgets to load his guns, falls off his horse, and carries his guitar everywhere. Piling on the spoof of the wholesome and ostensibly celibate singing cowboy, he tells the leading lady, "Us westerners aren't the marrying kind. We just go riding off into the sunset."

While the Three Stooges' brand of simple plots, physical comedy, sight gags, and cartoonish violence was tailor-made for two-reelers, their feature films are less memorable. *Gold Raiders* (United Artists, 1951) is a case in point: too much conventional story, not enough slapstick. It does, however, include some rare-at-the-time glimpses of coded Jews in the Wild West. Larry, Moe, and Shemp head west in a peddler's wagon painted with "Three Aces Emporium, Coast to Coast." Caught in cowboy-outlaw gunfire, Moe tells Larry, "The men out here are rough and they love to battle." Larry replies, "Well, I'm weak and soft and I love the Bronx." Arriving in town, they set up their wares in a saloon and Larry announces, "You can't go shopping in the big city, we bring the big city to you." The trio turn out to be scheming merchants: dishonest swindlers and junk salesmen who by the end of the movie are selling insurance.

The Outlaws Is Coming (Columbia, 1965) is the Stooges' sixth and final feature film. The title spoofs the tagline of Alfred Hitchcock's *The Birds* (Universal, 1963), "The birds is coming," thereby ruffling the feathers of many English teachers.[52] Cowritten, directed, and produced by Moe's son-in-law, Norman Maurer, the movie latched onto the Stooges' renewed popularity at the time, bringing together Larry and Moe, then in their sixties, and DeRita, who was in his mid-fifties. The Stooges are bumbling Boston newspaper printers sent to Wyoming in 1871 with reporter Ken Cabot (Adam West). They uncover a plan by Rance Roden (Don Lamond) to kill off all the buffalo, thereby stirring the Natives to riot and destroy the U.S. Cavalry. On their wagon heading west, Curly Joe brings out an animal horn resembling a shofar to "whip up a buffalo call." Moe warns against blowing "those screechy notes," but DeRita plays along to a melodious trumpet track, something that would have amused Jewish viewers familiar with Moe's impression of the horn. Unlike the Stooges' previous Westerns, this one includes Native Americans. While they are, as might be expected, dripping with offensive stereotypes, they break type when the chief's bespectacled son, who has studied at the University of Alabama and speaks with a southern twang, tells Roden to "cut out that broken English and that cornball pantomime." Roden recruits to his gang legendary outlaws Wyatt Earp, Bat Masterson, Cole Younger, Jesse James, Johnny Ringo, Wild Bill Hickok, Bob Dalton, Belle Starr, and Billy the Kid, all of whom are played by children's television hosts from around the country whose shows featured the Stooges' shorts and contributed to their resurgent popularity.[53] Before the outlaws have a chance to do damage, the Stooges sneak into the baddies' hideout while they sleep and glue their guns into their holsters. The next day, they convince the humiliated outlaws to change their ways. At one point in the action, Moe tells the cavalry colonel, "We thought you were going to be late," to which the colonel repeats the classic line, "Sir, never in the history of motion pictures has the United States Cavalry ever been late." At the end of the movie, Curly Joe announces, "Just like in the big budget Westerns, we get to ride into the sunset," cuing a freak thunderstorm.

Bugs Bunny and Yosemite Sam

There is debate about whether Looney Tunes star Bugs Bunny should be viewed as a Jew. On the one hand, non-Jew Tex Avery is generally credited with introducing the character in the 1940 Merrie Melodies short, *A Wild Hare* (Warner Bros.). On the other hand, Bugs was largely based on Groucho Marx and received much of his personality from legendary Jewish voice man Mel Blanc, who based the bunny's accent on a nasally Flatbush mix of Brooklyn whimsicality and Bronx realism.[54] Bugs's brashness and temper might be Irish stereotypes, but his fluid transformation from cop to woman to old man can be read as Jewish immigrant vaudevillians' "ability to become someone else with a simple change of costume," which, according to Jewish studies scholar Andrea Most, "helped them navigate the perilous landscape of American racial ideology both on and off stage."[55] In *Baton Bunny* (Warner Bros., 1959), Bugs's shape-shifting ears twist to form a ten-gallon cowboy hat, a Native headdress, and a cap of a cavalry officer rushing to his own rescue. Yet when Bugs recollects growing up on Manhattan's Lower East Side in *A Hare Grows in Manhattan* (Warner Bros., 1947), he references Betty Smith's 1943 novel, *A Tree Grows in Brooklyn*, about an Irish-Austrian immigrant family, not a Jewish one.[56] And while Bugs is hardly an underdog—his brazenness, violent proclivities, and incontestable command of all situations suggest a godlike string-puller—he nonetheless resonated with self-perceived underdogs in the audience.[57] A 1943 issue of *Showmen's Trade Review* quipped, "The average person, in life a hard-working introvert striving to get along, found in [Bugs Bunny] the nerve and bluster, the boldness and self-assurance, he himself would like to possess."[58]

Western-themed Bugs Bunny shorts were popular throughout the 1940s and 1950s, coinciding with the immense popularity of the Western genre. *Hiawatha's Rabbit Hunt* (Warner Bros., 1941) includes a role reversal in which Bugs breaks free of his Native pursuer's ropes, ties him to a tree, and does a mocking "Indian dance" that morphs into a Latin conga line. In *Wacky Wabbit* (Warner Bros., 1942), he drives prospector Elmer Fudd to pull out his own gold tooth. *Unruly Hare* (Warner Bros., 1945), another Fudd story, shows Bugs retaliating against his adversary through a series of impersonations: female, fireman, baseball catcher, and hobo. *A Feather in His Hair* (Warner Bros., 1948) has a Native American with glasses, prominent nose, broken English, and a New York inflection, suggesting a tongue-in-cheek Hebraic Indian spoof. In these and other stories, Bugs's clever (possibly Jewish) mind gets him out of situations where brawn would be the Wild West's go-to method.

Bugs Bunny's main cowboy villain is, of course, Yosemite Sam, the pint-sized, hotheaded outlaw whose bluster, hypercharged emotions, and high-volume barks (supplied by Blanc) overcompensate for his bumbling ineptness. Never a serious match for Bugs, Yosemite Sam, whose appearance was based on red-haired, five-foot-four Jewish animator and director Isadore "Friz" Freleng, has the residue of the try-and-fail Jewish cowboy sendups of vaudeville and early film. Preceded in type, size, and hair color by the Red Hot Ryder, "Brooklyn's tiniest cowboy," in the 1944 short *Buckaroo Bugs* (Warner Bros.), Yosemite Sam made his first appearance the following year in *Hare Trigger* (Warner Bros.). The short's writer, Michael Maltese, remembers how he settled on the character's name: "I was going to call him Texas Tiny . . . Wyoming Willie . . . Denver Dan. We were deliberately going for a location to make it Western. So I called him 'Yosemite Sam.' I had never been to Yosemite, but 'Yosemite Sam' sounded right."[59]

The euphonious name spurred decades of speculation about Yosemite Sam's real identity, including the possible play on words *Yo-Semite*. Finally, in "Daffy Duck, Esquire," a 2013 episode of *The Looney Tunes Show* (Cartoon Network), Sam is introduced in court as Samuel Rosenbaum. Whether any of this makes Yosemite Sam canonically Jewish is an open question, but a certain Jewishness underpins the character and the broader Looney Tunes universe.

Blazing Saddles (1974)

The plot of Mel Brooks's *Blazing Saddles* is intentionally straightforward: a crooked politician, Hedley Lamarr (Harvey Korman), conspires with Governor William J. Le Petomane (Brooks) to displace the townsfolk of Rock Ridge, grab the land, and profit from its sale to the railroad. The two men try to make the inhabitants leave by assigning them a new sheriff, Bart (Cleavon Little), a Black man whose appearance will have them running for the hills. Instead, the sheriff and his sidekick, the Waco Kid (Gene Wilder), a worn-out, alcoholic former gunfighter, gradually win over the townspeople. Bart, a debonair urbanite who brings 1974 threads and lingo to 1874, overcomes racial vitriol in a "triumph of humanity over its inherent prejudices."[60] For some critics, neither the laughs nor the message landed: Pauline Kael called it a "comedy of chaos, with a surfeit of chaos and scarcity of comedy."[61] But most were more generous, agreeing with Gene Siskel that "whenever the laughs begin to run dry, Brooks and his quartet of gag writers splash about in a pool of obscenities that score belly laughs if your ears aren't sensitive and if you're hip to Western movie conventions being parodied."[62] Less often mentioned is the film's shared zeitgeist with Black cinema of the 1970s. For example, *Buck and the Preacher* (Columbia, 1972), Sidney Poitier's directorial debut, stars Poitier and Harry Belafonte as an ex-soldier wagon master and a con artist preacher who assist freed slaves dogged by violent agents sent by Louisiana plantation owners. Another film, *Thomasine and Bushrod* (Columbia, 1974), puts a Black Western spin on *Bonnie and Clyde* (Warner Bros., 1967), while the documentary *Black Rodeo* (Cinema Releasing, 1972) features an all-Black rodeo on New York City's Randall's Island. Like the best of the era's blaxploitation films, *Blazing Saddles* heroicizes a fashionable inner-city Black and uses forceful storytelling to dismantle white myths of rugged individualism, the pioneer spirit, and racial tolerance.

Yet while Black audiences might see *Blazing Saddles* as a Black Western, Jews, including Brooks, view it as a Jewish one. When asked to name his favorite Jewish movies, Brooks cited *Schindler's List* (Universal, 1993), *Fiddler on the Roof* (United Artists, 1971), *The Frisco Kid* (Warner Bros., 1979), and two of his own: *The Producers* (Embassy, 1967) and *Blazing Saddles*.[63] The first three are stories with Jewish characters, Jewish events, and Jewish themes, but Brooks's movies are less overt. The Jewish identities of accountant Leo Bloom (Gene Wilder) and greedy producer Max Bialystock (Zero Mostel) are unstated in *The Producers*, about a scam to make a tasteless Broadway flop about Hitler that ends up being an inconvenient success.[64] Likewise, *Blazing Saddles* regularly appears on lists of great Jewish movies, but its conspicuous Jewish content is limited to Brooks's brief appearance as a Yiddish-speaking Native American chief. According to Brooks, his chief was not meant to spoof the Hebraic Indian myth or the cottage industry of Jewish actors playing Native Americans, such as Leonard Nimoy's Chief Black Hawk in *Old Overland Trail* (Republic, 1953) or Ed Ames's Mingo on four seasons of *Daniel Boone* (NBC, 1964–68). Instead, it came from an aversion to "Indian talk": "I didn't want him to do the clichéd Indian sounds—'Hi Yoyo'—and that sort of stuff. I was thinking that no one knew Yiddish so why not use it."[65] Posters for the movie prominently feature the chief's profile with Hebrew words on his headdress (*kosher l'Pesach*, or

Mel Brooks as the Native American chief in *Blazing Saddles* (Warner Bros., 1974).

kosher for Passover), adding to the lasting impression of *Blazing Saddles* as a Jewish movie.

Another reason for the film's perceived Jewishness is the casting of Wilder as the Waco Kid. Brooks had initially asked John Wayne to play the role (just as he was approached to play Tommy Lillard in *The Frisco Kid*), but Wayne said that his fans would protest. Dan Daily, whose Westerns included *A Ticket to Tomahawk* (Twentieth Century–Fox, 1950), also turned down the role. Gig Young, whose Western credits included *Lust for Gold* (Columbia, 1949) and *Slaughter Trail* (RKO, 1951), then took on the part, but his portrayal of the alcoholic was a little too real: he had to be removed from the set by ambulance for severe alcohol poisoning. Wilder was brought on in a pinch, with Brooks conceding, "I wanted an old alkie. I got a New York Jew."[66]

As a result of Wilder's casting as the nonracist sidekick to Little's Sheriff Bart, viewers received the film as a reminder of the Black-Jewish civil rights alliance, which by the late 1960s had eroded over identity politics and Black militants' objections to Zionism.[67] Behind the scenes, this alliance played out in the film's "gang of comedy writers" approach, adapted from Brooks's formative days in Sid Caesar's writing room. Along with fellow Jews Andrew Bergman and Norman Steinberg, Brooks recruited two Black writers, Alan Uger and young standup Richard Pryor, whom Brooks had wanted to play Sheriff Bart. Brooks was keen on the Black-Jewish solidarity subtext, which Wilder helped realize onscreen in a way Wayne or Young could not have. According to Brooks, the movie "comes from the feeling that, as a Jew and as a person, you don't fit into the mainstream of American society. It comes from the realization that even though you're better and smarter, you'll never belong."[68] More to the point, in Brooks's view, "If you want a comedy to last, there's a secret you must follow: You have to have an engine driving it. In *Blazing Saddles*, there's a very serious backstory. Racial prejudice is the engine that really drives the film and helps to make it work."[69]

This political consciousness is the real substance of the film's Jewish humor—or, as Brooks would call it, its New York Jewish humor.[70] None of the writers had ever lived in the West, and their only expertise in the genre came from watching Westerns as kids.[71] This perspective might explain the abundance of Western cinema references in the movie: the expanding railroad, quicksand, land snatching, wagon trains, hangings, a preacher, a mountain man who speaks "authentic frontier gibberish," a new sheriff, and the clichéd title words. The movie's genre genuineness came primarily from Frankie Laine, the popular singer of Western themes from the 1940s through the 1960s, who sang the film's opening song, and the casting of Slim Pickens as the dumb henchman Taggart. As producer Michael Hertzberg puts it, there were "a bunch of New York Jews doing this movie, a Western, and there's Slim Pickens, who's Mr. West."[72] Pickens roughed it in his Winnebago with his dog, campfire, beans, and rifle while the other cast and crew members lodged at a motel near the shooting location in Antelope Valley, California.

Some exaggerated authenticity also comes from the writers' outsider perspective. For the first time in mainstream film history, farts were heard onscreen when the cowboys sit around a campfire drinking black coffee and eating plates of beans. Brooks explains, "Surely there had to be one little sound from all those beans."[73] The gratuitous scene, which was turned silent when the movie aired on network TV (giving the impression of a "choreographed ballet"), has been described as "a barrage of farting that sounds like the gunfight at the O.K. Corral."[74] Brooks's character is named for a famous turn-of-the-twentieth-century French flatulist, Joseph Pujol, whose stage name was Le Pétomane.

Even more controversial is the copious use of the n-word in the film. Yet while comedically excessive, these are not frivolous utterances: everyone in the "peaceful town of Rock Ridge" using the word is an ignorant, racist buffoon. This blatant prejudice not only subverts the Western myth of frontier harmony—which, if present, typically extended only to those of European extraction—but also held a mirror to continued racial tensions of 1970s America (and beyond). As Wilder recalled, the writers "smash racism in the face, and the nose is bleeding, but they're doing it while you laugh."[75] The film's biting commentary includes Lamarr's quip that there are "200,000 acres of Indian territory which we have deemed unsafe for their use at this time," and the Waco Kid's reassurance to Bart after an old woman calls him the n-word, "You've got to remember, these are just simple farmers. These are people of the land. The common clay of the new West. You know—morons."

When *Blazing Saddles* was released, some critics were concerned that it spelled the end of Westerns. Not only was it wildly successful, but its box-office clout also helped sustain the genre, which was well past its prime. Social commentary aside, it was a love letter to Westerns written by people who had been raised on them, grew up to see their flaws, and still revered them in an irreverent way. To some observers, the film's simultaneous lampooning and recalling of genre signatures exemplifies Jewish humor's tendency to throw shade at power rather than to try to overthrow it. As Lawrence Epstein points out, "If America is considered the object being spoofed and Jews those who do the spoofing, then Jews can be seen as mocking the wider society but with no revolutionary intent, no desire to change it. Additionally, spoofing provides Jews with an aesthetic distance from America, the object being spoofed, so as not to be absorbed by the country. In Brooks' conception, then, an American Jewish identity makes Jews permanently partial insiders and simultaneously permanently partial outsiders. This identity allows Jews a connection to the country without disappearing in it, though the tenuous nature of the dual identity is never explored in Brooks' films."[76]

In 1975, Andrew Bergman made a pilot for CBS called *Black Bart*, written by screenwriters Michael Elias and Frank Shaw, who had sold a first draft of *The Frisco Kid* (called *No-Knife*) in 1971. The implicit Black-Jewish partnership was preserved with the casting of Louis Gossett Jr. as Bart and Steve Landesberg as Reb Jordan, an ex-Confederate soldier whose name suggests both *rebel* and the Yiddish honorific *reb* (rabbi). Although the racial humor was toned down for TV, the failed show continued the film's fight against corruption and bigotry in the Old West and has a few nice touches, like Bart's white horse whose name is Whitey.

Three Amigos (1986)

Three Amigos (Orion, 1986), helmed by Jewish director John Landis and cowritten by Steve Martin and two Jews, *Saturday Night Live* producer Lorne Michaels and singer-songwriter Randy Newman, is a reflexive comedy about a trio of urban greenhorns who are unwittingly thrown into the "rougher masculinity" of lawless Mexico.[77] The movie is a reapplication of the Three Stooges formula, with dimwitted silent film cowboy actors Lucky Day (Steve Martin), Dusty Bottoms (Chevy Chase), and Ned Nederlander (Martin Short) even doing their version of the Stooges' salute from *Horses' Collars*. The title plays off The Four Amigos, a 1960s Puerto Rican musical quartet that specialized in Spanish-language versions of American hits. It is also a nod to the Westerns' many trios, such as *The Three Mesquiteers* (Republic, 1936), *Three on the Trail* (Paramount, 1936), *Three Texas Steers* (Republic, 1939), *Three in the Saddle* (Producers Releasing, 1945), *Three Young Texans* (Twentieth Century–Fox, 1954), *The Three Outlaws* (Associated Film, 1956), *Three Violent People* (Paramount, 1957), and perhaps especially *The Three Caballeros* (Disney, 1944), one of the first feature-length movies to combine traditional animation with live-action actors.

The Amigos, who play Spanish vaqueros onscreen, are invited to "perform" in the remote Mexican village of Santa Poco only to learn that they have been recruited to fight real-life bandits led by El Guapo (Alfonso Arau) the "infamous," which the actors think means "more than famous." Recently fired from Goldsmith Pictures by studio head Harry Flugelman (Joe Mantegna)—a caricature of the era's tyrannical Jewish movie moguls—the actors reprise the vaudeville conceit of (coded) cowboy Jews who lack the toughness and know-how to make it as real cowboys. But instead of returning to "civilization" with their heads hanging low, the Amigos fend off the imposing bad guys, ultimately transforming from schlemiels to heroes.

The Amigos arrive in Mexico and enter a saloon that had been shot up moments before by ruthless German arms dealers on their way to visit El Guapo. (This plot element mirrors the 1969 revisionist Western *The Wild*

Bunch, in which Germans similarly deliver crates of guns to the Mexican villain.) Before leaving, the Germans warn that their German friends, who are also arriving in town, would not be as kind. Petrified, the dirt-covered, gun-toting patrons mistake the goofy, mariachi/charro-dressed Amigos for those "friends." The Amigos ask the bartender for beers but instead get tequila, sending them into zany contortions again borrowed from the Three Stooges. Believing the silent patrons to be starstruck, the Amigos launch into an effeminate song-and-dance routine, highlighting the absurdity of Hollywood's singing cowboys in an "authentic" Western setting and vaguely recalling the emasculated Jewishness of Cantor's Henry Williams.

El Guapo and his men finally confront the Amigos in Santa Poco, where they think they are starring in a Wild West show. Their gimmicks are interrupted when Lucky Day is shot from his horse. "Real bullets!" The Amigos burst into tears: "We're not going to get paid." "El Guapo only kills men," the villain scoffs. "He does not kill crying women." The Amigos ride off, leaving the villagers vulnerable to El Guapo's gang. After much soul-searching in the desert, the Amigos eventually decide to return to the village to help.

Lucky Day (Steve Martin, bottom) and Ned Nederlander (Martin Short) in *Three Amigos* (Orion, 1986).

"Ned, we could get killed," Dusty Bottoms says. "Back there," Ned replies, "the Three Amigos are already dead. Here, we could be the Three Amigos for real."

Despite the comic tone and requisite suspension of disbelief, the ensuing escapades are surprisingly grounded. At no point do the Amigos transform into classic cowboy heroes. Instead, they rely on their acting backgrounds and cleverness to navigate the action sequences. In the end, the hapless, self-centered actors become heroes on their own terms, using Hollywood ingenuity to defeat rugged masculinity. Recalling one of their silent films, *Amigos, Amigos, Amigos*, the trio turns the villagers' sewing skills against El Guapo and his gang, creating facsimiles of the Amigos' flashy charro outfits and overwhelming the bandits with what appear to be dozens of Amigos in all shapes and sizes—men, women, children, and elderly. Leading up to this climactic scene, Lucky Day stirs the villagers with his imitation of an inspirational cowboy speech: "In a way, all of us have an El Guapo to face someday. For some, shyness might be their El Guapo. For others, a lack of education might be their El Guapo. For us, El Guapo is a big, dangerous guy who wants to kill us. But as sure as my name is Lucky Day, the people of Santa Poco can conquer their own personal El Guapo, who also happens to be the actual El Guapo."

City Slickers (1991) and *City Slickers II: The Legend of Curly's Gold* (1994)

Another iteration of three urban dwellers in the "authentic West" is *City Slickers* (Columbia, 1991), a contemporary Western directed by Ron Underwood and cowritten by Jewish screenwriters Lowell Ganz and Babaloo Mandel. It continues a theme identified by pop culture scholar John G. Cawelti: the protagonists "win our interest and sympathy not by courage and heroic deeds but by bemused incompetence, genial cowardice and the ability to face the worst with buoyancy and wit."[78] The film follows three friends, Mitch Robbins (Billy Crystal), Phil Berquist (Daniel Stern), and Ed Furillo (Bruno Kirby), on their midlife-crisis adventure involving a two-week cattle drive from New Mexico to Colorado. Ed, an Italian, is called a macho lunatic, while his two friends, thinly veiled Jews, see themselves as sheep. The extended cast of pay-to-play dude ranchers includes Jewish ice cream entrepreneurs Ira and Barry Shalowitz (David Paymer and Josh Mostel), inspired by Ben and Jerry's Ben Cohen and Jerry Greenfield.

The New Yorkers' ill-suitedness for the task is established in a series of vignettes: a montage of them trying on cowboy clothes, a scene of them nursing their saddle-sore crotches, and Mitch's admission at the start of the cattle drive, "I feel like a schmuck," to which Phil replies, "Oh yeah, big schmuck. Yee-haw!" Their frequent references to Western entertainment—singing the *Bonanza* and *Rawhide* themes, quoting John Wayne's "Move 'em out!" from *Red River* (United Artists, 1948), and the like—highlight their unpreparedness for the actual hardships of the cattle drive. When the wisecracking Mitch tells leathery trail boss Curly, played by Western mainstay Jack Palance, "It's just my way," Curly responds, "I don't know that way," highlighting the distance between the verbose city Jew and the silent cowboy type. "We're a dying breed," Curly later laments. "You city folk, you worry about a lot of shit, don't you?" In truth, the sarcastic city dwellers are more believable than the authenticity they perceive in Curly, "one of the last real men." Curly is a squinting, stoic, cowboy loner, a mythic figure about whom the friends fantasize becoming.[79]

When Curly dies halfway through the film, the Old West seems to die with him. The friends must now complete the drive to Colorado, braving a heavy storm and finally shedding their cushy white-collar lives and First World problems in a physical struggle against nature. When they reach Colorado, they are disappointed to learn that the herd is destined for meat. "I've got to stop being a schmuck," sighs an exasperated Phil. Mitch adopts a calf, Norman, whose life he had saved earlier in the film, and the city slickers return home transformed. All of this is predictable, and much of it is contrived. However, as Roger Ebert pointed out, "There are so many ways this movie could have gone wrong—with gratuitous action scenes, forced dialogue or contrived showdowns—that it's sort of astonishing, how many ways it finds to go right."[80]

The same cannot be said for the sequel, *The Legend of Curly's Gold* (Columbia, 1994). Comparing it to the original, Ebert wrote, "The [first] movie was a comedy, yes, but it was also rich in human values, and in their talks around the campfire the men confided secrets and worries that we could identify with. The movie was so special that Crystal said he didn't want to do a sequel until he had exactly the right screenplay. He should have waited longer."[81] Crystal shares writing credits with Ganz and Mandel on the picture. The MacGuffin is a lost gold mine outside of Las Vegas that turns out to be a phony gimmick for a treasure-hunt adventure business. The movie introduces Curly's twin brother, Duke, played by Palance, and Mitch's black-sheep brother, Glen Robbins (Jon Lovitz), who takes Ed's place. The movie not only recycles elements of Western classics (most notably *The Treasure of the Sierra Madre* [Warner Bros., 1948]) but also, in the tradition of bad sequels, poorly rehashes its predecessor. Mitch and Phil have no reason to look for the supposed treasure; they are now rich and happy. Despite having a more Jewish cast, with Lovitz joining Crystal and Stern as the third Amigo, the Jewish signaling from the first film fades behind the flavorless comedy. A few moments foreground the city-rural culture clash, as when the three city slickers invite Duke to snuggle up with them for warmth on a stormy night and he responds, "I'm up here with a goddamn musical," but the comments lack the weight and charm of the original. Ebert correctly assessed that the movie "makes the mistake of thinking we care more about the gold than about the city slickers. . . . It is a lesson easily said, but learned with difficulty, that in a good movie the plot should be at the service of the characters, and not the other way around."[82]

CHAPTER 7

Revisionist Sensibility

Searching for historical fidelity in Westerns is usually a fruitless endeavor. It is neither the intention nor the capacity of these films to tell what really happened. Still, some movies are more sensitive to historical realities than others. Within the constraints and conventions of consumer-focused entertainment, they strive to highlight neglected aspects and forgotten features of the Wild West, all through a presentist lens. In this regard, they resonate with elements of New Western History, which recovers stories of the American West from the point of view of the oppressed, conquered, and marginalized; questions the triumphalism of westward expansion; and critiques the white ethnocentrism of Turner's frontier thesis.[1]

Westerns, like all facets of culture, are products of their time and place. Not only are the filmmakers themselves engaged in the events and attitudes of their day, but to appeal to audiences, their films must also tap into general trends, tastes, and expectations. Westerns are in a sense current-day snapshots of the past, revealing more about the society the storytellers and intended viewers inhabit than about the world depicted onscreen. This was as true for the earlier romanticizing of rugged individualism and implicit white Christian supremacy as it was for later films that critiqued those notions.

As narrative presentations of a useful past, Westerns frame and reframe historical periods (usually post–Civil War to the turn of the twentieth century), historical figures (for example, Wyatt Earp and Billy the Kid), and historical events (such as Native American wars and gold rushes) to make sense in—and make sense of—the present. A Western's merits depend not on accurate depictions of the Old West but on how those depictions thrill, entertain, and move the audience. Westerns, especially during the genre's heyday from the postwar 1940s through the 1950s, almost always portrayed cowboys, lawmen, and outlaws—both bad-guy and Robin Hood types—as white, despite the racial and ethnic diversity of the real people on whom those characters are based (Mexicans, Blacks, and Jews among them). The American cowboy actually has Spanish roots, frontier towns were multicultural, and Native Americans were, of course, victims rather than villains. Even the depiction of the frontier as lawless and excessively dangerous does not accord with the historical record: there was more violence in some established eastern cities and more vigilantism in the South than in the western states and territories.[2] As Scott Simmon writes in *The Invention of the Western Film*, "Indeed, the types of murder that Western legends claim as so distinctive to the West—personal quarrels, barroom gunfights, killing over insults—remain statistically much more common in the South than in any other region, including the West." But to acknowledge "gunplay as in any way 'southern' would be to admit how much [the Western] looks not forward but backward toward a defeated traditionalism."[3]

A major turning point for the American Western was the abandonment of the Production Code, freeing filmmakers to draw on the prevailing antiestablishment zeitgeist and the (counter)culture's rejection of simplistic morality. Westerns had already lost their Hollywood dominance by the early 1960s. Changing times, shifting tastes, and growing cynicism made untenable the simplistic portrayals of white-hatted heroes and black-hatted villains and fights between virtuous cowboys and evil Native Americans. The Vietnam War cast doubt on the morality of expansionism, and various social protest and ethnic/racial pride movements called for new representations. The few classical Westerns that remained on television, on the big screen, or in advertising archetypes were a small remnant of the genre's heyday. Between 1953 and 1963, Hollywood Westerns dropped from 27 percent of films to just 9 percent.[4] What gradually emerged in their place were revisionist Westerns: critical, conscientious, contrarian retellings that added shades of gray to black-and-white stories, stripped violence of its redemptive value, offered sympathetic depictions of Natives and other mis- and underrepresented groups, and generally upended Western themes and character types. In these postclassical Westerns or anti-Westerns, societal reassessments of the late 1960s and beyond were projected onto the mythic West.

Dirt was and remains a key feature of these films, a symbol of realism that marks these stories as unsanitized.[5] Equating unclean lifestyles and harsh conditions with moral ambiguity, they literally and figuratively soil traditional genre signifiers. The vantage points of women, Native Americans, Mexicans, Blacks, Chinese, and other marginalized groups likewise make a mess of clear-cut formulas. Notable contributions include Sergio Leone's antihero spaghetti Westerns, *A Fistful of Dollars* (United Artists, 1964), *For a Few Dollars More* (United Artists, 1965), and *The Good, the Bad, and the Ugly* (United Artists, 1966); Sam Peckinpah's *The Wild Bunch* (Warner Bros., 1969) and *Pat Garrett and Billy the Kid* (MGM, 1973), which killed the Western mystique with crude characters and excessive violence; Clint Eastwood's *The Outlaw Josey Wales* (Warner Bros., 1973), which abandoned the upstanding portrait of Unionists; and a number of 1990s "pro-Native" entries, such as Kevin Costner's *Dances with Wolves* (Orion, 1990), Walter Hill's *Geronimo: An American Legend* (Columbia, 1993), and Jim Jarmusch's *Dead Man* (Miramax, 1995). Still, what exactly constitutes a revisionist Western is not easy to pinpoint. For example, according to Native American history scholar Raul S. Chavez, regardless of the reputation of *Dances with Wolves*, it is "an unabashed defender of White Supremacist doctrine," with Lieutenant John J. Dunbar/Dances with Wolves (Costner) as the paternalistic defender of "good Indians" against "bad Indians," who are shown as "hideous creatures warranting extermination."[6] Cultural historian Richard Slotkin adds that revisionism is often superficial in that it uses "a (mainly) White agenda of cultural revision" to assuage an inherited sense of guilt rather than going deeper in terms of cultural competency or righting wrongs.[7]

In addition to debates about the effectiveness and motives of revisionism is the issue of periodization. Although the revisionist perspective is generally viewed as a post-Code phenomenon informed by academic and countercultural historiographical movements, aspects of revisionism sometimes appear earlier. To cite examples already covered in this book, *Cimarron* (1931) challenged the myth of interethnic harmony on the frontier, *Harlem on the Prairie* (1937) populated the West with multifaceted Black characters, *Forty Guns* (1957) gave a woman the role of iron-fisted taskmaster, and *Cat Ballou* (1965) made the female lead an active and independent force. Director John Ford, who was instrumental in codifying classical Westerns, changed course in the mid-1950s with *The Searchers*, arguably setting the new countertendency in motion. John Wayne's character, Ethan Edwards, is an outdated, openly bigoted relic of earlier norms. Ford's final Western, *Cheyenne Autumn* (Warner Bros., 1964), based on the Northern Cheyenne Exodus of 1878–79, in which Northern Cheyenne attempted to flee Indian Territory for their Montana homeland, is likewise considered an apology for Ford's anti–Native American track record. To these we might add a fistful of films from the 1940s and 1950s that critique the John Wayne–style macho bravado, such as Howard Hawks's *Red River* (United Artists, 1948), starring the Duke himself, and several that transpose archetypal male traits—powerful, gunslinging, self-reliant, always in control—onto confident female leads, including *Arizona* (Columbia, 1940), *Duel in the Sun* (Selznick, 1946), *Yellow Sky* (Twentieth Century–Fox, 1948), *Hellfire* (Republic, 1949), *Rawhide* (Twentieth Century–Fox, 1951), and *Rancho Notorious* (RKO, 1952).

Some critics identify revisionism based on how much the stories interrogate or overturn norms, excluding examples where reflexive and reflective elements are seen as tangential. But even then, such measurements are subjective. The determination of which movies have genre manipulation as their primary focus ultimately lies with film criticism, not with the movies themselves.[8] A single scene might be considered revisionist, as is the case with the campfire flatulence schtick in *Blazing Saddles*. Although exaggerated for comic effect, the farting adds a touch of realism lacking in cinematic depictions of rural frontier diets. California Gold Rush accounts, for example, depict badly prepared meals cooked by inexperienced men who ignited cooking fires with gunpower, put rice over flames without first adding water, ate whatever they could find, and used unclean frying pans, pots, plates, and utensils.[9] Scientifically, Mel Brooks had it right: flatulence is a byproduct of intestinal bacterial metabolism, a natural process exacerbated when food is difficult to digest. In the case of *Blazing Saddles,* the men eat copious amounts of unsanitary baked beans containing undigestible carbohydrates.

A looser approach would grant the revisionist label to any Western "that in whole or part interrogate[s] aspects of the genre such as its traditional representations of history and myth, heroism and violence, masculinity and minorities."[10] Virtually all Westerns made since the 1960s fit this description, whether they are driven by a social agenda or are merely keeping the genre fresh for contemporary audiences. This group includes a number of

Jewish-made projects. The TV series *Branded* (NBC, 1965–66), created by Larry Cohen, centers on a blacklisted ex-cavalry captain thrown out of the military for alleged cowardice. *The Misfits* (United Artists, 1961), a neo-Western penned by Arthur Miller, shows cowboy culture out of sync with modern times. *The Professionals* (Columbia, 1966), written and directed by Richard Brooks, tells of a Texas millionaire who hires four mercenaries to rescue his wife from a notorious Mexican bandit, only to find that she does not want to return. *Tell Them Willie Boy Is Here* (Universal, 1969), directed by Abraham Polonsky, draws on the true story of a Chemehuevi man hunted by a posse for killing his lover's father in self-defense. *A Man Called Horse* (National General, 1970), directed by Elliot Silverstein, climaxes with Native warriors massacring white invaders bent on annihilating them. *The Ballad of Little Jo* (Fine Line, 1993), written and directed by Maggie Greenwald, has a society woman going west and living as a man to escape the stigma of having a child out of wedlock. *Bad Girls* (20th Century Fox, 1994), cowritten by Ken Friedman and directed by Jonathan Kaplan, imbues female outlaws with the toughness, tenacity, and violence traditionally ascribed to masculinity.

Finding a specifically Jewish angle in this almost universal approach is difficult. From a certain perspective, any Western made by a Jewish director and/or writer is in some sense Jewish. But what exactly distinguishes a Jewish revisionist sensibility? Straightforwardly Jewish themes and characters are generally absent from these films unless, for example, we include *The Frisco Kid* or *Fievel Goes West* as revisionist for restoring Jews to the westward expansion narrative. But sensibility suggests an identifiable outlook: a point of view unique to the individual filmmakers (there is no one-size-fits-all, monolithic Jewish viewpoint) but still broadly consistent with an outsider, questioning, deconstructive perspective rooted in the dialogical culture of a historically marginalized diaspora people.

Perhaps instead of searching for distinctly Jewish aspects in these revisionist projects, it is enough to highlight the Jews' experience as oppressed minorities and their disproportionate involvement in liberal and radical leftist politics since the Jewish Enlightenment (Haskalah)—which picked up steam during the 1800s and into the early 1900s, resurged with the 1960s and 1970s counterculture, and continues to the present—as sources of cinematic identification with and empathy for other marginalized peoples. There is also the natural affinity between revisionism and rabbinic midrash (the age-old process of imaginatively retelling and filling gaps in biblical texts). Talmud scholar Ithamar Gruenwald describes this interpretive impulse as the "midrashic condition," or a "mental attitude or disposition in which the interpretative attention expressed entails more than a concern for lexicological or plain-sense meaning of a text or piece of information. What really matters . . . is not the mere act of understanding texts, but the creation of the meaning that is attached to them."[11] For filmmakers engaged in revisionist Westerns, deciphering meanings or values from earlier movie "texts" is less important than using the old structures and settings to create new meanings and alternative themes. Just as in scripture-based Jewish storytelling, there is the text (Western tropes and clichés), the retelling of the text, and the retelling of the retelling, each with its own set of questions and emphases that makes it relevant. Of course, this does not mean that Jews invented revisionist Westerns or are the only ones capable of engaging in the process. The long list of revisionist Westerns says otherwise. Rather, revisionism fits comfortably in Jewish midrashic culture. Others have noted resemblances between classical rabbinic midrash and contemporary creative activities such as fan fiction and popular media content.[12] As Geoffrey H. Hartman and Sanford Budick acknowledge in their anthology, *Midrash and Literature*, similar tendencies drive modern-day reappraisals and reformulations of long-established genres, a group that includes Westerns made by Jewish filmmakers.[13]

The Devil's Doorway (1950)

Six years before *The Searchers*, director Anthony Mann broke narrative and stylistic ground with *The Devil's Doorway* (MGM, 1950). Mann's mother was a Jewish drama teacher, while his father was a Catholic academic. When he was young the family moved from San Diego to New York, where he developed a penchant for acting and theater at the Young Men's Hebrew Association.[14] In the late 1940s, Mann made a series of crime films, including *Desperate* (RKO, 1947) and *Raw Deal* (Eagle-Lion, 1948), that fused a noir style with elements of Hollywood's "tolerance cycle"—exposing antisemitism in *Crossfire* (RKO, 1947) and *Gentlemen's Agreement* (Twentieth Century–Fox, 1947) and anti-Black racism in *Pinky* (Twentieth Century–Fox, 1949) and *Intruder in the Dust* (MGM, 1949). *The Devil's Doorway*,

Mann's first Western, is an intriguing transition that features a takedown of cherished Western tropes.

The Devil's Doorway centers on Lance Poole (Robert Taylor), a prosperous Shoshone chief who returns from Union Army service in the Civil War to find his Wyoming ranch taken over by racists. Realizing that his assimilation into white society was in vain, Poole sheds his Euro-American attire, reclaims his long hair and bandana, and defends a piece of land with fellow Shoshone. When the white oppressors kill Poole, he is wearing a Union Army uniform, Congressional Medal of Honor, and traditional headdress, symbolizing the country's many broken promises to Native Americans and, as media professor Julian Petley argues, exposing "with merciless logic that the purpose of (white) law is repression and exploitation, and that political power does indeed flow from the barrel of a gun"—an allusion to Mao's famous dictum.[15]

Set against the establishment of the Wyoming Territory (1868) and the Homestead Act (enacted in 1862), which legalized land-grabbing, the film was ahead of its time in portraying racism as systemic, not individual: the true villains are colonialism, the United States, and the law. Poole's two white defenders, the local marshal and a female lawyer, are presented as sympathetic but not salvific. The lawyer, Orrie Masters (Paula Raymond), although anachronistic (there is no record of women lawyers in Wyoming before 1874), accentuates the film's central message: her interracial romance with Poole remains taboo, her "typically female" optimism is dashed, and her faith in justice is obliterated when she invites the U.S. Cavalry to negotiate a truce only to see the military men side with the white antagonists and kill Poole.[16]

The Devil's Doorway is based on a short story by Guy Trosper, "The Drifter," about a conflict between a small-time rancher and a ruthless cattle baron.[17] Though in the story, both men are white, Mann's film transforms the protagonist into a well-to-do Indigenous landowner whose "sin" was thinking he could integrate at the top. According to film and media scholar Joanna Hearne, this rewriting made the story an allegory for early civil rights struggles, laying bare the cruelty and hypocrisy of segregation but avoiding the ire of conservative audiences, the Production Code office, and McCarthyism. "The threat of 'miscegenation' in *Devil's Doorway*," writes Hearne, "is one of native integration into white family structures, of native claims to property, and of native permanence rather than disappearance."[18] The film traces American racism to its economic roots, with one of Poole's friends reminding him that "nobody likes a rich Indian." Its unvarnished critique of the capitalist system earned it recognition as Film of the Year in the Communist Party USA's *Daily Worker*.

From a twenty-first-century point of view that is sensitive to cultural appropriation, the casting of matinee idol Taylor as the Shoshone protagonist seems off. However, his presence earned sympathy from white viewers, and the movie would not have been made otherwise. Mann may have felt uneasy with casting a white actor as a Native, a decision that clashed with his intention of giving voice to the oppressed. The casting is somewhat rectified when Poole escorts Orrie Masters and her mother home and they encounter a group of Shoshone elders, women, and children, played by Native Americans speaking their own language, who are fleeing brutal conditions on the reservation.

The Devil's Doorway is mostly forgotten. It was overshadowed at the box office by another film that year, *Broken Arrow* (Twentieth Century–Fox, 1950), directed by Delmer Daves and penned by Jewish screenwriter Albert Maltz, that less effectively (and more sentimentally) addresses the question of whether whites and Natives can get along.[19] Mann is better remembered for a string of Westerns starring James Stewart, including *Winchester '73* (Universal, 1950), *Bend of the River* (Universal, 1952), *The Naked Spur* (MGM, 1953), *The Far Country* (Universal, 1954), and *The Man from Laramie* (Columbia, 1955), that despite being "rather too neatly self-contained" brought a distinct psychological complexity to the genre.[20] *The Furies* (Paramount, 1950), starring Barbara Stanwyck, introduced a Freudian element to the story of a woman's struggles with her father's legacy and the ranch she will inherit. With these and other Westerns, Mann skewed the genre toward bleak narratives and tormented protagonists, influencing John Ford and other directors and foreshadowing the revisionist Westerns to come. Mann was not always as successful as he was with *The Devil's Doorway* and his fistful of classics. He also directed the widely panned 1960 remake of *Cimarron*, a misfire that, according to critic David Thomson, shows Mann's ability as an "utterly refined" and "master craftsman" but is "devoid of personality, as if he hardly knew an outside world to compare with his films."[21]

High Noon (1952)

High Noon (United Artists, 1952), which takes place in a small town in the New Mexico Territory in 1898, was helmed by influential Jewish Polish-born director Fred Zinnemann, a visual stylist who meticulously researched, sketched, and annotated his shots. Will Kane (Gary Cooper) is a former marshal trying to start afresh with his violence-abhorring Quaker bride, Amy Fowler (Grace Kelly). When an ex-convict from Kane's past, Frank Miller (Ian MacDonald), is coming to town to settle the score, the former lawman is torn between breaking his vow of nonviolence and facing Miller or leaving to avoid a shootout. Kane chooses to stay but struggles to assemble a posse in a series of escalating scenes counting down to Miller's arrival at high noon. The judge who sentenced Miller asks Kane, "Why must you be stupid?" before fleeing on horseback. At the saloon, Kane is told, "You must be crazy coming in here to raise a posse. Frank has friends in here, you know that." More concerned for their own well-being—and the town's economic growth—the townspeople convince themselves that this is merely a personal conflict between Miller and Kane and that a posse is unnecessary because their taxes support local law enforcement. During a meeting at a church, Kane is urged to leave town: "It's better for you and it's better for us." A friend of Kane's agrees to be deputized but backs out when he realizes he is the only volunteer, sighing, "I got no stake in this." Former marshal Martin Howe (Lon Chaney Jr.) tells Kane, "You risk your skin catching killers and the juries turn 'em lose so that they can come back and shoot at you again. If you're honest, you're poor your whole life. And in the end, you wind up dying all alone on some dirty street. For what? For nothing. For a tin star. . . . People gotta talk themselves into law and order before they do anything about it. Maybe because deep down, they don't care. They just don't care." In the end, Kane and his previously pacifist wife defeat Miller and his gang. As they leave town, Kane throws his tin star in the dirt. There is no rejoicing.

High Noon was scripted by the socially conscious Carl Foreman, who came from a working-class Chicago Jewish family. During the film's production, Foreman was summoned to appear before the House Un-American Activities Committee. He testified that he had once been a member of the American Communist Party but became disillusioned and quit ten years earlier. Refusing to name other party members, Foreman was classified as an "uncooperative witness" and was blacklisted by the Hollywood studios.[22] Partly for this reason, *High Noon* has been branded a left-wing Western "damning Hollywood's moral cowardice in the face of the witch hunters."[23] Foreman himself suggested this allegory, writing scenes questioning the supposed goodness and purity of the townsfolk and their (capitalist) desire for personal comfort over the social good.[24] It was a Western cinematic norm for the community to band together to resist villains, even in the face of overwhelming odds. In *High Noon*, not only do the people turn their backs on Kane, but, in the end, he also rejects them in disgust. Kane had risked all defending a town unworthy of his defense.[25]

Even more radical is the film's portrayal of Helen Ramírez (Katy Jurado) as a strong, independent, savvy businesswoman in a patriarchal town, countering stereotypes of Mexican harlots in the mythical West. "I hate this town," she tells Amy, "I always hated it. To be a Mexican woman in this town—" She thus says all that needs to be said about gender and racial prejudice in "idyllic" Western settings. Through Ramírez, we hear a Jewish concern for the oppressed via filmmakers Foreman, Zinnemann, and producer Stanley Kramer.

John Wayne, the archetypal conservative Western star and avowed anticommunist, declared the film "unmanly" and "un-American."[26] Kane admits his fear, is saved by his wife in a gunfight, and lets moral reflection spoil an old-fashioned shootout.[27] Zinnemann's approach countered Wayne's exteriorized machismo: "That kind of interior drama is to me very exciting because, among other things, I feel that the fact that somebody shoots a gun is of no interest. What I want to know is why he shoots it and what the consequences are—which means that external action is less important than the inner motive through which you get to know what the person's about."[28] Wayne's role in *Rio Bravo* (Warner Bros., 1959)—an unwavering lawman who refuses assistance and holds the accused murderers in jail despite threats to his life—was a rebuttal to *High Noon*'s attack on "the single-handed hero myth."[29] Howard Hawks, *Rio Bravo*'s director, said that his film constituted a furious response to Kane "running around like a chicken with his head cut off asking for help."[30]

High Noon's critique of America's Cold War–era insistence on moral exceptionalism was not obvious to all. Between 1954 and 1986, it was the most-watched film in the White House, shown whenever presidents felt they were leading the country without sufficient support.[31] Although mired in controversy for its political themes, whatever communist message it had was hidden or subtextual enough to make the film an instant classic. It was nominated for seven Academy Awards, winning four (actor, editing, score, and song), and took home four Golden Globes (actor, supporting actress, score, and black-and-white cinematography). *High Noon* also informed later revisionist Westerns, which similarly exposed the shakiness of America's moral center and the fragility of "law and order" democracy.

Butch Cassidy and the Sundance Kid (1969)

Written by Jewish novelist, playwright, and screenwriter William Goldman, *Butch Cassidy and the Sundance Kid* (Twentieth Century–Fox, 1969) exemplifies what Leslie Fiedler called the New Western: a subgenre that assumes familiarity with Western literary/cinematic conventions but subverts them through edgy satire and/or bloody violence to expose what they generally elide.[32] Fiedler associated the New Western with Jewishness, arguing that once Jewish novelists/screenwriters had entered the establishment, they critiqued it, making them both successful assimilators and challengers of that establishment.[33] John Cawelti similarly links the New Western to Jewish identity, explaining that the heroes of these stories are "Jewish cowboys," although not in any overt or vaudevillian sense:

> In its treatment of violence as an expression of aggressive drives toward destruction in the pioneer spirit, in its negative and guilt-ridden assessment of the winning of the West and its reversal of traditional valuations of the symbolic figures and groups of the Western story, this new formula has a great deal in common with another recent form which I have labeled, rather facetiously, the legend of the Jewish cowboy. The hero of this type of Western is not literally Jewish, though often played by Jewish actors like Paul Newman. Actually, I suspect that Jews are likely to be the last of the ethnic groups to insist on donning the mantle of the cowboy hero.[34]

The example of Newman refers specifically to *Butch Cassidy and the Sundance Kid*, in which he plays Cassidy, the likeable, clever, talkative, almost pacifistic leader of the outlaw Hole in the Wall Gang. Calling such types "six-gun schlemiels" and "urban existentialists," Cawelti sees them as behaving "more like characters transported from the pages of Saul Bellow or Bernard Malamud into the legendary West than they do like the traditional Western hero. They win our interest and sympathy not by courage and heroic deeds but by bemused incompetence, genial cowardice, and the ability to face the worst with buoyancy and wit."[35] Moreover, their enemy is not the Native American or the black-hatted villain but the corporations and modernizing industrial society that threaten their leisurely, old-fashioned way of life. In *Butch Cassidy and the Sundance Kid*, this is encapsulated in the carefree bicycle ride to "Raindrops Keep Falling on My Head," a countertraditional but somehow appropriate song by Jewish singer-songwriter Burt Bacharach.[36]

Goldman's screenplay is loosely based on real outlaws Robert LeRoy Parker, known as Butch Cassidy, and his loyal partner, Harry Longabaugh, the Sundance Kid. Newman's Cassidy and Robert Redford's stoic Sundance Kid carry out a string of train robberies, are tracked by an elite posse, flee to Bolivia with Sundance's lover, Etta Place (Katharine Ross), learn enough Spanish to rob the local banks, and are eventually cornered and gunned down by Bolivian soldiers.

Set at the turn of the twentieth century, the movie opens with faux silent film footage of the "real" Hole in the Wall Gang, symbolically grounding the action in both old Western cinema and American history. But when the film transitions to sound and color, the New Western takes over. Early on, Harvey Logan (played by Ben Cassidy, the six foot nine actor best known for playing Lurch on *The Addams Family* [ABC, 1964–66]) challenges Butch to a knife fight for leadership of the gang. Like David in his bout with Goliath, the underdog Butch turns to alternative means, approaching Harvey to discuss the rules of engagement only to deliver what the screenplay calls "*the most aesthetically exquisite kick in the balls in the history of the modern American cinema.*"[37] Butch's quick thinking and aversion to brutality set him apart from the typical Western hero/antihero and suggests a classically Jewish dexterity of brain over brawn.

During the gang's second encounter with Woodcock (George Furth), the messenger in charge of the train's express car, Butch pleads, "You can't want to get blown up again." Woodcock replies, "Butch, you know if it were my money, there is nobody that I would rather have steal it than you.

But, you see, I am still in the employment of E. H. Harriman of the Union Pacific Railroad." In another scene, the local sheriff tells the duo, "I never met a soul more affable than you, Butch, or faster than the Kid, but you're still nothing but two-bit outlaws on the dodge." Their likeability is so intense that the marshal is unable to gather a posse to hunt down the Hole in the Wall Gang, necessitating the hiring of a crack team.

After arriving in Bolivia, Butch and the Kid briefly try going straight, working as payroll guards on a dangerous route plagued by bandits. During a tense confrontation with robbers, Butch confesses, "I never shot anybody before," recalling the stereotype of the Jew's aversion to firearms and reinforcing perceptions of Butch as a Jewish cowboy. More generally, the pair's nonconformity, challenging to authority, and desire to live outside the system and by their own rules tapped into the late-1960s countercultural ethos and made it the top-grossing film of 1969.

There Was a Crooked Man . . . (1970)

There Was a Crooked Man . . . (Warner Bros., 1970) offers a more cynical take on the Western. Cowritten by David Newman and Robert Benton as a follow-up to their classic neo-noir, *Bonnie and Clyde* (Warner Bros., 1967), and directed by Joseph L. Mankiewicz, a Jewish director, screenwriter, and producer whose diverse Hollywood career spanned forty years, the film plays fast and loose with mood, style, and substance. Its severe revisionist sensibility is captured in Western novelist and scriptwriter Brian Garfield's derision of the film as "nauseating" and "monumentally distasteful."[38]

The story centers on Paris Pitman Jr., played by Jewish actor Kirk Douglas, a hyperintelligent, manipulative charmer whose cunning wit reflects the darker side of the scheming (coded Jewish) city slicker who conquers the Old West with urban-honed skills. He is, in a sense, the anti–Butch Cassidy. In 1883, Pitman and his gang break into the home of a wealthy rancher and steal $500,000, sparking a shootout between the family and Pitman's gang, during which Pitman guns down several of his men before fleeing and hiding the money in a desert rattlesnake pit. Soon thereafter, Pitman is arrested and sentenced to ten years at a prison camp in the Arizona Territory. Pitman wins the trust of his cellmates, who include a couple of con artists, a young man who killed his girlfriend's father with a billiard ball, an oafish gunman who shot a sheriff in the leg, a silent Chinese immigrant, and a seasoned train robber. The brutal warden Francis E. LeGoff, played by Martin Gabel (who guest starred as Nathan Shotness on *Have Gun—Will Travel*), agrees to let Pitman break free for an even split of the loot. The plan is foiled when LeGoff is killed during an inmate uprising. The well-intentioned Woodward Lopeman (Henry Fonda), a limping sheriff who was shot by the gunman imprisoned in the camp, becomes the new reformist warden. Intending to imbue the prisoners with self-respect, Lopeman abolishes hard labor and cruel punishment. He recruits the silver-tongued and outwardly agreeable Pitman to supervise the construction of a dining hall. Behind the scenes, Pitman convinces the inmates to help him stage a breakout and collect a share of the hidden money. While the governor is visiting to see the fruits of Lopeman's reform campaign, Pitman sparks a riot, leading to the death of several inmates, with Pitman shooting two of his comrades. Pitman's devious exploits prove futile when he reaches the rattlesnake pit, opens the bag of money, and is fatally bitten. Lopeman arrives shortly thereafter, deposits Pitman's body at the prison, and rides off with the money.

A late-career entry for Mankiewicz, *There Was a Crooked Man . . .* was his first and only Western. He saw the film as "a chance to try some muscles I haven't used before" and a case of what he called "cocking the snook." "What I like to do," he told critic Gordon Gow, "is put my tongue halfway

Kirk Douglas (center) as Paris Pitman Jr. in *There Was a Crooked Man . . .* (Warner Bros., 1970).

in my cheek. Here I'm having a little fun with the mythology of the Wild West."[39] The result is less of a clear-cut Western and more of a hangout picture or prison film, with laid-back scenes of quirky characters working, playing, and chatting; doses of comedy; and plenty of violence thrown in. Some critics smear the film's jagged jumps between broad humor, social commentary, and cutthroat cruelty. Mat Brewster of *Cinema Sentries* writes that "unlike Arthur Penn who seems to have completely understood what Newman and Benton were going for with *Bonnie and Clyde*, Mankiewicz seems completely befuddled. The tone of this film is so off-kilter, so all over the place, one wonders if it wasn't made by two or three directors."[40] Pauline Kael was even less charitable, citing the film as an "example of commercialized black-comedy nihilism [that] seems to have been written by an evil 2-year-old" and directed in a mass-produced, low-quality style of filmmaking.[41]

These criticisms, highlighting the film's jaggedness and unredemptive message, overlook the method to Mankiewicz's madness. *There Was a Crooked Man . . .* is an intentionally crooked film, a demolition of a genre the director and many others had grown weary of watching. That the outlandish and unpredictable ride makes for disjointed viewing seems to be the point. With his own scripts, most notably *All about Eve* (Twentieth Century–Fox, 1950) and *The Barefoot Contessa* (United Artists, 1954), Mankiewicz developed a reputation for writing sarcastic dialogue, juggling multiple characters, and balancing complicated storylines that comment on the surrounding world.[42] All of that is on display here. Pitman's affable demeanor and bookish looks (enhanced by a pair of phony glasses) hide an anarchic sociopath whose crookedness infects everyone around him, exposing the facade of justice, virtue, and loyalty in American Westerns, contemporary society, and specifically the prison system.

Revisionist elements are peppered throughout, chipping away at Western icons. Early on, we see an exhausted and disgruntled Black maid put on her bandana, grab a plate of chicken, force a smile, and serve her white masters with a minstrelesque "Mmm-mmm," conveying the pain and hopelessness lurking beneath the smiles of menial laborers and narratively foreshadowing the idea that appearances are deceiving. During a prison riot, an imposing Chinese inmate, played by Olympic decathlon silver-medal winner C. K. Yang, breaks the back of the racist warden, acting out a revenge fantasy for those tired of being called "Chinks" or worse and giving us a glimpse of a powerful Chinese character in a genre that rarely portrays Asians and when it does so depicts them as weak and anonymous. The replacement warden, Lopeman, a devout Christian committed to reform, not only is undone by Pitman's duplicity and treachery but also becomes criminally corrupt by the end of the film, riding off to Mexico with the hidden treasure and living happily ever after. This twist eviscerates long-standing assurances of the Western lawman's invincibility and the moral strength of his religion. There are also diverse gay characters, ranging from a vicious prison guard to the "old married couple" con artists Dudley Whinner (Hume Cronyn) and John Randolph (Cyrus McNutt), whose intimate relationship and emotional complexity, while played mostly for laughs, stand out in a film from 1970 and particularly in a macho prison-Western hybrid.

By watching the film, the audience is made crooked through association, hypnotized by Pitman's carefree nature and unable to root against him even as he shoots his allies in the back and makes a mockery of earnest efforts to rehabilitate the inmates. Without viewers noticing, he becomes the reflection of the collective antiauthoritarian id.

Little Big Man (1970)

Little Big Man (National General, 1970), directed by Arthur Penn, a descendant of Russian Jews, uses a comic-ironic tone to invert myths of the American frontier. A follow-up to his American New Wave–defining *Bonnie and Clyde*, *Little Big Man* is told from the perspective of 121-year-old Jack Crabb/Little Big Man (Dustin Hoffman), who was rescued and raised by members of the Cheyenne tribe, worked as a snake-oil salesman, had a stint as a gunslinger, skinned mules under General George Armstrong Custer, and was purportedly the only white survivor of the Battle of Little Bighorn. The movie is at once a string of tall tales about a coded Jewish chameleon and a serious reconsideration of the impact of westward expansion on Native Americans. Adapted from Thomas Berger's 1964 novel of the same name, the movie makes Crabb more congenial and gives the Cheyenne more amiable personas. The film's lightheartedness makes the weighty themes of greed, racial intolerance, environmental destruction, and "the moral emptiness of American society" easier to swallow.[43] And although

Custer's exaggerated lunacy and deranged vanity might suggest that white Native killers were psychopathic outliers, *Little Big Man* vilifies all of white America.[44] Even Crabb, the hero, is a mostly passive observer who on several occasions is quick to reclaim his whiteness to save his life.

The story humorously plays on the Cheyenne calling themselves "human beings," implying that other Homo sapiens—and specifically whites—are not. Crabb says at one point, "I didn't figure" that going back to Cheyenne country "was dangerous, speaking Cheyenne and having once been a human being myself." This message rang clear in the context of inhumane military intervention in Vietnam and its countercultural pushback. Indeed, *Little Big Man* works on two levels: a "serious parody" that challenges the triumphalism of Western cinema and historiography, and a Vietnam allegory drawing parallels between past and present horrors. "The military atrocities of the Vietnam War inform new visions of a bloodthirsty, sadistic cavalry, indiscriminately mutilating and massacring women and children," writes David Lusted. "The disturbing reenactment of the Washita River Massacre of 1868 in *Little Big Man* in particular is part of a critique, both historical and contemporary. The historical revelation of a frontier atrocity also exposes a contemporary American foreign policy that destroyed Vietnamese villages—'in order to save them,' as one militarist of the time reportedly put it—in the name of democracy, and a military authority unable to control many of its units, as in the infamous massacre by American soldiers of an entire Vietnamese village, My Lai."[45]

The film also came against the backdrop of the American Indian Movement (founded in 1968) and the occupation of Alcatraz (1969), which drew attention to systemic poverty, discrimination, and police brutality suffered by Indigenous Americans. Moreover, *Little Big Man* heralded and possibly helped inspire the 1973 standoff between the FBI and followers of the American Indian Movement at Wounded Knee.[46] Meanwhile, American youth of different backgrounds were idealizing the "Native American way of life" as spiritually and ecologically sound, in contrast to the destructive consumerism and environmental devastation of modern society. The film inaccurately connects this youth movement with Cheyenne culture, showing communal lovemaking in a tepee à la 1960s hippies. In reality, Cheyenne women maintained strict rules of chastity, and courtship was conducted over a period of years under rigid guidelines.[47] Nevertheless, Crabb's adoption of an Indigenous lifestyle—"I wasn't just playing Indian, I was living Indian"—allowed white viewers to vicariously experience things from his vantage point as a fantasy version of themselves.

It is probably no coincidence that Dustin Hoffman, a well-known Jewish actor, was cast to play a white man who assumes a Native American identity, alluding to the long and problematic tradition of Jewish actors playing Native Americans onscreen. Philip French, writing in *Art in America* shortly after the film's release, noted that "the charge has been made that Cheyenne in Little Big Man are less Indians than New York Jews."[48] When Old Lodge Skins, played by Tsleil-Waututh Nation chief Dan George, fails to bring about his ceremonial death on a hilltop outside the Cheyenne village, he delivers a Borscht Belt line: "Well, sometimes the magic works, sometimes it doesn't." Even the Cheyenne concept of human being recalls the Yiddish *mensch*, literally meaning "person" but referring to someone who is honorable, upright, decent, and dignified and who possesses a "sense of what is right, responsible, decorous."[49]

Hints of Jewish humor also appear elsewhere in the film. For example, when Crabb is temporarily adopted by a devout white Christian couple after surrendering to cavalry soldiers and professing his whiteness, the wife tells him, "Moses was a Hebrew, but Jesus was a Gentile like you and me." The remark is doubly ironic: Hoffman is Jewish, and so was Jesus. (The woman later becomes a brothel worker—a not-so-subtle jab at the pretensions of Christian virtue.) Less humorously, the cavalry's brutal attack on the Cheyenne village, which had My Lai as its immediate reference point, also plays as a pogrom analogy fueled by racial mania.[50]

Less successful is the portrayal of Little Horse (Robert Little Star) as a Two Spirit, with one reviewer calling the depiction "an offensive limp-wrist drag queen from a Manhattan Hallowe'en ball."[51] In one scene, Little Horse tells Crabb, "You look tired, Little Big Man. Would you like to come in my teepee and rest on soft furs? Come and live with me, and I'll be your wife!" Nevertheless, according to Crabb's narration, the Cheyenne revere the Two Spirit's gender, and Little Horse's refusal to join the attack on the cavalry is accepted because no one is forced to fight, thereby adding further civility to the Cheyenne, especially when compared to the Vietnam draft.

The Quick and the Dead (1995)

As far as revisionist Westerns go, *The Quick and the Dead* (Sony, 1995) is in some ways as standard as it gets. The story revolves around a quick-draw contest in the remote and dusty town of Redemption, Arizona, ruled by merciless outlaw John Herod (Gene Hackman), whose surname alludes to the notorious Jewish Roman client king of Judea (ruled 37–4 BCE). Herod, who controls Redemption through intimidation, brutality, and rapacious taxation, sits on an ornate throne and drinks from a goblet. He announces a gladiator-like single-elimination quick-draw tournament with four rules: any contestant may challenge any other; no challenge can be refused; each contestant must fight once per day; and the duel continues until one contestant yields or dies.

Director Sam Raimi, who was raised in a Jewish household and was at the time best known for a trilogy of cult supernatural horror films *The Evil Dead* (New Line, 1981), *Evil Dead II* (Rosebud, 1987), and *Army of Darkness* (Universal, 1992), applied his knack for gore, camp, and stylistic flourishes (Dutch angles, extreme closeups, black backdrops, split diopters) to a spaghetti Western–inspired story. The film ends with Ellen, "The Lady" (Sharon Stone's tribute to Clint Eastwood's "Man with No Name"), exacting revenge on Herod in an homage to Sergio Leone's *Once upon a Time in the West* (Paramount, 1968). In both the Leone and Raimi films, the heroes were forced as children to participate in the hanging of a family member (a brother in Leone's film and a father in Raimi's), devote their lives to a revenge quest, and withhold their identity from the perpetrator until the climactic showdown, letting a memento do the revealing instead of words. In The Lady's case, it is a badge that belonged to her father, a local marshal whom Herod killed.

The most obvious revisionist aspect of *The Quick and the Dead* is the hero's gender. The film opens with a clichéd image of a long-coated cowboy riding across a dry valley. The twist is that the cowboy is a cowgirl: The Lady. As the story progresses, our acclimation to her stoic "Woman with No Name" presence is itself thwarted. She lets out cathartic tears and shouts of anger and sadness, reminding us that the movie cowboy's usual repression of emotions is an unrealistic and unhealthy byproduct of a contrived masculinity. The town of Redemption is also refreshingly diverse. Within the movie's first ten minutes, we see Blacks and Mexicans occupying various roles in the town as well as a celebration of Día de Los Muertos. Without explicitly saying so, the film suggests that Herod has scheduled the tournament to coincide with the death-themed Mexican holiday.

The film also introduces and dispatches with a lineup of Western archetypes, both heroes and villains, any of whom could have been the stars of their own stories. There is a self-assured Buffalo Soldier, Sergeant Clay Cantrell (Keith David), whom the townsfolk hired to defeat Herod in the tournament but who is instead killed by Herod. A Native American gunfighter, Spotted Horse (Jonothon Gill), claims that bullets cannot kill him and shows his many scars to prove it. He dies by a bullet fired by Cort (Russell Crowe), Herod's former henchman who has renounced violence to become a preacher but whom Herod tortures and forces into the tournament. Herod's son, The Kid, played by a young Leonardo DiCaprio, is talented, cocky, hotheaded, and ultimately killed by his father. Other archetypes include a flashy Wild West Show cowboy, Ace Hanlon (Lance Henriksen), whose boasts are bigger than his accomplishments; Scars (Mark Boone Junior), an uncouth criminal dressed in prison stripes; and Eugene Dred (Kevin Conway), an unsavory lowlife who rapes the saloon owner's young daughter and loses a shootout to The Lady, who then leaves town briefly to grapple with the triviality of violence and death. When she returns, she and Cort hatch a plan that involves faking her death, a series of surprise explosions, and the fulfillment of her revenge.

The plot is intentionally thin and overtly mythological, from the biblical name of the villain to the title, which is taken from the King James Bible: "judge the quick and the dead" (Acts 10:42; 2 Tim. 4:1; 1 Pet. 4:5). Roger Ebert, who was right not to take the film too seriously, remarked, "You'd think contestants would have to be pretty hard up to enter a contest where the odds are about 10-to-1 in favor of their being killed. But there's no shortage of entrants."[52] The disconnect between the audience and the characters onscreen gives the film a meta quality: we know that most of these characters will die, but they are absolutely sure they will not. This makes *The Quick and the Dead* more than a highlight reel of archetypes from innumerable Western movies. By pitting Western icons against each other and having them kill off each other, it mirrors the death (or near death) of the genre itself. While as many as 140 Westerns were released annually between 1940 and 1960, only 148 Westerns were made during the entire 1990s.[53]

True Grit (2010) and *The Ballad of Buster Scruggs* (2018)

Two Westerns by Ethan and Joel Coen round out our revisionist tour: *True Grit* (Paramount, 2010), previously adapted to film in 1969, with its tough, independent, quick-thinking girl alongside an aging (and less capable) male hero archetype, and *The Ballad of Buster Scruggs* (Netflix, 2018), an anthology of six loosely connected existentialist meditations on mortality and the absurdities of life. Both films occupy bleak, blood-soaked, harshly beautiful landscapes where black humor disrupts Western conventions and expectations. While the Coen Brothers are no strangers to Jewish subjects or characters, Jews, implicit or otherwise, do not appear in these films. Still, they are in many ways midrashic Westerns: postmodern retellings that breathe new relevance and new questions into old texts.

Set in 1870s western Arkansas, *True Grit* follows a self-assured, hyperarticulate fourteen-year-old farm girl, Mattie Ross, played by Hailee Steinfeld in her debut feature role, and Jeff Bridges as a boozy, well-past-his-prime Deputy U.S. Marshal Rooster Cogburn. Mattie hires Cogburn to hunt down Tom Chaney (Josh Brolin), an outlaw who murdered her father. They are joined by Texas Ranger LaBoeuf (Matt Damon), who has been tracking Chaney for killing a state senator. More a faithful adaptation of Charles Portis's 1968 novel than a remake of the 1969 movie (which earned John Wayne his only Oscar for playing Cogburn), the Coen brothers restore Mattie to the leading role and reclaim her tough-as-nails, hard-to-get-along-with personality. In the earlier adaptation, Mattie is shown crying in a way she never would in the book, presumably because making her seem stronger than Wayne's Cogburn was unthinkable. The Coens also tap into the book's dark humor, applying their signature mix of sophisticated laughs and shocking violence to reclaim the human dimensions of a story that were sacrificed in the earlier film to adhere to a more traditional Western narrative. Perhaps the biggest difference between the films is Cogburn. In 1969, he was merely Wayne with an eye patch: a near-invincible force mowing down adversaries. In Bridges's handling, he is a falling-down drunk malcontent who seems ready to abandon the mission at any moment.

Undercutting is the film's primary revisionist technique. Unlike his heroic forbearers, Cogburn rarely lives up to the cowboy/marshal ideal. While he is intermittently able to shoot straight, showing glimpses of his former glory, he is more likely to miss (blaming "cheap shells"), spill cornbread from his saddlebag, and get caught up in his windblown coat. At the film's climax, Mattie shoots an unarmed Chaney with a rifle, blowing him off a ridge. The recoil jerks Mattie backward into a cave containing a rotting corpse, where she is bitten by a rattlesnake, necessitating the amputation of her arm. "Mattie's moment of triumph is immediately undercut," Pete Falconer writes in *The Afterlife of the Hollywood Western*, complicating notions of frontier justice and righteous vengeance and creating "an implicit contrast between how we might suppose events to play out and how they play out in practice."[54]

A more humorous bit of revisionism comes from the deliberate choice to avoid all contractions in the dialogue. At first glance, this feature seems to ground the film in an authentic past, when language was presumably more stilted and contractions had yet to catch on. Portis's book includes contractions but leaves certain words uncontracted. For example, "Well I killed the wrong man and that is why I am here. If I had killed the man I meant to I don't believe I would have been convicted."[55] The filmmakers took Portis's style a step further, drawing much of the dialogue from the novel but removing contractions altogether. Getting into the habit offscreen was key to making it work on camera: "It was a frequent occurrence on the set that an actor would use a contraction," Ethan Coen told NPR, "and we would ask them not to."[56] In another interview, he said (perhaps with a wink), "We've been told that the language and all that formality is faithful to how people talked in the period."[57] However, the constricted dialogue presents a false sense of authenticity. According to linguist Mark Lieberman, "Informal American speech in the 1870s was far from contractionless, and in fact I suspect that it had roughly the same proportion of contractions as it does today."[58] Proving the point, Lieberman cites the many contractions in Mark Twain's Missouri-based novel *Tom Sawyer* (1876). Still, as a revisionist detail, the odd vernacular rhetorically separates *True Grit* from other Westerns, situating it in a past that defies genre and language conventions and aligning it more with a Shakespearean play or a page from the King James Bible, which share themes of human frailty, interpersonal messiness, and the limits of human power.

With *The Ballad of Buster Scruggs*, the Coen brothers plunge deeper into the uncertainty of life and inevitability of death. If *A Serious Man* was the brothers' retelling of the Book of Job in 1960s Jewish suburbia (a claim they have denied), then *Buster Scruggs* is their meditation on Ecclesiastes/Kohelet.[59] Like the biblical book, the movie reminds us that life is random, uncontrollable, and fleeting: "Utter futility!—said Kohelet. Utter futility! All is futile! What real value is there for a man in all the gains he makes beneath the sun? One generation goes, another comes, but the earth remains the same forever" (Eccl. 1:2–4).

An anthology of six Old West vignettes purportedly taken from the pages of a (fictitious) 1873 book, the film presents misadventures exposing harsh realities of life, the pointlessness of our intentions, and the unavoidability of death—all linked together to the tune of "Streets of Laredo," a song about a dying cowboy's regret of a life wasted on drink, gambling, and women.[60] The Coen brothers began writing the shorts for their own amusement, not knowing what to do with them. They eventually recognized a unifying theme. According to Ethan, "At the point where we'd written three or four of them and thought we had almost enough to do as a feature, we started thinking consciously about what ties them together. And clearly that was death."[61]

While the movie seems to revel in violence, the dead are often shown lying down, eyes open, staring blankly at the sky, implying there is nothing noble or redemptive in their bloody demises. This alone is enough to make *Buster Scruggs* an anti-Western. The first chapter centers on the film's titular character: the clean-cut, white-clad singing cowboy Buster Scruggs (Tim Blake Nelson), whose small stature, affable composure, and trusty horse belie his true nature as a misanthropic gunfighter-sociopath. He is a devilish cross between Paris Pitman Jr., Gene Autry, and Bugs Bunny, narrating his own story, breaking the fourth wall, and shooting down mean-looking, dirt-covered ruffians without breaking a sweat. After a particularly cartoonish encounter at a saloon card table in which Scruggs stomps on a loose table plank, causing his opponent to shoot himself thrice in the forehead, Scruggs wins over the stunned patrons by singing "Surly Joe the gambler, he will gamble never more" as the scene morphs into an upbeat musical revue. The overconfident Scruggs finally meets his match when a mysterious harmonica-playing man in black arrives, seemingly out of a spaghetti Western. The stranger wins the duel, asserts himself as the new top gun, and sings a duet with Scruggs's disembodied spirit, allegorizing the end of the ostensibly wholesome singing cowboy and the arrival of a new, more vicious West.

In the second chapter, "Near Algodones," a cowboy (James Franco) botches a bank robbery and awakens with a noose around his neck. Fortunately for him, the hanging posse is attacked by Comanche, who leave him hanging from a tree, saddled on his horse. He is saved by a cattle rustler, only to be reapprehended by lawmen and noosed for a public hanging, this time successfully. The message: there is no cheating death.

Chapter 3, "Meal Ticket," is the grim tale of a traveling impresario (Liam Neeson) and Harrison (Harry Melling), an armless, legless orator who recites bits of Shakespeare, the Gettysburg Address, and other famous speeches. The performance is initially popular, but as the two travel, the crowds thin out and the profits dwindle. Desperate for cash, the impresario sees a large group watching a chicken that supposedly can count. Falling for the trick, he eagerly buys the chicken and tosses the helpless Harrison into a river before riding to the next town. This is a literal comment on the disposability of life: the impresario has to dress and spoon-feed the orator and help him use the bathroom and sees him as a financial liability rather than as a person; the chicken, who represents the ascendancy of low-level entertainment over highbrow oratory, is in some sense the death of culture.

"All Gold Canyon," the fourth chapter, stars musician Tom Waits as a grizzled prospector alone in a pristine mountain valley digging for gold. The story's twist comes after days of tireless toil, when he finally reaches a gold vein he dubs "Mr. Pocket" but is shot in the back by a man who had been lurking, waiting for him to strike gold. When the man jumps into the hole to collect the loot, the prospector springs back to life, wrestles away the man's gun, and fatally shoots him. The prospector then cleans his wound and determines it to be nonfatal: "It went clean through, he didn't hit nothin' important!" He finishes mining the gold, throws the man into the resulting hole, and goes on his way. This is the most hopeful of the film's segments in that the good guy wins, but it also repeats a familiar Coen brothers theme: pursuing money causes death.

In chapter 5, "The Gal Who Got Rattled," Alice Longabaugh (Zoe Kazan) and her inept older brother Gilbert (Jefferson Mays) join a wagon train heading to Oregon, where Gilbert insists he has a business partner who will marry Alice. Gilbert dies of cholera shortly after they embark. Alone and penniless, Alice attracts the young wagon leader, who proposes marriage. She pragmatically accepts. One morning on the trail, the senior wagon leader finds Alice wandering in a field. Spotting a Native American scout and war party, he prepares for a fight, giving Alice a pistol and instructing her that if he is killed, she should shoot herself to avoid capture. Mistakenly believing that the wagon leader has been killed, Alice shoots herself in the head, thereby short-circuiting what should have been the much-deserved happy next stage of her life and proving that "even good people trying to do the right thing can have fortune backfire on them."[62]

The final chapter, "The Mortal Remains," features five people on a stagecoach riding to Fort Morgan, Colorado: a Frenchman, an older society lady, a disheveled fur trapper, and two bounty hunters, an Englishman and an Irishman. The bounty hunters, played by Jonjo O'Neill and Brendan Gleeson, spook the others with their nonchalant self-descriptions as "reapers" and "harvesters of souls" and references to a corpse they are transporting as "cargo." They explain their method: while the English raconteur distracts the bounty with captivating stories, the Irish "thumper" does the deadly deed. The other passengers argue over the nature of humanity: the trapper sees people as no different than the ferrets he catches; the lady divides people into sinners and the righteous; the Frenchman believes people change depending on the circumstances. The bounty hunters remind their fellow travelers that whatever human beings might be, they inevitably die. When they finally reach Fort Morgan, the passengers are hesitant to stay in the same hotel as the bounty hunters.

This ending is fitting if enigmatic for a movie that brings unrelenting darkness to the formerly optimistic Old West. The six stories center on losers and nobodies—the sort of people who leave no paper trail and are generally omitted from heroic tales of westward expansion, both historical and cinematic. Far from inspiring visions of the American dream, they caution against such dreaming. As Kohelet says, "It is better to go to a house of mourning than to a house of feasting; for that is the end of every man, and the living should take it to heart" (Eccl. 7:2).

Conclusion

During an interview for my podcast/YouTube show *Amusing Jews*, I asked Valerie Estelle Frankel, a prolific pop culture historian and author of several volumes on Jews in science fiction and fantasy, if anything specific needs to be present for a work to be considered "Jewish science fiction." She told me that Steven H. Silver, who curates an online list of Jewish science fiction and fantasy, once asked her what percentage of a story has to be identifiably Jewish.[1] Her answer: "Maybe zero."[2]

Any cultural product created by a Jew will be infused with some degree of Jewishness, whether it is recognizable, subtextual, or simply in there somewhere as a result of the fact that creations invariably reflect their creators. As a case in point, Frankel mentioned Maurice Sendak's *Where the Wild Things Are*, which makes no direct reference to Jewish identity, history, or practice but is darker than many children's books as a consequence of the author-illustrator's post-Holocaust consciousness. Moreover, the Wild Things were based on Sendak's childhood memories of loud, hairy, slobbery Jewish relatives telling him, "We're going to eat you up, you're so cute!"

This inclusive, unwritten definition of what constitutes a Jewish work allows the possibility of the receiver's perspective: knowing that it came from a Jewish person invites us to discover its Jewishness regardless of the creator's intent. Yet while this view is conceptually sound and appropriately subjective—there is, after all, no one way for Jewishness to be conceived or expressed—it introduces many more potential examples than a study of Jewish science fiction or Jewish Westerns can attempt to cover.

This is particularly apparent when the topic turns to Jewish sensibility: an instinct or feeling that cannot be adequately put into words. Because there is no single way to be Jewish or experience things Jewishly or even one Judaism—there are Judaisms—the determining features are, more often than not, elusive or in the eyes of beholders rather than delineated on the page or screen.

This book has charted a middle course between restricting content to only that featuring recognizably Jewish characters or themes and the zero-percent rule of anything and everything made by a Jewish writer, director, producer, actor, scorer, editor, costume designer, makeup artist, cinematographer, and so forth. The book is less concerned with answering the big questions—What makes a movie "Jewish"? What counts as a "Jewish image"? How much of a film's "Jewishness" owes to the filmmakers, and how much to the viewer's interpretation?—than with filling in broad but still inherently limited categories.

Only a few Westerns—fewer than a fistful—contain explicitly Jewish stories or scenes, and very rarely do Old West tales involve identifiably Jewish characters, obvious or otherwise. This underrepresentation reflects a sentiment stated by a Jewish character in Mordecai Richler's 1971 novel, *St. Urbain's Horseman*: "When a Jew gets on a horse he stops being a Jew."[3] Yet while this presumption still rings true among the uninitiated who see *Jew* and *cowboy* as incongruous, it is patently false. One need only look at Artie Auerbach, a comic actor who found fame as the Yiddish-accented Mr. Kitzel on radio and television, including as a regular on *The Goldbergs* and *The Jack Benny Program*. In a profile published in the Omaha *Jewish Press* in 1949, Auerbach was described as "a loyal New Yorker who is a frustrated cowboy at heart. He owns two horses and a western outfit."[4]

What constitutes "Jewish" or a "Jewish Western" can be stretched beyond the immediately apparent—and well beyond the examples presented herein. This study is wide-ranging but is representative rather than maximalist. It would be tedious and distracting to list every possible iteration of a Jewish character or perspective in Western films or television shows or to analyze every possible Jewish idea in a Western made by Jewish filmmakers. Instead, I have taken a selective approach, examining specimens from a variety of Western eras and subgenres.

This volume is the first book-length treatment of Jews and Westerns, but it will hopefully not be the last. Although they have largely been ignored by fans, buffs, and historians of the genre, Jewish contributions, both in front of and behind the camera, have played defining roles throughout Wild West cinema history, from foundation-setting silent shorts to classical morality tales to Old West musicals and comedies to anti-Westerns.

Notes

Introduction

1. R. Philip Loy, *Westerns and American Culture, 1930–1955* (Jefferson, NC: McFarland, 2001), 1.

2. David Lusted, *The Western* (London: Pearson Longman, 2003), 4; Raul S. Chavez, *Childhood Indians: Television, Film and Sustaining the White (Sub)Conscience* (Scotts Valley, CA: CreateSpace, 2010), 4.

3. Josh Garrett-Davis, *What Is a Western? Region, Genre, Imagination* (Norman: University of Oklahoma Press, 2019), 5.

4. Pauline Kael, "The Current Cinema: The Street Western," *New Yorker*, February 25, 1974, 100; Pete Falconer, *The Afterlife of the Hollywood Western* (London: Palgrave Macmillan, 2020). Garrett-Davis, *What Is a Western?*, 11, notes that afterlife Westerns are sometimes called post-Westerns, ghost Westerns, or dead Westerns.

5. Ed Andreychuk, *The Golden Corral: A Roundup of Magnificent Western Films* (Jefferson, NC: McFarland, 1997), 151.

6. "The Passing of the Western Subject," *Nickelodeon*, February 18, 1911.

7. Falconer, *Afterlife of the Hollywood Western*, 4; Scott Simmon, *The Invention of the Western Film: A Cultural History of the Genre's First Half-Century* (New York: Cambridge University Press, 2003), 32–33.

8. Falconer, *Afterlife of the Hollywood Western*, 5. More than one hundred Western features were made each year from 1935 to 1943, in 1948, and from 1950 to 1952 (Falconer, *Afterlife of the Hollywood Western*, 4).

9. Falconer, *Afterlife of the Hollywood Western*, 5, 6.

10. Lusted, *The Western*, 12.

11. Andrew Patrick Nelson, *Still in the Saddle: The Hollywood Western, 1969–1980* (Norman: University of Oklahoma Press, 2015), 207.

12. Nina Metz, "The Stream Became a Binge," *Chicago Tribune*, April 21, 2022.

13. Lusted, *The Western*, 12.

14. Ted Jojola, "Absurd Reality II: Hollywood Goes to the Indians," in *Hollywood's Indian: The Portrayal of the Native American in Film*, edited by Peter C. Rollins and John E. O'Connor (Lexington: University Press of Kentucky, 2003), 19.

15. Ray Merlock, "Preface to *Hollywood's West: The American Frontier in Film, Television, and History*, edited by Peter C. Collins and John E. O'Connor (Lexington: University Press of Kentucky, 2005), xi.

16. Jeremy Agnew, *The Landscapes of Western Movies: A History of Filming on Location, 1900–1970* (Jefferson, NC: McFarland, 2020), 52.

17. Ruth Ellen Gruber, "Heym on the Range," *Tablet*, November 4, 2020, https://www.tabletmag.com/sections/arts-letters/articles/heym-on-the-range.

18. Alan Pergament, "'The Last Movie Stars' Is a Creative and Revealing Portrait of Newman and Woodward," *Buffalo News*, July 22, 2022.

19. Sarah J. Tracy, *Qualitative Research Methods: Collecting Evidence, Crafting Analysis, Communicating Impact*, 2nd ed. (New York: Wiley Blackwell, 2020), 2.

20. Christopher N. Poulos, *Essentials of Autoethnography* (Washington, DC: American Psychological Association, 2021), 27.

21. Richard Abel, "'Our Country'/Whose Country?: The 'Americanization' Project of Early Westerns," in *Back in the Saddle Again: New Essays on the Western*, edited by Edward Buscombe and Roberta Pearson (London: British Film Institute, 1998), 77–95.

22. Simmon, *Invention of the Western Film*, xiii.

23. Stephen Aron, *The American West: A Very Short Introduction* (New York: Oxford University Press, 2015), 112.

24. Jim Kitses, "Introduction: Post-Modernism and the Western," in *The Western Reader*, edited by Jim Kitses and Gregg Rickman (New York: Limelight, 1998), 19.

25. "John Wayne: Playboy Interview," *Playboy*, May 1971, 82.

26. Reagan quoted in Richard Drinnon, *Facing West: The Metaphysics of Indian Hating and Empire Building* (New York: Schocken, 1990), xiii.

27. Garrett-Davis, *What Is a Western?*, 11.

28. Pollock quoted in Anne Thompson, "Beyond-the-Pale Riders," *Film Comment* 28, no. 4 (1992): 53.

29. Chavez, *Childhood Indians*, 140.

30. See Richard Slotkin, *Gunfighter Nation: The Myth of the Frontier in Twentieth-Century America* (Norman: University of Oklahoma Press, 1998).

31. Chavez, *Childhood Indians*, 62–63; Kathleen A. McDonough, "Wee Willie Winkie Goes West: The Influence of the British Empire Genre on Ford's Cavalry Trilogy," in *Hollywood's West: The American Frontier in Film, Television, and History*, edited by Peter C. Rollins and John E. O'Connor (Lexington: University Press of Kentucky, 2005), 113; John E. O'Connor, "The White Man's Indian: An

Institutional Approach," in *Hollywood's Indian: The Portrayal of the Native American in Film*, edited by Peter C. Rollins and John E. O'Connor (Lexington: University Press of Kentucky, 2003), 28, 34.

32. Merryana Salem, "'Killers of the Flower Moon' Can't Escape Its Own White Gaze," *Junkee*, October 20, 2023, https://junkee.com/killers-of-the-flower-moon-white-gaze-racism/355061; David Smith, "'Hollywood Doesn't Change Overnight': Indigenous Viewers on *Killers of the Flower Moon*," *Guardian*, November 3, 2023, https://www.theguardian.com/film/2023/nov/03/indigenous-native-american-review-opinion-killers-flower-moon-movie.

33. Jojola, "Absurd Reality II," 12.

34. Elizabeth Fenton, *Old Canaan in a New World: Native Americans and the Lost Tribes of Israel* (New York: New York University Press, 2020), 4.

35. Juan Alonzo, *Badmen, Bandits, and Folk Heroes: The Ambivalence of Mexican American Identity in Literature and Film* (Tucson: University of Arizona Press, 2009); Sue Matheson, ed., *Women in the Western* (Edinburgh: Edinburgh University Press, 2020); Mia Mask, *Black Rodeo: A History of the African American Western* (Urbana: University of Illinois Press, 2023).

36. Michael R. Pitts, *Western Movies: A Guide to 5,105 Feature Films*, 2nd ed. (Jefferson, NC: McFarland, 2013).

37. Donn J. Moyer, *Cowboy Cliffhangers: A Listing of All Sound B-Western Chapter Plays from A to Z* (Tacoma, WA: Wild West, 1999).

38. Jon Tuska, *The Filming of the West* (Garden City, NY: Doubleday, 1976), xviii.

39. Hasia Diner, "American West, New York Jewish," in *Jewish Life in the American West*, edited by Ava F. Kahn (Los Angeles: Autry Museum of the American West, 2002), 37.

40. Leslie Fiedler, *To the Gentiles* (New York: Stein and Day, 1972), 102.

41. Helene Meyers, *Movie-Made Jews: An American Tradition* (New Brunswick, NJ: Rutgers University Press, 2021), 19.

42. Kenneth Turan, "Letting Jews Be Jews: Ethnicity and Hollywood, Its Fall and Rise," in *Jews in the Los Angeles Mosaic*, edited by Karen S. Wilson (Berkeley: University of California Press, 2013), 45–46.

43. Turan, "Letting Jews Be Jews," 48.

44. David Kaufman, *Jewhooing the Sixties: American Celebrity and Jewish Identity: Sandy Koufax, Lenny Bruce, Bob Dylan, and Barbra Streisand* (Waltham, MA: Brandeis University Press, 2012).

45. Lawrence J. Epstein, *American Jewish Films: The Search for Identity* (Jefferson, NC: McFarland, 2013), 7.

46. See Jane P. Tompkins, ed., *Reader-Response Criticism: From Formalism to Post-Structuralism* (Baltimore: Johns Hopkins University Press, 1980).

47. Gayle Wald, "Dreaming of Michael Jackson: Notes on Jewish Listening," in *The Song Is Not the Same: Jews and American Popular Music*, edited by Bruce Zuckerman, Josh Kun, and Lisa Ansell (West Lafayette, IN: Purdue University Press, 2011), 1–8.

48. Jon Stratton, *Coming Out Jewish: Constructing Ambivalent Identities* (New York: Routledge, 2003), 270–71.

49. Epstein, *American Jewish Films*, 7.

50. Epstein, *American Jewish Films*, 101.

51. Gabrielle Newman shared this concept with me on December 21, 2022, in a class I was teaching on Jewish music history.

52. Gruber cited in Lusted, *The Western*, 24.

53. John Shelton Lawrence, "Filmography," in *Hollywood's West: The American Frontier in Film, Television, and History*, edited by Peter C. Rollins and John E. O'Connor (Lexington: University Press of Kentucky, 2005), 301.

54. Pitts, *Western Movies*, 1.

55. Larry Langman, *A Guide to Silent Westerns* (Westport, CT: Greenwood, 1992).

56. Garrett-Davis, *What Is a Western?*, 89.

57. Garrett-Davis, *What Is a Western?*, 93.

58. Garrett-Davis, *What Is a Western?*

59. Mark Anthony Ayling, "White Saviours, Yellow Perils, and Green Eyes: John Carpenter's *Big Trouble in Little China*," *VHS Revival: A Retro Movie Magazine*, August 21, 2020, https://vhsrevival.com/2020/08/21/white-saviours-yellow-perils-and-green-eyes-john-carpenters-big-trouble-in-little-china/.

60. Simmon, *Invention of the Western Film*, 152–53.

61. Simmon, *Invention of the Western Film*, 180. See also "The West of the Mohicans," in Simmon, *Invention of the Western Film*, 89–93; Jeffrey Walker, "Deconstructing an American Myth: *The Last of the Mohicans* (1992)," in *Hollywood's Indian: The Portrayal of the Native American in Film*, edited by Peter C. Rollins and John E. O'Connor (Lexington: University Press of Kentucky, 2003), 170–86.

62. Amanda J. Cobb, "This Is What It Means to Say Smoke Signals: Native American Cultural Sovereignty," in *Hollywood's Indian: The Portrayal of the Native American in Film*, edited by Peter C. Rollins and John E. O'Connor (Lexington: University Press of Kentucky, 2003), 225.

63. Falconer, *Afterlife of the Hollywood Western*, 17, 207. See Thomas O. Beebee, *The Ideology of Genre: A Comparative Study of Generic Instability* (University Park: Pennsylvania State University Press, 1994).

64. In *Jacobellis v. Ohio*, 378 U.S. 184 (1964), Stewart wrote, "I shall not today attempt further to define the kinds of material I understand to be embraced

within that shorthand description ['hard-core pornography'], and perhaps I could never succeed in intelligibly doing so. But I know it when I see it, and the motion picture involved in this case is not that."

65. Werner Sollors, *Beyond Ethnicity: Consent and Descent in American Culture* (New York: Oxford University Press, 1987).

66. Lester D. Friedman, ed., *Unspeakable Images: Ethnicity and the American Cinema* (Urbana: University of Illinois Press, 1991); Marsha J. Hamilton and Eleanor S. Block, *Projecting Ethnicity and Race: An Annotated Bibliography of Studies on Imagery in American Film* (New York: Bloomsbury, 2003); Charles Ramírez Berg, *Latino Images in Film: Stereotypes, Subversion, and Resistance* (Austin: University of Texas Press, 2002); Peter X. Feng, ed., *Screening Asian Americans* (New Brunswick, NJ: Rutgers University Press, 2002); Michael Boyce Gillespie, *Film Blackness: American Cinema and the Idea of Black Film* (Durham, NC: Duke University Press, 2016); Joanna Hearne, *Native Recognition: Indigenous Cinema and the Western* (Albany, NY: SUNY Press, 2013).

Chapter 1. How the West Was Made

1. *Manischewitz Presents the Jewish Cowboy*, Manischewitz, 1958, EP.

2. Rachel S. Harris, "New Frontiers: Creating a Nation through the Israeli Western," in *Casting a Giant Shadow: The Transnational Shaping of Israeli Cinema*, edited by Lucy Fischer and Dan Chyutin (Bloomington: Indiana University Press, 2021), 83.

3. Oz Almog, *The Sabra: The Creation of the New Jew* (Berkeley: University of California Press, 2000); *Manischewitz Presents the Jewish Cowboy*.

4. See, for example, Edward Zerin, *Jewish San Francisco* (Charleston, SC: Arcadia, 2006); Jonathan L. Friedmann, *Jewish Gold Country* (Charleston, SC: Arcadia, 2020); Jonathan L. Friedmann, *Jewish Los Angeles* (Charleston, SC: Arcadia, 2020.

5. Jewish agricultural colonies were established in Kansas, North and South Dakota, Utah, California, Oregon, Louisiana, Michigan, Arkansas, Florida, New York, and New Jersey. See, for example, Everett L. Cooley, "Clarion, Utah: Jewish Colony in 'Zion,'" *Utah Historical Quarterly* 36, no. 2 (1968): 113–31; Janet E. Schulte, "'Proving and Moving Up': Jewish Homesteading Activity in North Dakota, 1900–1920," *Great Plains Quarterly* 10, no. 4 (1990): 228–44; Uri D. Herscher, *Jewish Agricultural Utopias in America, 1880–1910* (Detroit: Wayne State University Press, 1991); J. Sanford Rikoon, "The Jewish Agriculturalists' Aid Society of America: Philanthropy, Ethnicity, and Agriculture in the Heartland," *Agricultural History* 72, no. 1 (1998): 1–32.

6. Laura Wolff Scanlan, "Jewish Pioneers," *Humanities* 31, no. 1 (2010), https://www.neh.gov/humanities/2010/januaryfebruary/statement/jewish-pioneers.

7. See Debra Shein, "Isaac Raboy's *Der Yiddisher Cowboy* and Rachel Calof's *My Story*: The Role of the Western Frontier in Shaping Jewish American Identity," *Western American Literature* 36, no. 4 (2002): 359–80.

8. See M. L. Marks, *Jews among the Indians: Tales of Adventure and Conflict in the Old West* (Chicago: Benison, 1992). David S. Koffman's *The Jews' Indian: Colonialism, Pluralism, and Belonging in America* (New Brunswick, NJ: Rutgers University Press, 2019) offers a critical reappraisal of the oft-celebrated relationship between Jews and Native Americans, describing how Jewish class striving and civic belonging at times resulted in exploitative actions and attitudes akin to those of non-Jewish white settlers.

9. See Lynn Downey, *Levi Strauss: The Man Who Gave Blue Jeans to the World* (Amherst: University of Massachusetts Press, 2016); Penny Diane Wolin, *The Jews of Wyoming: Fringe of the Diaspora* (Cheyenne, WY: Crazy Woman Creek, 2000), 222; Bob Proehl, *Flying Burrito Brothers' "The Gilded Palace of Sin"* (New York: Bloomsbury, 2008), 163; Nick Kotz, *The Harness Maker's Dream: Nathan Kallison and the Rise of South Texas* (Fort Worth: Texas Christian University Press, 2013); and Hollace Ava Weiner, "Frances Rosenthal Kallison, 1908–2004: Cowgirl with a Jewish Conscience," *Western States Jewish History* 48, no. 1 (2015): 3–26.

10. The journal was published under the title *Western States Jewish Historical Quarterly* from 1968 to the summer of 1983, when it became *Western States Jewish History*. Early efforts at charting Jewish history in the western United States include W. Gunther Plaut, *The Jews in Minnesota: The First Seventy-Five Years* (New York: American Jewish Historical Society, 1959); Allen D. Breck, *A Centennial History of the Jews of Colorado, 1859–1959* (Denver: Hirschfeld, 1960); Norton B. Stern, *California Jewish History: A Descriptive Bibliography* (Glendale, CA: Clark, 1967); Max Vorspan and Lloyd P. Gartner, *History of the Jews of Los Angeles* (San Marino, CA: Huntington Library, 1970); Robert E. Levinson, *The Jews in the California Gold Rush* (New York: Ktav, 1978); Moses Rischin, ed., *The Jews of the West: The Metropolitan Years* (Berkeley, CA: Magnes, 1979); Fred Rochlin and Harriet Rochlin, *Pioneer Jews: A New Life in the Far West* (Boston: Houghton Mifflin, 1984).

11. Natalie Ornish, *Pioneer Jewish Texans* (College Station: Texas A&M University Press, 2011), xii.

12. See, for example, Hollace Ava Weiner and Kenneth D. Roseman, eds., *Lone Stars of David: The Jews of Texas* (Waltham, MA: Brandeis University Press, 2007); Bryan Edward Stone, *The Chosen Folks: Jews on the Frontiers of Texas* (Austin: University of Texas Press, 2010).

13. See Kenneth Libo and Irving Howe, *We Lived There, Too: In Their Own Words and Pictures—Pioneer Jews and the Westward Movement of America, 1630–1930* (New York: St. Martin's, 1985). For recent applications of New Western History to

Jewish topics, see Naomi Sandweiss, "Ethnic Homesteading in the Nineteenth-Century Midwest: A Historiography of Irish Catholic, African American, and Eastern European Jewish Settlements," *Western States Jewish History* 52, no. 1 (2021): 43–54; Ellen Eisenberg, ed., *Jewish Identities in the American West: Relational Perspectives* (Chicago: University of Chicago Press, 2022); Rebecca Clarren, *The Cost of Free Land: Jews, Lakota, and an American Inheritance* (New York: Penguin, 2023).

14. See, for example, Patricia Nelson Limerick, *The Legacy of Conquest: The Unbroken Past of the American West* (New York: Norton, 1987); Patricia Nelson Limerick, *Something in the Soil: Legacies and Reckonings in the New West* (New York: Norton, 2000).

15. Marc Lee Raphael, "Beyond New York: Challenges to Local History," in *Jews of the American West*, edited by Moses Rischin and John Livingston (Detroit: Wayne State University Press, 1991), 48–65.

16. Deverell, foreword, xii, xiii; Mickey Katz and His Kosher-Jammers, *Haim Afen Range (Home on the Range)/Yiddish Square Dance* (RCA Victor, 1947).

17. Jeremy Agnew, *The Old West in Fact and Film: History versus Hollywood* (Jefferson, NC: McFarland, 2012), 229.

18. Jane P. Tompkins, *West of Everything: The Inner Life of Westerns* (New York: Oxford University Press, 1993), 45.

19. Garrett-Davis, *What Is a Western?*, 12, 79; Jojola, "Absurd Reality II," 12; Paul Varner, *The A to Z of Westerns in Cinema* (Lanham, MD: Scarecrow, 2009), xxvii.

20. Shaina Hammerman, *Silver Screen, Hasidic Jews: The Story of an Image* (Bloomington: Indiana University Press, 2017), 21.

21. See Jody Rosen, "'Cohen Owes Me Ninety-Seven Dollars': Images of Jews from the Jewish Sheet-Music Trade," in *The Song Is Not the Same: Jews and American Popular Music*, edited by Bruce Zuckerman, Josh Kun, and Lisa Ansell (West Lafayette, IN: Purdue University Press, 2011), 89–114.

22. Aaron Manela, "Chosen Cowboy Mazl Tov: Tin Pan Alley and the Wild West Cowboy Jew," *Journal of Jewish Identity* 10, no. 1 (2017): 27.

23. Anthony Slide, *New York City Vaudeville* (Charleston, SC: Arcadia, 2006), 7.

24. Oliver Double, *Getting the Joke: The Inner Workings of Stand-Up Comedy* (London: Bloomsbury, 2014), 25. Boston's thirty-five-hundred-seat National Theatre, built in 1911, promoted itself as the "largest vaudeville theatre in the world" ("New National Theatre," *Journal of Education* [Boston], August 24, 1911).

25. David Nasaw, *Going Out: The Rise and Fall of Public Amusements* (New York: Basic, 1993), 51.

26. See Rosen, "Cohen Owes Me Ninety-Seven Dollars."

27. Rosen, "Cohen Owes Me Ninety-Seven Dollars," 12.

28. American Reform rabbis, led by Rabbi William Friedman of Denver, were particularly outspoken in criticizing Jewface. Details of their anti-stage-Jew campaign are recorded in "Report of the Committee on Church and State," *Year Book of the Central Conference of American Rabbis* 21 (1911): 79–81.

29. "Tobias Schanfarber in Chicago Israelite," *American Israelite* (Cincinnati), August 28, 1913. Neil Simon based his play *The Sunshine Boys* (1972) on the careers of Smith and Dale. In April 1913, Schanfarber, a representative of the Central Conference of American Rabbis, was a founder of the Anti–Stage Jew Vigilance Committee along with other leading Chicago Jews, most of whom came from Reform and Central European backgrounds. The other founders included Adolf Kraus of B'nai B'rith and Babette Mandel, Jennie Purvin, and Hannah Solomon of the National Council of Jewish Women. See M. Alison Kibler, *Censoring Racial Ridicule: Irish, Jewish, and African American Struggles over Race and Representation, 1890–1930* (Chapel Hill: University of North Carolina Press, 2015), 152.

30. Kelly Cooper, "From Challah to Chazantes: Jewish Women's Journey from the Kitchen to Bimah" (master's thesis, Academy for Jewish Religion California, 2022, https://www.tilb.org/wp-content/uploads/2022/05/CantorCooper_Thesis_Challah_to_Chazante.pdf), 33; Jody Rosen, liner notes to *Jewface* (Reboot Stereophonic, 2006, CD).

31. Nasaw, *Going Out*, 53.

32. Kibler, *Censoring Racial Ridicule*, 28.

33. Andrea Most, "'Big Chief Izzy Horowitz': Theatricality and Jewish Identity in the Wild West," *American Jewish History* 87, no. 4 (1999): 314.

34. Reproduced in Manela, "Chosen Cowboy Mazl Tov," 37–40.

35. Harry I. Robinson and Will J. Harris, *Yonkle the Cow-Boy Jew* (Chicago: Rossiter, 1907).

36. Manela, "Chosen Cowboy Mazl Tov," 41.

37. For an evaluation of Jews' relationship to nature from an urban Jewish standpoint, see Steven S. Schwarzschild, "The Unnatural Jew," in *Judaism and Environmental Ethics: A Reader*, edited by Martin D. Yaffe (Lanham, MD: Lexington, 2001), 267–82.

38. Robert Lynam, ed., *The Beecher Island Annual* (Wray, CO: Beecher Island Battle Memorial Association, 1930), 15, 20.

39. Edgar Leslie, Halsey K. Mohr, and Al Piantadosi, *I'm a Yiddish Cowboy ("Tough Guy Levi")* (New York: Barron, 1908); Rachel Rubinstein, *Members of the Tribe: Native America in the Jewish Imagination* (Detroit: Wayne State University Press, 2010), 45–46.

40. Ben Harrison and Manny Gould, dirs., *Rough Dough* (Columbia, 1931). Harrison wrote the film, Gould animated it, and Charles Mintz produced it.

41. Jeff T. Branen and Al Piantadosi, *Big Chief Dynamite* (Chicago: Piantadosi, 1909).

42. Rubinstein, *Members of the Tribe*, 52.

43. Rubinstein, *Members of the Tribe*, 53; Sandra Lea Rollins, "Jewish Indian Chief," *Western States Jewish Historical Quarterly* 1, no. 4 (1969): 151–63.

44. Leslie A. Fiedler, "The Demon of the Continent," in *The Pretend Indians: Images of Native Americans in the Movies*, edited by Gretchen M. Bataille and Charles L. P. Silet (Ames: Iowa State University Press, 1980), 10.

45. Ben Sidran, *There Was a Fire: Jews, Music, and the American Dream* (Madison, WI: Nardis, 2012), 29.

46. See Fenton, *Old Canaan in a New World*.

47. See Rachel Rubinstein, "Encountering Native Origins," in *The Cambridge History of Jewish American Literature*, edited by Hana Wirth-Nesher (New York: Cambridge University Press, 2016), 62–84.

48. Gretchen M. Bataille and Charles L. P. Silet, eds., *The Pretend Indians: Images of Native Americans in the Movies* (Ames: Iowa State University Press, 1980).

49. Neal Gabler, *An Empire of Their Own: How the Jews Invented Hollywood* (New York: Anchor, 1988), 206.

50. Turan, "Letting Jews Be Jews," 48; Simmon, *Invention of the Western Film*, 81.

51. Gabler, *Empire of Their Own*, 57–59.

52. Richard F. Shepard, "Film: Yiddish Cinema," *New York Times*, April 9, 1985; Phineas J. Biron, "Strictly Confidential," *Jewish Press*, August 30, 1940.

53. Alexandra Keller, "Generic Subversion as Counterhistory: Mario Van Peebles's *Posse*," in *Western Films through History*, edited by Janet Walker (New York: Routledge, 2001), 36.

54. Jon Winokur, *Encyclopedia Neurotica* (New York: St. Martin's, 2005), 222; Otto Friedrich, *City of Nets: A Portrait of Hollywood in the 1940s* (Berkeley: University of California Press, 1997), 356.

55. See Lary L. May and Elaine Tyler May, "Why Jewish Movie Moguls: An Exploration in American Culture," *American Jewish History* 72, no. 1 (1982): 6–25.

56. Turan, "Letting Jews Be Jews," 48.

57. Gabler, *Empire of Their Own*, 2.

58. Gabler, *Empire of Their Own*, 4–6.

59. J. Randolph Cox, "Dime Novels," in *The Oxford History of Popular Print Culture*, vol. 6, *US Popular Print Culture 1860–1920*, edited by Christine Bold (New York: Oxford University Press, 2011), 63–80; James G. Shoopman, *Patterns of American Popular Heroism: From Roman and Biblical Roots to Modern Media* (Jefferson, NC: McFarland, 2020), 142.

60. Robinson quoted in Gabler, *Empire of Their Own*, 1.

61. See Michael E. Birdwell, *Celluloid Soldiers: The Warner Bros. Campaign against Nazism* (New York: New York University Press, 1999); David Thomson, *Warner Bros: The Making of an American Movie Studio* (New Haven: Yale University Press, 2017); Chris Yogerst, *The Warner Brothers* (Lexington: University Press of Kentucky, 2023).

62. Gary Baum, "How the Academy Museum's Jewish Exclusion Became Exhibit A," *Hollywood Reporter*, March 19, 2022, https://www.hollywoodreporter.com/movies/movie-features/academy-museum-jewish-exclusion-1235114988/.

63. Daniel Bernardi, *Classic Hollywood, Classic Whiteness* (Minneapolis: University of Minnesota Press, 2001), 6.

64. Theodore Roosevelt, *Winning the West*, vol. 3 (Lincoln: University of Nebraska Press, 1995), 30, 45; Roosevelt quoted in Martin E. Marty, *Righteous Empire: The Protestant Experience in America* (New York: Dial, 1970), 12.

65. Simmon, *Invention of the Western Film*, 156, 158–59.

66. Simmon, *Invention of the Western Film*, 157.

67. John Fiske, *American Political Ideas Viewed from the Standpoint of Universal History* (New York: Harper, 1885). Fiske built on the concept of manifest destiny, which is attributed to John O'Sullivan, "Annexation," *United States Magazine and Democratic Review* 17, no. 1 (1845): 5–10.

68. Chavez, *Childhood Indians*, 66.

69. Simmon, *Invention of the Western Film*, xv. "Colonizer mentality" is borrowed from Albert Memmi, *The Colonizer and the Colonized* (Boston: Beacon, 1965).

70. Michael J. Riley, "Trapped in the History of Film: *The Vanishing American*," in *Hollywood's Indian: The Portrayal of the Native American in Film*, edited by Peter C. Rollins and John E. O'Connor (Lexington: University Press of Kentucky, 2003), 58.

71. Frederick Jackson Turner, "The Significance of the Frontier in American History," *Annual Report of the American Historical Association* (1893): 197–227.

72. John E. O'Connor and Peter C. Rollins, "Introduction: The West, Westerns, and American Character," in *Hollywood's West: The American Frontier in Film, Television, and History*, edited by Peter C. Collins and John E. O'Conner (Lexington: University Press of Kentucky, 2005), 5.

73. Ray Allen Billington, foreword to *Jews on the Frontier: An Account of Jewish Pioneers and Settlers in Early America*, by I. Harold Sharfman (Chicago: Regnery, 1977), ix.

74. J. E. Smyth, "The New Western History in 1931: RKO and the Challenge of *Cimarron*," in *Hollywood's Indian: The Portrayal of the Native American in Film*,

edited by Peter C. Rollins and John E. O'Connor (Lexington: University Press of Kentucky, 2003), 38.

75. M. Gail Hamner, "Scorsese as a Critic of Modernity: The Woman Question," in *Scorsese and Religion*, edited by Christopher B. Barnett and Clark J. Elliston (Boston: Brill, 2019), 120.

76. Nelson, *Still in the Saddle*, 6.

77. Leah Williams, "How Hollywood Whitewashed the Old West," *Atlantic*, October 5, 2016, https://www.theatlantic.com/entertainment/archive/2016/10/how-the-west-was-lost/502850/.

78. Lusted, *The Western*, 70–71, 83, 75.

79. Loy, *Westerns and American Culture*, 11; Lusted, *The Western*, 86; Richard W. Slatta, *The Cowboy Encyclopedia* (New York: Norton, 1996), 128.

80. William K. Everson, *A Pictorial History of the Western Film* (New York: Citadel, 1969), 18.

81. Loy, *Westerns and American Culture*, 11.

82. Frederick Elkin, "The Psychological Appeal of the Hollywood Western," *Journal of Educational Sociology* 24 no. 2 (1950): 77.

83. Lane Roth and Tom W. Hoffer, "G. M. 'Broncho Billy' Anderson: The First Movie Cowboy Hero," in *Back in the Saddle: Essays on Western Film and Television Actors*, edited by Gary A. Yoggy (Jefferson, NC: McFarland, 1998), 14.

84. Jack Fischel and Susan M. Ortman, eds., *Encyclopedia of Jewish American Popular Culture* (Santa Barbara, CA: ABC-CLIO, 2008), 135. Jeremy Geltzer remarks succinctly, "Essanay's director-star Broncho Billy Anderson concealed his own Jewish heritage" (*Dirty Words and Filthy Pictures: Film and the First Amendment* [Austin: University of Texas Press, 2015], 30).

85. See Peter Wegele, *Max Steiner: Composing, Casablanca, and the Golden Age of Film Music* (Lanham, MD: Rowman and Littlefield, 2014).

86. Dorothy Lamb Crawford, *A Windfall of Musicians: Hitler's Émigrés and Exiles in Southern California* (New Haven: Yale University Press, 2009), ix.

87. See Jonathan L. Friedmann, "Was Max Steiner a Jew?," *Journal of Film Music* 9, nos. 1–2 (2016): 94–106; Jonathan L. Friedmann, "The Jewish Roots of Hollywood Music," *Western States Jewish History* 45, no. 1 (2012): 47–54.

88. Kathryn Kalinak, Introduction to *Music in the Western: Notes from the Frontier*, edited by Kathryn Kalinak (New York: Routledge, 2012), 2.

89. James V. D'Arc, "Music to Match the Movies, and a Ride into the Sunset" (liner notes to *Saddles, Sagebrush, and Steiner*, Brigham Young University Film Music Archive, 2019, CD), 5.

90. Steven C. Smith, *Music by Max Steiner: The Epic Life of Hollywood's Most Influential Composer* (New York: Oxford University Press, 2020), 225.

91. Max Steiner, "Scoring the Film," in *We Make the Movies*, edited by Nancy Naumburg (New York: Norton, 1937), 225.

92. Charles Leinberger, "The Dollars Trilogy: 'There Are Two Kinds of Western Heroes, My Friend!,'" in *Music in the Western: Notes from the Frontier*, edited by Kathryn Kalinak (New York: Routledge, 2012), 132.

93. Kalinak, introduction, 1.

94. Mariana Whitmer, *Elmer Bernstein's "The Magnificent Seven": A Film Score Guide* (Lanham, MD: Rowman and Littlefield, 2017), 1.

95. Whitmer, *Elmer Bernstein's "The Magnificent Seven,"* 3; Bernstein quoted in Sue Fox, "Music That Changed Me," *BBC Magazine*, September 2002, https://elmerbernstein.com/articles/music-that-changed-me-elmer-bernstein/.

96. Mariana Whitmer, "Reinventing the Western Film Score: Jerome Moross and *The Big Country*," in *Music in the Western: Notes from the Frontier*, edited by Kathryn Kalinak (New York: Routledge, 2012), 51.

97. Whitmer, "Reinventing the Western Film Score," 51; Whitmer, *Elmer Bernstein's "The Magnificent Seven,"* 1.

98. Whitmer, "Reinventing the Western Film Score," 53.

99. Paul Griffiths, notes to *Copland: Dance Symphony, El Salón México, Four Episodes from Rodeo, Fanfare for the Common Man* (Polygram, 1982, LP). See also Donald C. Meyer, "Music Cue Archetypes in the Film Scores of Elmer Bernstein" (paper presented at From Nineteenth-Century Stage Drama to Twenty-First-Century Film Score: Musicodramatic Practice and Knowledge Organization symposium, April 15, 2012).

100. See Elizabeth Bergman Crist, *Music for the Common Man: Aaron Copland during the Depression and War* (New York: Oxford University Press, 2009).

101. Beth E. Levy, *Frontier Figures: American Music and the Mythology of the American West* (Berkeley: University of California Press, 2012), 322.

102. Copland quoted in *Keeping Score*, season 1, episode 3, "Copland and the American Sound," aired November 16, 2006, on PBS, https://www.pbs.org/keepingscore/copland-american-sound.html.

103. Bernstein quoted in Jon Burlingame, "Hollywood's Score Keeper," *Los Angeles Times*, November 8, 2001.

104. Gayle Murchison, *The American Stravinsky: The Style and Aesthetics of Copland's New American Music, the Early Works, 1921–1938* (Ann Arbor: University of Michigan Press, 2012), 132.

105. Aaron Copland, "Looking Back with Aaron Copland," *Los Angeles Times*, September 9, 1984. See Hans Nathan, ed., *Israeli Folk Music: Songs of the Early Pioneers* (Madison, WI: A-R, 1994). Others recruited for the project included Ernst Toch, Paul Dessau, Darius Milhaud, Arthur Honegger, Stefan Wolpe, Erich Walter Sternberg, and Kurt Weill.

106. Levy, *Frontier Figures*, 332, 301.

107. See Ildar Khannanov, "*High Noon*: Dimitri Tiomkin's Oscar-Winning Ballad and Its Russian Sources," *Journal of Film Music* 2, nos. 2–4 (2009): 225–48.

108. Dimitri Tiomkin interviewed on *Arthur Godfrey Time* (CBS Radio, June 20, 1962).

109. Phillip Drummond, *High Noon* (London: British Film Institute, 1997), 62–63.

110. Goldsmith quoted in Mauricio Dupuis, *Jerry Goldsmith: Music Scoring for American Movies* (Vicenza, Italy: DMG, 2014), 120.

Chapter 2. Pre-Code Westerns

1. Turan, "Letting Jews Be Jews," 45.

2. Turan, "Letting Jews Be Jews," 46.

3. Turan, "Letting Jews Be Jews," 46. Cagney shows off his impeccable Yiddish, which he learned in childhood, in the Warner Bros. film *Taxi!* (1932).

4. Felicia Herman, "Jewish Leaders and the Motion Picture Industry," in *California Jews*, edited by Ava F. Kahn and Marc Dollinger (Waltham, MA: Brandeis University Press, 2003), 95.

5. Kibler, *Censoring Racial Ridicule*, 147.

6. Kibler, *Censoring Racial Ridicule*, 137.

7. Herman, "Jewish Leaders," 95–96.

8. For the Catholic role in pushing motion picture censorship, see Gregory D. Black, *The Catholic Crusade against the Movies, 1940–1975* (New York: Cambridge University Press, 1998).

9. Herman, "Jewish Leaders," 101.

10. "A Brief History of Film Censorship," National Coalition against Censorship, accessed August 12, 2004, https://ncac.org/resource/a-brief-history-of-film-censorship.

11. Herman, "Jewish Leaders," 102.

12. Lenny Bruce, *How to Talk Dirty and Influence People: An Autobiography* (1965; Boston: Da Capo, 2016), xvii.

13. Patricia Erens, *The Jew in American Cinema* (Bloomington: Indiana University Press, 1984), 30, 33.

14. Hasia Diner, *Roads Taken: The Great Jewish Migrations to the New World and the Peddlers Who Forged the Way* (New Haven: Yale University Press, 2015), 48.

15. Alexandra Keller, "Historical Discourse and American Identity in Westerns since the Reagan Era," in *Hollywood's West: The American Frontier in Film, Television, and History*, edited by John E. O'Connor and Peter C. Rollins (Lexington: University Press of Kentucky, 2009), 255.

16. Erens, *The Jew in American Cinema*, 35 (citing *Motion Picture World*, September 11, 1909), 34.

17. Erens, *Jew in American Cinema*, 38 (citing *Motion Picture World*, August 14, 1909), 39.

18. Erens, *Jew in American Cinema*, 39–40.

19. Langman, *Guide to Silent Westerns*, 343, 356.

20. "Zane Grey on Film: A Listing of Movies Made from Zane Grey's Writings," *Zane Grey's West Society*, accessed August 12, 2024, https://www.zgws.org/zgmovies.php. More than one hundred movies have been made from Grey's novels; *The Light of Western Stars* was the first of the sound era.

21. "Critical Comments on Current Films," *Screenland*, August 1930, 87.

22. "The Light of Western Stars (1930) Review, with Richard Arlen and Mary Brian," *Pre-Code.com*, September 9, 2022, https://pre-code.com/the-light-of-western-stars-1930-review-with-richard-arlen-and-mary-brian/.

23. Susan Courtney, *Hollywood Fantasies of Miscegenation: Spectacular Narratives of Gender and Race* (Princeton: Princeton University Press, 2021), 113–15.

24. Edward D. Berkowitz, *Mass Appeal: The Formative Age of the Movies, Radio, and TV* (New York: Cambridge University Press, 2010), 7.

25. Friedmann, *Jewish Los Angeles*, 49.

26. Simmon, *Invention of the Western Film*, 186; Matt Singer, "The Worst Oscar Best Picture Winners Ever," *Screen Crush*, March 8, 2022, https://screencrush.com/worst-oscar-best-picture-winners/.

27. Paul Monaco, *A History of American Movies: A Film-by-Film Look at the Art, Craft, and Business of Cinema* (Lanham, MD: Scarecrow, 2010), 34.

28. Julie Goldsmith Gilbert, *Ferber: Edna Ferber and Her Circle, a Biography* (New York: Applause, 1999), 42.

29. Smyth, "New Western History in 1931," 42

30. Monaco, *History of American Movies*, 34.

31. Smyth, "New Western History in 1931," 58.

32. Paul Miles Schneider, "The Best Picture Project: A Film Lover's Journey through Every Oscar-Winning Best Picture in Chronological Order: Cimarron (1930–31)," *www.paulmilesschneider.com*, March 20, 2015, www.paulmilesschneider.com/bestpictureproject/cimarron-1930-31/.

33. H. Wayne Morgan, *Oklahoma: A History* (New York: Norton, 1977), xviii.

34. See Ann R. Shapiro, "Edna Ferber, Jewish American Feminist," *Shofar* 20, no. 2 (2002): 52–60.

35. Henry J. Tobias, *The Jews in Oklahoma* (Norman: University of Oklahoma Press, 1980), 10, 13.

36. See Russell Cobb, *The Great Oklahoma Swindle: Race, Religion, and Lies in America's Weirdest State* (Lincoln: University of Nebraska Press, 2020), 87–97.

37. Tobias, *Jews in Oklahoma*, 56, 62.

38. Edna Ferber, *Cimarron* (London: Heinemann, 1930), 181.

39. Janet Burstein, "Edna Ferber," *Jewish Women's Archive*, February 27, 2009, https://jwa.org/encyclopedia/article/ferber-edna.

40. Edna Ferber, *A Peculiar Treasure* (New York: Doubleday, 1960).

41. Ferber, *Cimarron*, 186.

Chapter 3. Code-Era Westerns

1. Meyers, *Movie-Made Jews*, 21, 22.

2. Meyers, *Movie-Made Jews*, 23.

3. Slotkin, *Gunfighter Nation*, 461.

4. David Thomson, *A Biographical Dictionary of Film* (New York: Morrow, 1976), 185.

5. Pauline Kael, *5001 Nights at the Movies* (New York: Holt, 1991), 662.

6. Brian Spittles, *John Ford* (New York: Routledge, 2004), 95.

7. Robert B. Pippin, "What Is a Western?: Politics and Self-Knowledge in John Ford's *The Searchers*," *Critical Inquiry* 35, no. 2 (2009): 243.

8. Koffman, *Jews' Indian*, 12.

9. Rochlin and Rochlin, *Pioneer Jews*, 69–70.

10. Nancy Schoenberger, *Wayne and Ford: The Films, the Friendship, and the Forging of an American Hero* (New York: Anchor, 2018), 118.

11. Pippin, "What Is a Western?," 243.

12. Ken Nolley, "The Representation of Conquest: John Ford and the Hollywood Indian, 1939–1964," in *Hollywood's Indian: The Portrayal of the Native American in Film*, edited by Peter C. Rollins and John E. O'Connor (Lexington: University Press of Kentucky, 2003), 85.

13. Tag Gallagher, *John Ford: The Man and His Films* (Berkeley: University of California Press, 1986), 465.

14. For more on negotiations Jews undertook on their westward journey, see Shari Rabin, *Jews on the Frontier: Religion and Mobility in Nineteenth-Century America* (New York: New York University Press, 2017).

15. Stephen Vider, "Riding Shotgun," *Tablet*, May 18, 2005, https://www.tabletmag.com/sections/arts-letters/articles/riding-shotgun.

16. Simmon, *Invention of the Western Film*, 276.

17. Martin Scorsese, Foreword to *A Third Face: My Tale of Writing, Fighting, and Filmmaking*, by Samuel Fuller (New York: Knopf, 2002), xi.

18. David Meuel, *The Noir Western: Darkness on the Range, 1943–1962* (Jefferson, NC: McFarland, 2015), 82; Simmon, *Invention of the Western Film*, 276.

19. Nicholas Garnham, *Samuel Fuller* (New York: Viking, 1971), 100.

20. Peter Travers, "Forty Guns (1957)," in *The B List: The National Society of Film Critics on the Low-Budget Beauties, Genre-Bending Mavericks, and Cult Classics We Love*, edited by David Sterritt and John Anderson (Cambridge, MA: Da Capo, 2008), 141.

21. Carson Lund, "Blu-Ray Review: Samuel Fuller's *Forty Guns* on the Criterion Collection," *Slant*, January 10, 2019, https://www.slantmagazine.com/dvd/forty-guns-bd/.

22. Garnham, *Samuel Fuller*, 100.

23. Samuel Fuller, *A Third Face: My Tale of Writing, Fighting, and Filmmaking* (New York: Knopf, 2002), 358.

24. Chaim Waxman, *American Jews* (Philadelphia: Temple University Press, 1983), 50.

25. Ava F. Kahn, ed., *Jewish Voices of the California Gold Rush: A Documentary History, 1849–1880* (Detroit: Wayne State University Press, 2002), 7.

26. Lund, "Blu-Ray Review."

27. Macy Nulman, *The Encyclopedia of Jewish Prayer* (Northvale, NJ: Aronson, 1996), 7.

28. Bosley Crowther, "Screen: New 'Cimarron,'" *New York Times*, February 17, 1961.

29. "Cinema: Oklacoma: *Cimarron*," *Time*, February 24, 1961.

30. This phrase is borrowed from William Friedman (1880–1939), a prominent Denver-based rabbi and standard-bearer of the Americanizing Jewish Reform movement. See Ferenc Morton Szasz, *Religion in the Modern American West* (Tucson: University of Arizona Press, 2000), 59.

31. "Cinema: Oklacoma."

32. Leonard Maltin, Luke Sader, and Mike Clark, eds., *Leonard Maltin's 2009 Movie Guide* (New York: Penguin, 2008), 247.

33. Erens, *Jew in American Cinema*, 32.

34. Samantha Baskind, *The Warsaw Ghetto in American Art and Culture* (University Park: Pennsylvania State University Press, 2018), 111.

35. "Books: Back to the Wall," *Time*, June 2, 1961.

36. Rachel Leket-Mor, "My Heart Is in the West but I Am on the Eastern Edge: Hebrew Pulp Westerns and the Sabra Cowboy," in *The Western in the Global Literary Imagination*, edited by Christopher Conway, Marek Paryz, and David Rio (Boston: Brill, 2022), 254.

37. Gary Fishgall, *Gregory Peck: A Biography* (New York: Scribner, 2002), 282.

38. Rita Keshena, "The Role of American Indians in Motion Pictures," in *The Pretend Indians: Images of Native Americans in Movies*, edited by Gretchen M. Bataille and Charles L. P. Silet (Ames: Iowa State University Press, 1980), 109–10.

39. Keshena, "Role of American Indians," 110.

Chapter 4. Television Westerns

1. Poyntz Tyler, ed., *Television and Radio* (New York: Wilson, 1961), 140.

2. Vincent Brook, *Something Ain't Kosher Here: The Rise of the "Jewish" Sitcom* (New Brunswick, NJ: Rutgers University Press, 2003), 44.

3. See Michael Barrett, "*The Goldbergs*: The Most Jewish Show on Television," *Pop Matters*, April 27, 2020, https://www.popmatters.com/goldbergs-most-jewish-television-show.

4. Tyler, *Television and Radio*, 140.

5. Harry Golden, *Forgotten Pioneer* (New York: World, 1963), 23, 21, 20, 16, 28.

6. Oscar Handlin, *Adventure in Freedom* (New York: McGraw-Hill, 1954), 85–88.

7. Hasia Diner, "Entering the Mainstream of Modern Jewish History: Peddlers and the American Jewish South," *Southern Jewish History* 8 (2005): 22.

8. Diner, "Entering the Mainstream," 9.

9. *Jewish Progress*, April 10, 1896, quoted in Norton B. Stern and William M. Kramer, "Anti-Semitism and the Jewish Image in the Early West," *Western States Jewish Historical Quarterly* 6, no. 2 (1974): 129.

10. Stern and Kramer, "Anti-Semitism and the Jewish Image," 139–40.

11. Diner, "Entering the Mainstream," 19–20.

12. Rabin, *Jews on the Frontier*, 84.

13. Diner, "Entering the Mainstream," 12.

14. Diner, *Roads Taken*, 127.

15. Golden, *Forgotten Pioneer*, 15.

16. Everett Aaker, *Television Western Players, 1960–1975: A Biographical Dictionary* (Jefferson, NC: McFarland, 2017), 46.

17. "Shimon Wincelberg," *Variety*, October 1, 2004.

18. Brook, *Something Ain't Kosher Here*, 44.

19. Yehuda Slutsky, "Cantonists," in *Encyclopaedia Judaica*, 2nd ed., edited by Fred Skolnik and Michael Berenbaum (Detroit: Macmillan, 2007), 4:437–39.

20. Joseph A. Levine, *Rise and Be Seated: The Ups and Downs of Jewish Worship* (Northvale, NJ: Aronson, 2000), 264.

21. Diner, "Entering the Mainstream," 19–20.

22. Brook, *Something Ain't Kosher Here*, 47.

23. Daniel Goldmark, *Tunes for 'Toons: Music and the Hollywood Cartoon* (Berkeley: University of California Press, 2005), 32.

24. Koffman, *Jews' Indian*, 46.

25. Jonathan Pearl and Judith Pearl, *The Chosen Image: Television's Portrayal of Jewish Themes and Characters* (Jefferson, NC: McFarland, 1999), 196.

26. Pearl and Pearl, *Chosen Image*, 196.

27. Koffman, *Jews' Indian*, 41.

28. Peter Y. Medding, Gary A. Tobin, Sylvia Barack Fishman, and Mordechai Rimor, "Jewish Identity in Conversionary and Mixed Marriages," *American Jewish Yearbook* 92 (1992): 3.

29. Gruber, "Heym on the Range."

30. John P. Marschall, *Jews in Nevada: A History* (Reno: University of Nevada Press, 2008), 24, 71.

31. Amory quoted in Gary A. Yoggy, *Riding the Video Range: The Rise and Fall of the Western on Television* (Jefferson, NC: McFarland, 1995), 226.

32. Beringia Zen, "Rod Serling," *Dictionary of Unitarian and Universalist Biography*, September 16, 2001, https://uudb.org/articles/rodserling.html.

33. Robert J. Serling (Rod Serling's older brother) quoted in Marc Scott Zicree, *The Twilight Zone Companion*, 3rd ed. (Los Angeles: Silman-James, 2018), 2; Koren Shadmi, *The Twilight Man: Rod Serling and the Birth of Television* (Los Angeles: Humanoids, 2019), 117.

34. Zicree, *Twilight Zone Companion*, 10–11.

35. Tony Albarella, "'Noon on Doomsday' (1956) Reviewed," Rod Serling Memorial Foundation, https://rodserling.com/noon-on-doomsday-1956-reviewed/.

36. Oscar Handlin, "New Paths in American Jewish History," *Commentary*, January 8, 1948, 388–94.

37. Louis Jacobs, *A Concise Companion to the Jewish Religion* (New York: Oxford University Press, 1999), 10.

38. Rebecca Lesses, "Lilith," *Jewish Women's Archive*, March 20, 2009, https://jwa.org/encyclopedia/article/lilith.

39. Susan Ackerman, "Astarte: Bible," February 27, 2009, *Jewish Women's Archive*, https://jwa.org/encyclopedia/article/astarte-bible.

40. Don Presnell, *Wandering "The Wild Wild West": A Critical Analysis of the CBS Television Series* (Jefferson, NC: McFarland, 2021), 42.

41. While Rickles's onscreen performance was a departure for the comedian, Senensky recounts that behind the scenes, Rickles was thoroughly himself, "merciless, but funny. Everyone on the set was his potential next victim" (Ralph Senensky, "*The Wild Wild West*: 'The Night of the Druid's Blood,'" *Ralph's Cinema Trek: A Journey in Film*, accessed August 12, 2024, https://senensky.com/the-night-of-the-druids-blood/).

42. Most, "Big Chief Izzy Horowitz," 313–14.

43. Norton B. Stern, a trailblazing historian of Jews in the American West, noted that Louis Phillips (1829–1900) was "one of the very few Jewish pioneers of the American West who made his living as a working rancher" (Norton B. Stern, "Louis Phillips of the Pomona Valley: Rancher and Real Estate Investor," *Western States Jewish History* 16, no. 1 [1983]: 54).

44. Laura Manischewitz Alpern, *Manischewitz, the Matzo Family: The Making of an American Jewish Icon* (Jersey City, NJ: KTAV, 2008), 186.

45. See Lila Corwin Berman, "Sociology, Jews, and Intermarriage in Twentieth-Century America," *Jewish Social Studies* 14, no. 2 (2008): 32–60.

46. Louis A. Berman, *Jews and Intermarriage: A Study in Personality and Culture* (New York: Yoseloff, 1968); Jennifer H. Thompson, *Jewish on Their Own Terms: How Intermarried Couples Are Changing American Judaism* (New Brunswick, NJ: Rutgers University Press, 2013), 33.

47. Marshall Sklare, *America's Jews* (New York: Random House, 1971), 193.

48. See, for example, Leslie A. Fiedler, *Fiedler on the Roof: Essays on Literature and Jewish Identity* (Boston: Godine, 1991), xii.

49. See William Toll, "Intermarriage and the Urban West: A Religious Context for Cultural Change," in *Jews of the American West*, edited by Moses Rischin and John Livingstone (Detroit: Wayne State University Press, 1991), 164–89.

50. Riley Moffat, *Population History of Western U.S. Cities and Towns, 1850–1990* (Lanham, MD: Scarecrow, 1996), 332.

51. Don Franks, *Entertainment Awards: A Music, Cinema, Theatre and Broadcasting Guide, 1928 through 2003*, 3rd ed. (Jefferson, NC: McFarland, 2014), 408.

52. Elliot Gertel, *Over the Top Judaism: Precedents and Trends in the Depiction of Jewish Beliefs and Observances in Film and Television* (Lanham, MD: University Press of America, 2003), 199–200.

53. James Loeffler, *The Most Musical Nation: Jews and Culture in the Late Russian Empire* (New Haven: Yale University Press, 2010), 164.

54. Egon Mayer and Carl Sheingold, *Intermarriage and the Jewish Future: A National Study in Summary* (New York: American Jewish Committee, 1979), 30.

55. Abraham W. Binder, ed., *Union Hymnal: Songs and Prayers for Jewish Worship* (New York: Central Conference of American Rabbis, 1932). The Shema setting appears eleven times in the volume, ten times described as "traditional" and once attributed to Sulzer. The melody does not appear in earlier volumes and may have been invented or adapted from memory by Binder.

56. Josephine Sarah Marcus Earp, *I Married Wyatt Earp: The Recollections of Josephine Sarah Marcus Earp*, collected and edited by Glenn G. Boyer (Tucson: University of Arizona Press, 1976).

57. Tony Ortega, "I Varied Wyatt Earp," *Phoenix New Times*, March 4, 1999; Tony Ortega, "How the West Was Spun," *Phoenix New Times*, December 24, 1998.

58. Kate Morrison, "She Lied about Everything, Except Marrying Wyatt Earp," *Messy Nessy*, March 15, 2017, https://www.messynessychic.com/2017/03/15/she-lied-about-everything-except-marrying-wyatt-earp/.

59. Brian Dervin Dillon and David Erin Dillon, "Wyatt and Josie Earp: Fact, Fiction, and Myth," *Western States Jewish History* 48, no. 1 (2015): 32.

60. Rochlin and Rochlin, *Pioneer Jews*, 173.

61. See Breck, *Centennial History*, 149.

62. See Matthew Wills, "Nittel Nacht: The Jewish Christmas Eve," *JSTOR Daily*, December 16, 2020, https://daily.jstor.org/nittel-nacht-the-jewish-christmas-eve/.

63. Ann Haber Stanton, *Deadwood's Jewish Pioneers: A Gold Rush Odyssey* (n.p.: Prairie Hills, 2019), 171.

64. Stanton, *Deadwood's Jewish Pioneers*, 72, 171–72, 173, 178, 182, 188.

65. Stanton, *Deadwood's Jewish Pioneers*, 172; Mike Runge, *Deadwood's Mount Moriah Cemetery* (Charleston, SC: Arcadia, 2017), 77.

66. Trevor Lane, "Deadwood: Comparing the Lead Characters and Their Real World Counterparts," *What Culture*, May 20, 2020, https://whatculture.com/tv/deadwood-comparing-the-lead-characters-and-their-real-world-counterparts.

67. Stanton, *Deadwood's Jewish Pioneers*, 7, 52, 53.

68. G. W. G. Hyde and William Stoddard, eds., *History of the Great Northwest and Its Men of Progress* (Minneapolis: Minneapolis Journal, 1901), 219.

69. Vider, "Riding Shotgun."

70. Stanton, *Deadwood's Jewish Pioneers*, 201–2.

Chapter 5. Post-Code Westerns

1. Marsha Bryan Edelman, "Continuity, Creativity, and Conflict: The Ongoing Search for 'Jewish' Music," in *You Should See Yourself: Jewish Identity on Postmodern American Culture*, edited by Vincent Brook (New Brunswick, NJ: Rutgers University Press, 2006), 121.

2. Joel Rosenberg, "Jewish Experience on Film—An American Overview," *American Jewish Yearbook* 96 (1996): 39; Nathan Abrams, *The New Jew in Film: Exploring Jewishness and Judaism in Contemporary Cinema* (New Brunswick, NJ: Rutgers University Press, 2012), 8.

3. Desirée J. Garcia, *The Migration of Musical Film: From Ethnic Margins to American Mainstream* (New Brunswick, NJ: Rutgers University Press, 2014), 187; Barry Rubin, *Assimilation and Its Discontents* (New York: Random House, 1995).

4. Meyers, *Movie-Made Jews*, 74.

5. Turan, "Letting Jews Be Jews," 50.

6. Meyers, *Movie-Made Jews*, 27.

7. Michael Elias, interview by author, telephone, September 24, 2021.

8. Molly Haskell, *Steven Spielberg: A Life in Films* (New Haven: Yale University Press, 2017), 21.

9. Much of this discussion comes from Jonathan L. Friedmann, "*The Frisco Kid* Revisited: Sources and Themes in the Original Screenplay," *Western States Jewish History* 52, no. 2 (2022): 35–58.

10. Epstein, *American Jewish Films*, 7.

11. Elias, interview by author.

12. Rabin, *Jews on the Frontier*, 143.

13. Elias, interview by author.

14. Hasia Diner, "The Study of American Jewish History: In the Academy, in the Community," *Polish American Studies* 65, no. 1 (2008): 54.

15. The Trappist monastery is a historical inaccuracy. See "Trappist Monasteries in North America," *GCatholic.org*, accessed August 14, 2024, http://www.gcatholic.org/churches/list/USA-Trappist.htm. Robert Grossbach, *The Frisco Kid* (New York: Warner, 1979), 210, invents a Trappist monastic mission, San Scholastica de Nursia, placing it near Sonora in the heart of California's gold country.

16. Michael Elias and Frank Shaw, *No-Knife*, second draft, Warner Bros., October 1977, 105.

17. Erens, *Jew in American Cinema*, 335.

18. Pitts, *Western Movies*, 116.

19. Roger Ebert, review of *The Frisco Kid*, January 1, 1979, https://www.rogerebert.com/reviews/the-frisco-kid-1979.

20. Alain Silver and James Ursini, *What Ever Happened to Robert Aldrich?: His Life and His Films* (New York: Limelight, 1995), 167–69.

21. Hammerman, *Silver Screen, Hasidic Jews*, 21.

22. Gene Wilder, *Kiss Me Like a Stranger: My Search for Love and Art* (New York: St. Martin's, 2005), 174.

23. Abigail Pogrebin, *Stars of David: Prominent Jews Talk about Being Jewish* (New York: Broadway, 2005), 96. According to Rabbi Stephen Robbins, who was a religion consultant for the film, Wilder learned the prayer chants from Rabbi Baruch Cohon, a cantor who served with Robbins at Temple Emanuel of Beverly Hills. Wilder also studied Hebrew texts with Robbins and picked up a Yiddish accent from Mel Brooks (Stephen Robbins, interview by author, telephone, April 18, 2022).

24. Pogrebin, *Stars of David*, 95. Brooks also described his humor as more New York than Jewish: "Jewish comedy was softer and sweeter. New York comedy was tougher and more explosive" (Michael Schulman, "Mel Brooks Writes It All Down," *New Yorker*, November 28, 2021, https://www.newyorker.com/culture/the-new-yorker-interview/mel-brooks-writes-it-all-down).

25. Terry Gross, "Mel Brooks Says His Only Regret as a Comedian Is the Jokes He Didn't Tell," *Fresh Air*, NPR, December 7, 2021, https://www.npr.org/2021/12/07/1061836388/mel-brooks-all-about-me.

26. Silver and Ursini, *What Ever Happened to Robert Aldrich?*, 169.

27. Elias, interview by author.

28. Pogrebin, *Stars of David*, 96.

29. Elias and Shaw, *No-Knife*, 31–36, 69–75.

30. Wendy Zierler, "Fools on the American Road: 'Gimpel the Fool,' *The Frisco Kid*, and *Forrest Gump*," in *Hit the Road Jack: Essays on the Culture of the American Road*, edited by Gordon E. Slethaug and Stacey Ford (Montreal: McGill–Queen's University Press, 2012), 218.

31. Saul Bellow, "On Jewish Storytelling," in *What Is Jewish Literature?*, edited by Hanna Wirth-Nesher (Philadelphia: Jewish Publication Society, 1994), 16–17.

32. Zierler, "Fools on the American Road," 223.

33. The novelization also includes a version of this scene, suggesting that it was a late omission. See Grossbach, *Frisco Kid*, 21–34.

34. Silver and Ursini, *What Ever Happened to Robert Aldrich?*, 169; Shari Rabin, "Fact-Checking *The Frisco Kid*: A Historian's Take on a Jewish Classic," *Jewish Book Council*, December 21, 2017, https://www.jewishbookcouncil.org/pb-daily/fact-checking-the-frisco-kid-a-historians-take-on-a-jewish-classic.

35. Laura Hodes, "Why We Need to Remember Gene Wilder in 'The Frisco Kid,'" *Forward*, September 2, 2016, https://forward.com/culture/349138/why-we-need-to-remember-gene-wilder-in-the-frisco-kid/.

36. B. C. Wallin, "The Delightful Orthodox Representation in 'The Frisco Kid,'" *Hey Alma*, July 27, 2021, https://www.heyalma.com/the-delightful-orthodox-representation-in-the-frisco-kid/.

37. Elias, interview by author.

38. Epstein, *American Jewish Films*, 99.

39. Elias, interview by author. Leon Uris, *Exodus* (New York: Doubleday, 1958).

40. Barbara Kirshenblatt-Gimblett, "Sounds of Sensibility," *Judaism* 47, no. 1 (1998): 52, calls the "heritage music" of *Fiddler on the Roof* and other revivalist efforts "a mode of cultural production that gives the disappearing and gone a second life as an exhibit of itself."

41. Garrett-Davis, *What Is a Western?*, 33–35.

42. Zierler, "Fools on the American Road," 222.

43. Elias, interview by author.

44. Formally Yerba Buena, the city was officially named San Francisco on January 30, 1847, by chief magistrate Washington Bartlett, who later served as the twentieth mayor of San Francisco (1883–87) and the sixteenth governor of California from January 1887 until his death on September 12, 1887. Bartlett was the state's first Jewish governor and to date remains the only Jew to hold that office. San Francisco and the rest of Alta California became a U.S. military territory in 1848 as part of the Treaty of Guadalupe Hidalgo, which ended the Mexican-American War. Shortly after California became a state on September 9, 1850, San Francisco was chartered as both a city and a county. Grossbach, *Frisco Kid*, 45,

describes the rapid transformation of Yerba Buena into the bustling city of San Francisco: "In 1846, the white population of Yerba Buena was seven hundred (half of them American), with 150 residents of other races. Three years later, forty thousand people arrived by sea and an equal number by land across the Great Basin, or north, from Mexico."

45. Elias and Shaw, *No-Knife*, 4, 10. Wagon trains from Missouri to California (roughly two thousand miles) took about six months.

46. Garrett-Davis, *What Is a Western?*, 34. See Philip L. Fradkin, *Stagecoach: Wells Fargo and the American West* (New York: Simon and Schuster, 2002). Grossbach, *Frisco Kid*, 220, calls it the "Overland Mail" office, reflecting the author's general concern for chronological accuracy. The original screenplay uses Wells Fargo (Elias and Shaw, *No-Knife*, 105–6).

47. See Norton B. Stern, "Toward a Biography of Isaias W. Hellman: Pioneer Builder of California," *Western States Jewish Historical Quarterly* 2, no. 1 (1969): 27–43.

48. Joyce G. Saricks, *The Readers' Advisory Guide to Genre Fiction* (Chicago: American Library Association, 2009), 315.

49. Elias, interview by author.

50. Garrett-Davis, *What Is a Western?*, 34; Edgar F. Kahn, "The Saga of the First Fifty Years of Congregation Emanu-El, San Francisco," *Western States Jewish Historical Quarterly* 3, no. 3 (1971): 129–47.

51. In 1854, Congregation Emanu-El hired Julius Eckman, a Posen-born, German-trained rabbi who had spent three years in London as a teenager and thus was fluent in English. In 1857, Rabbi Henry A. Henry, a Londoner of Polish-Prussian ancestry, was hired to serve Congregation Sherith Israel.

52. Elias and Shaw, *No-Knife*, 11–12.

53. Alan Silverstein, *Alternatives to Assimilation: The Response of Reform Judaism to American Culture, 1840–1930* (Waltham, MA: Brandeis University Press, 1995), 10–12.

54. Norton B. Stern and William M. Kramer, "The Major Role of Polish Jews in the Pioneer West," *Western States Jewish Historical Quarterly* 8, no. 4 (1976): 334.

55. Grossbach, *Frisco Kid*, 7. During the Hapsburg period, Jews comprised roughly one-third of the population of Kołomyja. See Paul Robert Magocsi, "Galicia: A European Land," in *Galicia: A Multicultural Land*, edited by Chris Hann and Paul Robert Magocsi (Toronto: University of Toronto Press, 2005), 11.

56. Garrett-Davis, *What Is a Western?*, 33.

57. Elias, interview by author.

58. David Desser and Lester D. Friedman, *American Jewish Filmmakers*, 2nd ed. (Urbana: University of Illinois Press, 2004), 306.

59. Joshua Louis Moss, *Why Harry Met Sally: Subversive Jewishness, Anglo-Christian Power, and the Rhetoric of Modern Love* (Austin: University of Texas Press, 2017), 202.

60. John Logie, "*Maus* (W)holes: Reflections on (and in) the Digitization of Art Spiegelman's *Maus*," in *Perspectives on Digital Comics: Theoretical, Critical, and Pedagogical Essays*, edited by Jeffrey S. J. Kirchoff and Mike P. Cook (Jefferson, NC: McFarland, 2019), 149. See Art Spiegelman, *Maus: A Survivor's Tale* (New York: Pantheon, 1986); Art Spiegelman, *Maus II: A Survivor's Tale: And Here My Troubles Began* (New York: Pantheon, 1991).

61. Sam B. Girgus, *Generations of Jewish Directors and the Struggle for America's Soul: Wyler, Lumet, and Spielberg* (Cham, Switzerland: Palgrave Macmillan, 2021), 37.

62. Jerry Beck, *The Animated Movie Guide* (Chicago: A Capella, 2005), 17; Joseph McBride, *Steven Spielberg: A Biography*, 2nd ed. (Jackson: University Press of Mississippi, 2010), 20.

63. Abigail Weil, "Revisiting 'An American Tail,' a Deeply Jewish Immigration Story," *Hey Alma*, September 20, 2021, https://www.heyalma.com/revisiting-an-american-tail-a-deeply-jewish-immigration-story/.

64. Beck, *Animated Movie Guide*, 17.

65. See Herman J. Levine and Benjamin Miller, *The American Jewish Farmer in Changing Times* (New York: Jewish Agricultural Society, 1966).

66. Jon Raymond, *The Half-Life: A Novel* (New York: Bloomsbury, 2008).

67. Jon Raymond and Kelly Reichardt, *First Cow* (Webster, TX: Filmscience, 2018), https://deadline.com/wp-content/uploads/2021/02/FIRST-COW-screenplay.pdf.

68. "Meek's Cutoff," *Rotten Tomatoes*, https://www.rottentomatoes.com/m/meeks_cutoff.

69. Stephanie Zacharek, "Kelly Reichardt's *First Cow* Is a Tranquil Reflection on Masculine Tenderness," *Time*, March 6, 2020, https://time.com/5797867/first-cow-review/.

70. Karen Gordon, "*First Cow*: An Anti-Mythic Tale of the Old West, Fabulous Fritters, Lactic Larceny and Larger Themes," *Original CIN*, March 11, 2020, https://www.original-cin.ca/posts/2020/3/11/first-cow-a-less-than-mythic-tale-of-the-old-west-fabulous-fritters-lactic-larceny-and-bigger-themes.

71. K. Austin Collins, "*First Cow* Is a Rich, Satisfying Tale of Frontier Friendship," *Vanity Fair*, March 6, 2020, https://www.vanityfair.com/hollywood/2020/03/first-cow-movie-review.

72. Falconer, *Afterlife of the Hollywood Western*, 83.

73. Falconer, *Afterlife of the Hollywood Western*, 83.

74. Yerba Buena's population in the 1830s numbered only a few hundred, including immigrants from Spain, England, Scotland, France, Holland, Germany, and the Pacific Islands as well as migrants from the United States (Mick Sinclair, *San Francisco: A Cultural and Literary History* [Oxford: Signal, 2004], 7).

75. See the Jewish Museum of the American West website, https://www.jmaw.org/.

76. Collins, "*First Cow* Is a Rich, Satisfying Tale."

Chapter 6. Comedic Sensibility

1. Epstein, *American Jewish Films*, 99.

2. Vanessa L. Ochs, "Ten Jewish Sensibilities," *Sh'ma: A Journal of Jewish Ideas*, December 1, 2003, http://shma.com/ten-jewish-sensibilities/.

3. William Novak and Moshe Waldoks, eds., *The Big Book of Jewish Humor* (New York: Morrow, 2006), xx–xi.

4. See Jeremy Dauber, *Jewish Comedy: A Serious History* (New York: Norton, 2017).

5. "A Portrait of Jewish Americans," Pew Research Center, October 1, 2013, https://www.pewresearch.org/religion/2013/10/01/jewish-american-beliefs-attitudes-culture-survey/Pew.

6. Nathan Abrams, "A Secular Talmud: The Jewish Sensibility of *Mad* Magazine," *Studies in Jewish Humor* 3, no. 30 (2014): 111.

7. Benjamin Blech, *The Complete Idiot's Guide to Jewish Culture and History*, 2nd ed. (New York: Alpha, 2004), 19.

8. See Anna Dubai and Nick Hopkins, "Humour Is Serious: Minority Group Members' Use of Humour in Their Encounters with Majority Group Members," *European Journal of Social Psychology* 50, no. 2 (2020):448–62.

9. Adele Berlin, "Esther: Introduction," in *The Jewish Study Bible*, edited by Adele Berlin and Marc Zvi Brettler (New York: Oxford University Press, 1999), 1623–25.

10. Gross, "Mel Brooks Says His Only Regret as a Comedian Is the Jokes He Didn't Tell."

11. Varner, *A to Z of Westerns in Cinema*, xxii.

12. Falconer, *Afterlife of the Hollywood Western*, 5.

13. Lawrence, "Filmography," 300.

14. Matthew R. Turner, "Cowboys and Comedy: The Simultaneous Deconstruction and Reinforcement of Generic Conventions in the Western Parody," in *Hollywood's West: The American Frontier in Film, Television, and History*, edited by Peter C. Rollins and John E. O'Connor (Lexington: University Press of Kentucky, 2005), 223.

15. Jeff Lenburg, Joan Howard Maurer, and Greg Lenburg, *The Three Stooges Scrapbook* (Chicago: Chicago Review, 2012), 194.

16. Beverly Gray, *Seduced by Mrs. Robinson: How "The Graduate" Became the Touchstone of a Generation* (Chapel Hill, NC: Algonquin, 2017), 233.

17. Caryl Flinn, "A Tale of Two Cowgirls: Songs, Western Novelty Acts, and 1950s Hollywood," in *Music in the Western*, edited by Kathryn Kalinak (New York: Routledge, 2012), 97.

18. Josh Kun, *Audiotopia: Music, Race, and America* (Berkeley: University of California Press, 2005), 54.

19. David Weinstein, *The Eddie Cantor Story: A Jewish Life in Performance and Politics* (Waltham, MA: Brandeis University Press, 2018), 91.

20. Henry Sapoznik, *The Compleat Klezmer* (Cedarhurst, NY: Tara), 66.

21. Weinstein, *Eddie Cantor Story*, 44; Ruth Wisse quoted in Janet Tassel, "Mame-loshn at Harvard," *Harvard Magazine*, July 1, 1997, https://www.harvardmagazine.com/1997/07/mame-loshn-at-harvard.

22. Most, "Big Chief Izzy Horowitz," 327.

23. Michael Wex, *Born to Kvetch: Yiddish Language and Culture in All Its Moods* (New York: St. Martin's, 2005).

24. Most, "Big Chief Izzy Horowitz," 325–26.

25. Most, "Big Chief Izzy Horowitz," 320.

26. Weinstein, *Eddie Cantor Story*, 92. See Ben Urwand's virulently antistudio *The Collaboration: Hollywood's Pact with Hitler* (Cambridge: Belknap Press of Harvard University Press, 2013); Thomas Doherty's more measured *Hollywood and Hitler, 1933–1939* (New York: Columbia University Press, 2013); and Steven J. Ross's *Hitler in Los Angeles: How Jews Foiled Nazi Plots against Hollywood and America* (New York: Bloomsbury, 2017), which convincingly debunks Urwand's argument, showing that the situation was far more complex than simply caving to Hitler for economic reasons.

27. Most, "Big Chief Izzy Horowitz," 320.

28. Wheeler Winston Dixon, "Fast Worker: The Films of Sam Newfield," *Senses of Cinema* 45 (2007), http://www.sensesofcinema.com/2007/feature-articles/sam-newfield/.

29. Curtis quoted in Edwin M. Bradley, *Hollywood Musicals You Missed: Seventy Noteworthy Films from the 1930s* (Jefferson, NC: McFarland, 2020), 140.

30. Cynthia J. Miller, "Tradition, Parody, and Adaptation: Jed Buell's Unconventional West," in *Hollywood's West: The American Frontier in Film, Television, and History*, edited by Peter C. Rollins and John E. O'Connor (Lexington: University Press of Kentucky, 2005), 67.

31. Richard Crouse, *The 100 Best Movies You've Never Seen* (Toronto: ECW, 2003), 213; emphasis added.

32. Loren Miller, "Hollywood's New Negro Films," *The Crisis*, January 1938, 8.

33. Stephanie Leigh Batiste, *Darkening Mirror: Imperial Representation in Depression-Era African American Performance* (Durham, NC: Duke University Press, 2011), 58.

34. S. Torriano Berry and Venise T. Berry, *The 50 Most Influential Black Films: A Celebration of African-American Talent, Determination, and Creativity* (New York: Kensington, 2001), 47.

35. Julia Leyda, *American Mobilities: Geographies of Class, Race, and Gender in US Culture* (Bielefeld, Germany: Transcript, 2016), 147.

36. *The New York Times Film Reviews*, vol. 3, 1939–48 (New York: Arno, 1970), 1772; "Reviews of the New Films," *Film Daily*, December 11, 1940.

37. Pitts, *Western Movies*, 127.

38. Matthew R. Turner, "Cowboys and Comedies," 222.

39. William Fischer, "The Story behind the Marx Brothers' Downfall," *Collider*, March 19, 2023, https://collider.com/marx-brothers-irving-thalberg/.

40. Matthew R. Turner, "Cowboys and Comedies," 220.

41. Parrin quoted in Groucho Marx and Richard J. Anobile, *The Marx Bros. Scrapbook* (New York: Darien House, 1973), 214.

42. Lusted, *The Western*, 46.

43. Daniel J. Boorstin, *The Americans: The Democratic Experience* (New York: Vintage, 1974), 285.

44. "Paramount, Newark," *Variety*, February 28, 1940.

45. Lenburg, Maurer, and Lenburg, *Three Stooges Scrapbook*, 93.

46. Benjamin Ivry, "Were the Three Stooges a Lot More Jewish Than We Realized?," *Forward*, July 19, 2022, https://forward.com/culture/510651/three-stooges-jewish-yiddish-nazi-charlie-chaplin-great-dictator-mad-magazine/.

47. Epstein, *American Jewish Films*, 50.

48. Ivry, "Were the Three Stooges a Lot More Jewish?"

49. Epstein, *American Jewish Films*, 95.

50. White quoted in Ted Okuda and Edward Watz, *The Columbia Comedy Shorts: Two-Reel Hollywood Film Comedies, 1933–1958* (Jefferson, NC: McFarland, 1986), 25.

51. "Horses' Collars," *The Three Stooges*, October 3, 2023, https://threestooges.com/horses-collars/.

52. "Hal Frayer," *Prabook*, accessed August 12, 2024, https://prabook.com/web/hal.fryar/2327178.

53. Tim Hollis, *Hi There, Boys and Girls!: America's Local Children's TV Programs* (Jackson: University Press of Mississippi, 2010), 8.

54. Joel Dinerstein, "The Lost World of Jewish Flatbush," in *Nonstop Metropolis: A New York City Atlas*, edited by Rebecca Solnit and Joshua Jelly-Schapiro (Berkeley: University of California Press, 2016), 74.

55. Most, "Big Chief Izzy Horowitz," 314.

56. Benjamin Ivry, "On Bugs Bunny's 80th Birthday, How Jewish Is That Wascally Wabbit Anyway?," *Forward*, July 26, 2020, https://forward.com/culture/449550/on-bugs-bunnys-80th-birthday-how-jewish-is-that-wascally-wabbit-anyway/.

57. As a Jewish child, Stephen Miller saw both God and Bugs Bunny as supernaturally cruel but appreciated that at least Bugs had a sense of humor (Stephen Miller, "God and Bugs Bunny," *Sewanee Review* 119, no. 2 [2011]: 256–68).

58. Joe Adamson, *Bugs Bunny: Fifty Years and Only One Grey Hare* (New York: Holt, 1990), 18.

59. Adamson, *Bugs Bunny*, 108.

60. Mel Brooks, "Back in the Saddle," *Blazing Saddles*, directed by Mel Brooks, Warner Bros., 2004, DVD.

61. Kael, *5001 Nights at the Movies*, 80.

62. Gene Siskel, "Shootout at 'Cockeyed Corral,'" *Chicago Tribune*, March 1, 1974.

63. Ivor Davis, "A Conversation with Mel Brooks," *Tablet*, June 27, 2016, https://www.tabletmag.com/sections/arts-letters/articles/a-conversation-with-mel-brooks.

64. Pogrebin, *Stars of David*, 95.

65. Davis, "Conversation with Mel Brooks."

66. Mel Brooks, *All about Me!: My Remarkable Life in Show Business* (New York: Ballantine, 2021), 217, 218; Brooks, "Back in the Saddle."

67. Andrew Silow-Carroll, "In 'Blazing Saddles,' Gene Wilder Helped Recall a Fading Black-Jewish Alliance," *Haaretz*, August 30, 2016.

68. Marc Brodsky, "'Blazing Saddles' Still Stands as One of the Great Comedies—And the Mel Brooks Film Teaches Lessons, Too," *Jewish Telegraph Agency*, April 8, 2020, https://www.jta.org/2020/04/08/culture/blazing-saddles-still-stands-as-one-of-the-great-comedies-and-the-mel-brooks-film-teaches-lessons-too.

69. Brooks, *All about Me!*, 209.

70. Aaron Howard, "The Jewish Comedy of Mel Brooks, Disobedient Jew," *Jewish Herald-Voice*, December 29, 2022.

71. Brooks, *All about Me!*, 207.

72. Michael Hertzberg, "Back in the Saddle," *Blazing Saddles*, directed by Mel Brooks, Warner Bros., 2004, DVD.

73. Brooks, *All about Me!*, 220.

74. Hertzberg, "Back in the Saddle"; Jim Dawson, *Who Cut the Cheese?: A Cultural History of the Fart* (Berkeley, CA: Ten Speed, 1999), 118.

75. Gene Wilder, "Back in the Saddle," *Blazing Saddles*, directed by Mel Brooks, Warner Bros., 2004, DVD.

76. Epstein, *American Jewish Films*, 95–96.

77. Lusted, *The Western*, 232.

78. John G. Cawelti, "Reflections on the New Western Films: The Jewish Cowboy, the Black Avenger, and the Return of the Vanishing American," in *The Pretend Indians: Images of Native Americans in the Movies*, edited by Gretchen M. Bataille and Charles L. P. Silet (Ames: Iowa State University Press, 1980), 113.

79. Falconer, *Afterlife of the Hollywood Western*, 202–3.

80. Roger Ebert, review of *City Slickers*, June 7, 1991, https://www.rogerebert.com/reviews/city-slickers-1991.

81. Roger Ebert, review of *City Slickers II: The Legend of Curly's Gold*, June 10, 1994, https://www.rogerebert.com/reviews/city-slickers-ii-the-legend-of-curlys-gold-1994/.

82. Ebert, review of *City Slickers II*.

Chapter 7. Revisionist Sensibility

1. See Forrest G. Robinson, ed., *The New Western History: The Territory Ahead* (Tucson: University of Arizona Press, 1998).

2. See Roger D. McGrath, *Gunfighters, Highwaymen, and Vigilantes: Violence on the Frontier* (Berkeley: University of California Press, 1987).

3. Simmon, *Invention of the Western Film*, 147.

4. Agnew, *Landscapes of Western Movies*, 185.

5. Falconer, *Afterlife of the Hollywood Western*, 83.

6. Chavez, *Childhood Indians*, 175.

7. Slotkin, *Gunfighter Nation*, 630.

8. Lusted, *The Western*, 231.

9. Gary Noy, *Hellacious California!: Tales of Rascality! Revelry! Dissipation! and Depravity! and the Birth of the Golden State* (Berkeley, CA: Sierra College Press, 2020), 56–57.

10. Jim Kitses and Gregg Rickman, eds., *The Western Reader* (New York: Limelight, 1998), 19.

11. Ithamar Gruenwald, "Midrash and the 'Midrashic Condition': Preliminary Considerations," in *The Midrashic Imagination: Jewish Exegesis, Thought, and History*, edited by Michael Fishbane (Albany, NY: SUNY Press, 1993), 7.

12. See Rachel Barenblat, "Transformative Work: Midrash and Fanfiction," *Religion and Literature* 43, no. 2 (2011): 171–77; Jonathan L. Friedmann, *Goliath as Gentle Giant: Sympathetic Portrayals in Popular Culture* (Lanham, MD: Lexington, 2022).

13. Geoffrey H. Hartman and Sanford Budick, eds., *Midrash and Literature* (New Haven: Yale University Press, 1986), x.

14. William Darby, *Anthony Mann: The Film Career* (Jefferson, NC: McFarland, 2009), 5.

15. Julian Petley, "Mann of the West," *Movie* 4, no. 53 (1980): 1048.

16. Simmon, *Invention of the Western Film*, 272.

17. Joanna Hearne, "The 'Ache for Home': Assimilation and Separatism in Anthony Mann's *Devil's Doorway*," in *Hollywood's West: The American Frontier in Film, Television, and History*, edited by Peter C. Rollins and John E. O'Connor (Lexington: University Press of Kentucky, 2005), 129.

18. Hearne, "Ache for Home," 154 n. 26.

19. Simmon, *Invention of the Western Film*, 271.

20. Thomson, *Biographical Dictionary of Film*, 355.

21. Thomson, *Biographical Dictionary of Film*, 355.

22. Jon Pareles, "Carl Foreman, Producer and 'River Kwai' Screenwriter, Dies," *New York Times*, June 27, 1984.

23. Michael Coyne, *The Crowded Prairie: American National Identity and the Hollywood Western* (London: Tauris, 1997), 99.

24. O'Connor and Rollins, "Introduction," 22.

25. O'Connor and Rollins, "Introduction," 28.

26. Stephen Whitfield, *The Culture of the Cold War*, 2nd ed. (Baltimore: Johns Hopkins University Press, 1996), 149.

27. Whitfield, *Culture of the Cold War*, 149.

28. George Stevens Jr., *Conversations with the Great Moviemakers of Hollywood's Golden Age at the American Film Institute* (New York: Vintage, 2007), 415.

29. Simmon, *Invention of the Western*, 261.

30. Joseph McBride, ed., *Hawks on Hawks* (Berkeley: University of California Press, 1982), 130.

31. O'Connor and Rollins, "Introduction," 22.

32. Leslie Fiedler, *The Return of the Vanishing American* (New York: Stein and Day, 1968).

33. Rubinstein, *Members of the Tribe*, 135.

34. Cawelti, "Reflections on the New Western Films," 113.

35. Cawelti, "Reflections on the New Western Films," 113.

36. Cawelti, "Reflections on the New Western Films," 113.

37. William Goldman, *Four Screenplays with Essays* (New York: Applause, 1995), 27.

38. Brian Garfield, *Western Films: A Complete Guide* (New York: Rawson, 1982), 314.

39. Gordon Gow, "Cocking a Snook," *Films and Filming*, November 1970, reprinted in Brian Dauth, ed., *Joseph L. Mankiewicz: Interviews* (Jackson: University Press of Mississippi, 2008), 39.

40. Mat Brewster, "*There Was a Crooked Man* . . . Blu-Ray Review: Revisionist Western Could Have Used a Few More Revisions," *Cinema Sentries*, July 12, 2021, https://cinemasentries.com/there-was-a-crooked-man-blu-ray-review-revisionist-western-could-have-used-a-few-more-revisions/.

41. Kael, *5001 Nights at the Movies*, 752.

42. Thomson, *Biographical Dictionary of Film*, 354.

43. Margo Kasden and Susan Tavernetti, "Native Americans in a Revisionist Western: *Little Big Man* (1970)," in *Hollywood's Indian: The Portrayal of the Native American in Film*, edited by Peter C. Rollins and John E. O'Connor (Lexington: University Press of Kentucky, 2003), 129.

44. Chavez, *Childhood Indians*, 170; Kasden and Tavernetti, "Native Americans in a Revisionist Western," 130.

45. Lusted, *The Western*, 197.

46. Vincent Brook, "A Wave of Their Own: How Jewish Filmmakers Invented the New Hollywood," in *New Wave, New Hollywood: Reassessment, Recovery, and Legacy*, edited by Nathan Abrams and Gregory Frame (New York: Bloomsbury, 2023), 63.

47. Kasden and Tavernetti, "Native Americans in a Revisionist Western," 132.

48. Philip French, "The Indian in the Western Movie," in *The Pretend Indians: Images of Native Americans in the Movies*, edited by Gretchen M. Bataille and Charles L. P. Silet (Ames: Iowa State University Press, 1980), 105.

49. Leo Rosten, *The New Joys of Yiddish* (New York: Three Rivers, 2001), 233.

50. Dan Georgakas, "They Have Not Spoken: American Indians in Film," in *The Pretend Indians: Images of Native Americans in the Movies*, edited by Gretchen M. Bataille and Charles L. P. Silet (Ames: Iowa State University Press, 1980), 138.

51. Georgakas, "They Have Not Spoken," 139.

52. Roger Ebert, review of *The Quick and the Dead*, February 10, 1995, https://www.rogerebert.com/reviews/the-quick-and-the-dead-1995.

53. Noah Gittell, "What the Western Means Now," *Atlantic*, June 17, 2014, https://www.theatlantic.com/entertainment/archive/2014/06/the-return-of-the-western/372871/.

54. Falconer, *Afterlife of the Hollywood Western*, 63, 65.

55. Charles Portis, *True Grit: A Novel* (New York: Abrams, 2002), 19.

56. Terry Gross, "The Coen Bros. Reflect on Making a 'Gritty' Western," *Fresh Air*, NPR, February 11, 2011, https://www.npr.org/2011/02/11/133652721/the-coen-bros-reflect-on-making-a-gritty-western.

57. David Ansen, "Joel and Ethan Coen on 'True Grit,'" *Newsweek*, December 24, 2010, https://www.newsweek.com/joel-and-ethan-coen-true-grit-68909.

58. Mark Lieberman, "*True Grit* Isn't True," *Language Log*, December 29, 2010, https://languagelog.ldc.upenn.edu/nll/?p=2873.

59. See David Tollerton, "Job of Suburbia?: A Serious Man and Viewer Perceptions of the Biblical," *Journal of Religion and Film* 15, no. 2 (2011), https://digital commons.unomaha.edu/jrf/vol15/iss2/7.

60. "Streets of Laredo" was first published in John A. Lomax, *Cowboy Songs and Other Frontier Ballads* (New York: Sturgis and Walton, 1910), 74, and is descended from a late-eighteenth-century Irish ballad, "The Unfortunate Rake."

61. Josh Rottenberg, "The Coen Brothers on Their Western Anthology Film 'The Ballad of Buster Scruggs,' Netflix and the Future of Moviegoing," *Los Angeles Times*, November 14, 2018.

62. John Orquiola, "The Ballad of Buster Scruggs: All 6 Endings Explained," *Screen Rant*, March 3, 2023, https://screenrant.com/ballad-buster-scruggs-endings-explained/.

Conclusion

1. Steven H. Silver, "Jewish Science Fiction and Fantasy," *Stevenhsilver.com*, accessed August 12, 2024, http://www.stevenhsilver.com/jewishsf.html.

2. Jonathan L. Friedmann and Joey Angel-Field, "Jewish Science Fiction, Fantasy, and Fandom—With author Valerie Estelle Frankel," *Amusing Jews*, May 29, 2023, https://www.youtube.com/watch?v=V4LUSNBoRrs.

3. Mordecai Richler, *St. Urbain's Horseman* (Toronto: McClelland and Stewart, 1971), 35.

4. Leon Gutterman, "Our Film Folk," *Jewish Press*, January 28, 1949.

Bibliography

Aaker, Everett. *Television Western Players, 1960–1975: A Biographical Dictionary*. Jefferson, NC: McFarland, 2017.

Abel, Richard. "'Our Country'/Whose Country?: The 'Americanization' Project of Early Westerns." In *Back in the Saddle Again: New Essays on the Western*, edited by Edward Buscombe and Roberta Pearson, 77–95. London: British Film Institute, 1998.

Abrams, Nathan. *The New Jew in Film: Exploring Jewishness and Judaism in Contemporary Cinema*. New Brunswick, NJ: Rutgers University Press, 2012.

Abrams, Nathan. "A Secular Talmud: The Jewish Sensibility of *Mad* Magazine." *Studies in Jewish Humor* 3, no. 30 (2014): 111–22.

Ackerman, Susan. "Astarte: Bible." *Jewish Women's Archive*, February 27, 2009. https://jwa.org/encyclopedia/article/astarte-bible.

Adamson, Joe. *Bugs Bunny: Fifty Years and Only One Grey Hare*. New York: Holt, 1990.

Agnew, Jeremy. *The Landscapes of Western Movies: A History of Filming on Location, 1900–1970*. Jefferson, NC: McFarland, 2020.

Agnew, Jeremy. *The Old West in Fact and Film: History versus Hollywood*. Jefferson, NC: McFarland, 2012.

Albarella, Tony. "'Noon on Doomsday' (1956) Reviewed." *Rod Serling Memorial Foundation*, accessed August 12, 2024. https://rodserling.com/noon-on-doomsday-1956-reviewed/.

Almog, Oz. *The Sabra: The Creation of the New Jew*. Berkeley: University of California Press, 2000.

Alonzo, Juan. *Badmen, Bandits, and Folk Heroes: The Ambivalence of Mexican American Identity in Literature and Film*. Tucson: University of Arizona Press, 2009.

Alpern, Laura Manischewitz. *Manischewitz, the Matzo Family: The Making of an American Jewish Icon*. Jersey City, NJ: KTAV, 2008.

Andreychuk, Ed. *The Golden Corral: A Roundup of Magnificent Western Films*. Jefferson, NC: McFarland, 1997.

Ansen, David. "Joel and Ethan Coen on 'True Grit.'" *Newsweek*, December 24, 2010. https://www.newsweek.com/joel-and-ethan-coen-true-grit-68909.

Aron, Stephen. *The American West: A Very Short Introduction*. New York: Oxford University Press, 2015.

Ayling, Mark Anthony. "White Saviours, Yellow Perils, and Green Eyes: John Carpenter's *Big Trouble in Little China*." *VHS Revival: A Retro Movie Magazine*, August 21, 2020. https://vhsrevival.com/2020/08/21/white-saviours-yellow-perils-and-green-eyes-john-carpenters-big-trouble-in-little-china/.

Barenblat, Rachel. "Transformative Work: Midrash and Fanfiction." *Religion and Literature* 43, no. 2 (2011): 171–77.

Barrett, Michael. "*The Goldbergs*: The Most Jewish Show on Television." *Pop Matters*, April 27, 2020. https://www.popmatters.com/goldbergs-most-jewish-television-show.

Baskind, Samantha. *The Warsaw Ghetto in American Art and Culture*. University Park: Pennsylvania State University Press, 2018.

Bataille, Gretchen M., and Charles L. P. Silet, eds. *The Pretend Indians: Images of Native Americans in the Movies*. Ames: Iowa State University Press, 1980.

Batiste, Stephanie Leigh. *Darkening Mirror: Imperial Representation in Depression-Era African American Performance*. Durham, NC: Duke University Press, 2011.

Baum, Gary. "How the Academy Museum's Jewish Exclusion Became Exhibit A." *Hollywood Reporter*, March 19, 2022. https://www.hollywoodreporter.com/movies/movie-features/academy-museum-jewish-exclusion-1235114988/.

Beck, Jerry. *The Animated Movie Guide*. Chicago: A Capella, 2005.

Beebee, Thomas O. *The Ideology of Genre: A Comparative Study of Generic Instability*. University Park: Pennsylvania State University Press, 1994.

Bellow, Saul. "On Jewish Storytelling." In *What Is Jewish Literature?*, edited by Hana Wirth-Nesher, 16–17. Philadelphia: Jewish Publication Society, 1994.

Berg, Charles Ramírez. *Latino Images in Film: Stereotypes, Subversion, and Resistance*. Austin: University of Texas Press, 2002.

Berkowitz, Edward D. *Mass Appeal: The Formative Age of the Movies, Radio, and TV*. New York: Cambridge University Press, 2010.

Berlin, Adele. "Esther: Introduction." In *The Jewish Study Bible*, edited by Adele Berlin and Marc Zvi Brettler, 1623–25. New York: Oxford University Press, 1999.

Berman, Lila Corwin. "Sociology, Jews, and Intermarriage in Twentieth-Century America." *Jewish Social Studies* 14, no. 2 (2008): 32–60.

Berman, Louis A. *Jews and Intermarriage: A Study in Personality and Culture*. New York: Yoseloff, 1968.

Bernardi, Daniel. *Classic Hollywood, Classic Whiteness*. Minneapolis: University of Minnesota Press, 2001.

Berry, S. Torriano, and Venise T. Berry. *The 50 Most Influential Black Films: A Celebration of African-American Talent, Determination, and Creativity*. New York: Kensington, 2001.

Billington, Ray Allen. Foreword to *Jews on the Frontier: An Account of Jewish Pioneers and Settlers in Early America*, by I. Harold Sharfman, ix–xii. Chicago: Regnery, 1977.

Binder, Abraham W., ed. *Union Hymnal: Songs and Prayers for Jewish Worship*. New York: Central Conference of American Rabbis, 1932.

Birdwell, Michael E. *Celluloid Soldiers: The Warner Bros. Campaign against Nazism*. New York: New York University Press, 1999.

Biron, Phineas J. "Strictly Confidential." *Jewish Press*, August 30, 1940.

Black, Gregory D. *The Catholic Crusade against the Movies, 1940–1975*. New York: Cambridge University Press, 1998.

Blech, Benjamin. *The Complete Idiot's Guide to Jewish Culture and History*. 2nd ed. New York: Alpha, 2004.

"Books: Back to the Wall." *Time*, June 2, 1961.

Boorstin, Daniel. *The Americans: The Democratic Experience*. New York: Vintage, 1974.

Bradley, Edwin M. *Hollywood Musicals You Missed: Seventy Noteworthy Films from the 1930s*. Jefferson, NC: McFarland, 2020.

Branen, Jeff T., and Al Piantadosi. *Big Chief Dynamite*. Chicago: Piantadosi, 1909.

Breck, Allen D. *A Centennial History of the Jews of Colorado, 1859–1959*. Denver: Hirschfeld, 1960.

Brewster, Mat. "*There Was a Crooked Man . . .* Blu-ray Review: Revisionist Western Could Have Used a Few More Revisions." *Cinema Sentries*, July 12, 2021. https://cinemasentries.com/there-was-a-crooked-man-blu-ray-review-revisionist-western-could-have-used-a-few-more-revisions/.

"A Brief History of Film Censorship." National Coalition against Censorship, accessed August 12, 2024. https://ncac.org/resource/a-brief-history-of-film-censorship.

Brodsky, Marc. "'Blazing Saddles' Still Stands as One of the Great Comedies—And the Mel Brooks Film Teaches Lessons, Too." *Jewish Telegraph Agency*, April 8, 2020. https://www.jta.org/2020/04/08/culture/blazing-saddles-still-stands-as-one-of-the-great-comedies-and-the-mel-brooks-film-teaches-lessons-too.

Brook, Vincent. *Something Ain't Kosher Here: The Rise of the "Jewish" Sitcom*. New Brunswick, NJ: Rutgers University Press, 2003.

Brook, Vincent. "A Wave of Their Own: How Jewish Filmmakers Invented the New Hollywood." In *New Wave, New Hollywood: Reassessment, Recovery, and*

Legacy, edited by Nathan Abrams and Gregory Frame, 59–78. New York: Bloomsbury, 2023.

Brooks, Mel. *All about Me!: My Remarkable Life in Show Business*. New York: Ballantine, 2021.

Brooks, Mel. "Back in the Saddle." *Blazing Saddles*, directed by Mel Brooks. Warner Bros., 2004. DVD.

Bruce, Lenny. *How to Talk Dirty and Influence People: An Autobiography*. 1965. Boston: Da Capo, 2016.

Burlingame, Jon. "Hollywood's Score Keeper." *Los Angeles Times*, November 8, 2001.

Burstein, Janet. "Edna Ferber." *Jewish Women's Archive*, February 27, 2009. https://jwa.org/encyclopedia/article/ferber-edna.

Cawelti, John G. "Reflections on the New Western Films: The Jewish Cowboy, the Black Avenger, and the Return of the Vanishing American." In *The Pretend Indians: Images of Native Americans in the Movies*, edited by Gretchen M. Bataille and Charles L. P. Silet, 112–14. Ames: Iowa State University Press, 1980.

Chavez, Raul S. *Childhood Indians: Television, Film and Sustaining the White (Sub) Conscience*. Scotts Valley, CA: CreateSpace, 2010.

"Cinema: Oklacoma: *Cimarron*." *Time*, February 24, 1961.

Clarren, Rebecca. *The Cost of Free Land: Jews, Lakota, and an American Inheritance*. New York: Viking, 2023.

Cobb, Amanda J. "This Is What It Means to Say Smoke Signals: Native American Cultural Sovereignty." In *Hollywood's Indian: The Portrayal of the Native American in Film*, edited by Peter C. Rollins and John E. O'Connor, 207–28. Lexington: University Press of Kentucky, 2003.

Cobb, Russell. *The Great Oklahoma Swindle: Race, Religion, and Lies in America's Weirdest State*. Lincoln: University of Nebraska Press, 2020.

Collins, K. Austin. "*First Cow* Is a Rich, Satisfying Tale of Frontier Friendship." *Vanity Fair*, March 6, 2020. https://www.vanityfair.com/hollywood/2020/03/first-cow-movie-review.

Cooley, Everett L. "Clarion, Utah: Jewish Colony in 'Zion.'" *Utah Historical Quarterly* 36, no. 2 (1968): 113–31.

Cooper, Kelly. "From Challah to Chazantes: Jewish Women's Journey from the Kitchen to Bimah." Master's thesis, Academy for Jewish Religion California, 2022. https://www.tilb.org/wp-content/uploads/2022/05/CantorCooper_Thesis_Challah_to_Chazante.pdf.

Copland, Aaron. "Looking Back with Aaron Copland." *Los Angeles Times*, September 9, 1984.

Courtney, Susan. *Hollywood Fantasies of Miscegenation: Spectacular Narratives of Gender and Race*. Princeton: Princeton University Press, 2021.

Cox, J. Randolph. "Dime Novels." In *The Oxford History of Popular Print Culture*, vol. 6, *US Popular Print Culture, 1860–1920*, edited by Christine Bold, 63–80. New York: Oxford University Press, 2011.

Coyne, Michael. *The Crowded Prairie: American National Identity and the Hollywood Western*. London: Tauris, 1997.

Crawford, Dorothy Lamb. *A Windfall of Musicians: Hitler's Émigrés and Exiles in Southern California*. New Haven: Yale University Press, 2009.

Crist, Elizabeth Bergman. *Music for the Common Man: Aaron Copland during the Depression and War*. New York: Oxford University Press, 2009.

"Critical Comments on Current Films." *Screenland*, August 1930, 86–87.

Crouse, Richard. *The 100 Best Movies You've Never Seen*. Toronto: ECW, 2003.

Crowther, Bosley. "Screen: New 'Cimarron.'" *New York Times*, February 17, 1961.

Darby, William. *Anthony Mann: The Film Career*. Jefferson, NC: McFarland, 2009.

D'Arc, James V. "Music to Match the Movies, and a Ride into the Sunset." Liner notes to *Saddles, Sagebrush, and Steiner*, Brigham Young University Film Music Archive, 2019. CD.

Dauber, Jeremy. *Jewish Comedy: A Serious History*. New York: Norton, 2017.

Dauth, Brian, ed. *Joseph L. Mankiewicz: Interviews*. Jackson: University Press of Mississippi, 2008.

Davis, Ivor. "A Conversation with Mel Brooks." *Tablet*, June 27, 2016. https://www.tabletmag.com/sections/arts-letters/articles/a-conversation-with-mel-brooks.

Dawson, Jim. *Who Cut the Cheese?: A Cultural History of the Fart*. Berkeley, CA: Ten Speed, 1999.

Desser, David, and Lester D. Friedman. *American Jewish Filmmakers*. 2nd ed. Urbana: University of Illinois Press, 2004.

Deverell, William. Foreword to *Western States Jewish History* 41, no. 4 (2009): xii–xiii.

Dillon, Brian Dervin, and David Erin Dillon. "Wyatt and Josie Earp: Fact, Fiction, and Myth." *Western States Jewish History* 48, no. 1 (2015): 27–44.

Diner, Hasia. "American West, New York Jewish." In *Jewish Life in the American West*, ed. Ava F. Kahn, 33–51. Los Angeles: Autry Museum of the American West, 2002.

Diner, Hasia. "Entering the Mainstream of Modern Jewish History: Peddlers and the American Jewish South." *Southern Jewish History* 8 (2005): 1–30.

Diner, Hasia. *Roads Taken: The Great Jewish Migrations to the New World and the Peddlers Who Forged the Way*. New Haven: Yale University Press, 2015.

Diner, Hasia. "The Study of American Jewish History: In the Academy, in the Community." *Polish American Studies* 65, no. 1 (2008): 41–55.

Dinerstein, Joel. "The Lost World of Jewish Flatbush." In *Nonstop Metropolis: A New York City Atlas*, edited by Rebecca Solnit and Joshua Jelly-Schapiro, 74–76. Berkeley: University of California Press, 2016.

Dixon, Wheeler Winston. "Fast Worker: The Films of Sam Newfield." *Senses of Cinema* 45 (2007). http://www.sensesofcinema.com/2007/feature-articles/sam-newfield/.

Doherty, Thomas. *Hollywood and Hitler, 1933–1939*. New York: Columbia University Press, 2013.

Double, Oliver. *Getting the Joke: The Inner Workings of Stand-Up Comedy*. London: Bloomsbury, 2014.

Downey, Lynn. *Levi Strauss: The Man Who Gave Blue Jeans to the World*. Amherst: University of Massachusetts Press, 2016.

Drinnon, Richard. *Facing West: The Metaphysics of Indian Hating and Empire Building*. New York: Schocken, 1990.

Drummond, Phillip. *High Noon*. London: British Film Institute, 1997.

Dubai, Anna, and Nick Hopkins. "Humour Is Serious: Minority Group Members' Use of Humour in Their Encounters with Majority Group Members." *European Journal of Social Psychology* 50, no. 2 (2020): 448–62.

Dupuis, Mauricio. *Jerry Goldsmith: Music Scoring for American Movies*. Vicenza, Italy: DMG, 2014.

Earp, Josephine Sarah Marcus. *I Married Wyatt Earp: The Recollections of Josephine Sarah Marcus Earp*. Collected and edited by Glenn G. Boyer. Tucson : University of Arizona Press, 1976.

Ebert, Roger. Review of *City Slickers*, June 7, 1991. https://www.rogerebert.com/reviews/city-slickers-1991.

Ebert, Roger. Review of *City Slickers II: The Legend of Curly's Gold*, June 10, 1994. https://www.rogerebert.com/reviews/city-slickers-ii-the-legend-of-curlys-gold-1994/.

Ebert, Roger. Review of *The Frisco Kid*, January 1, 1979. https://www.rogerebert.com/reviews/the-frisco-kid-1979.

Ebert, Roger. Review of *The Quick and the Dead*, February 10, 1995, https://www.rogerebert.com/reviews/the-quick-and-the-dead-1995.

Edelman, Marsha Bryan. "Continuity, Creativity, and Conflict: The Ongoing Search for 'Jewish' Music." In *You Should See Yourself: Jewish Identity in Postmodern American Culture*, edited by Vincent Brook, 119–34. New Brunswick, NJ: Rutgers University Press, 2006.

Eisenberg, Ellen, ed. *Jewish Identities in the American West: Relational Perspectives*. Chicago: University of Chicago Press, 2022.

Elias, Michael. Interview by author, telephone, September 24, 2021.

Elias, Michael, and Frank Shaw. *No-Knife*, second draft. Warner Bros., October 1977.

Elkin, Frederick. "The Psychological Appeal of the Hollywood Western." *Journal of Educational Sociology* 24, no. 2 (1950): 72–86.

Epstein, Lawrence J. *American Jewish Films: The Search for Identity*. Jefferson, NC: McFarland, 2013.

Erens, Patricia. *The Jew in American Cinema*. Bloomington: Indiana University Press, 1984.

Everson, William K. *A Pictorial History of the Western Film*. New York: Citadel, 1969.

Falconer, Pete. *The Afterlife of the Hollywood Western*. London: Palgrave Macmillan, 2020.

Feng, Peter X., ed. *Screening Asian Americans*. New Brunswick, NJ: Rutgers University Press, 2002.

Fenton, Elizabeth. *Old Canaan in a New World: Native Americans and the Lost Tribes of Israel*. New York: New York University Press, 2020.

Ferber, Edna. *Cimarron*. London: Heinemann, 1930.

Ferber, Edna. *A Peculiar Treasure*. New York: Doubleday, 1960.

Fiedler, Leslie. "The Demon of the Continent." In *The Pretend Indians: Images of Native Americans in the Movies*, edited by Gretchen M. Bataille and Charles L. P. Silet, 9–15. Ames: Iowa State University Press, 1980.

Fiedler, Leslie. *Fiedler on the Roof: Essays on Literature and Jewish Identity*. Boston: Godine, 1991.

Fiedler, Leslie. *The Return of the Vanishing American*. New York: Stein and Day, 1968.

Fiedler, Leslie. *To the Gentiles*. New York: Stein and Day, 1972.

Fischel, Jack, and Susan M. Ortman, eds. *Encyclopedia of Jewish American Popular Culture*. Santa Barbara, CA: ABC-CLIO, 2008.

Fischer, William. "The Story Behind the Marx Brothers' Downfall." *Collider*, March 19, 2023. https://collider.com/marx-brothers-irving-thalberg/.

Fishgall, Gary. *Gregory Peck: A Biography*. New York: Scribner, 2002.

Fiske, John. *American Political Ideas Viewed from the Standpoint of Universal History*. New York: Harper, 1885.

Flinn, Caryl. "A Tale of Two Cowgirls: Songs, Western Novelty Acts, and 1950s Hollywood." In *Music in the Western*, edited by Kathryn Kalinak, 94–114. New York: Routledge, 2012.

Fox, Sue. "Music That Changed Me." *BBC Magazine*, September 2002. https://elmerbernstein.com/articles/music-that-changed-me-elmer-bernstein/.

Fradkin, Philip L. *Stagecoach: Wells Fargo and the American West*. New York: Simon and Schuster, 2002.

Franks, Don. *Entertainment Awards: A Music, Cinema, Theatre and Broadcasting Guide, 1928 through 2003*. 3rd ed. Jefferson, NC: McFarland, 2014.

French, Philip. "The Indian in the Western Movie." In *The Pretend Indians: Images of Native Americans in the Movies*, edited by Gretchen M. Bataille and Charles L. P. Silet, 98–105. Ames: Iowa State University Press, 1980.

Friedman, Lester D., ed. *Unspeakable Images: Ethnicity and the American Cinema*. Urbana: University of Illinois Press, 1991.

Friedmann, Jonathan L. "*The Frisco Kid* Revisited: Sources and Themes in the Original Screenplay." *Western States Jewish History* 52, no. 2 (2022): 35–58.

Friedmann, Jonathan L. *Goliath as Gentle Giant: Sympathetic Portrayals in Popular Culture*. Lanham, MD: Lexington, 2022.

Friedmann, Jonathan L. *Jewish Gold Country*. Charleston, SC: Arcadia, 2020.

Friedmann, Jonathan L. *Jewish Los Angeles*. Charleston, SC: Arcadia, 2020.

Friedmann, Jonathan L. "The Jewish Roots of Hollywood Music." *Western States Jewish History* 45, no. 1 (2012): 47–54.

Friedmann, Jonathan L. "Was Max Steiner a Jew?" *Journal of Film Music* 9, nos. 1–2 (2016): 94–106.

Friedmann, Jonathan L., and Joey Angel-Field. "Jewish Science Fiction, Fantasy, and Fandom—With author Valerie Estelle Frankel." *Amusing Jews*, May 29, 2023. https://www.youtube.com/watch?v=V4LUSNBoRrs.

Friedrich, Otto. *City of Nets: A Portrait of Hollywood in the 1940s*. Berkeley: University of California Press, 1997.

Fuller, Samuel. *A Third Face: My Tale of Writing, Fighting, and Filmmaking*. New York: Knopf, 2002.

Gabler, Neal. *An Empire of Their Own: How the Jews Invented Hollywood*. New York: Anchor, 1988.

Gallagher, Tag. *John Ford: The Man and His Films*. Berkeley: University of California Press, 1986.

Garcia, Desirée J. *The Migration of Musical Film: From Ethnic Margins to American Mainstream*. New Brunswick, NJ: Rutgers University Press, 2014.

Garfield, Brian. *Western Films: A Complete Guide*. New York: Rawson, 1982.

Garnham, Nicholas. *Samuel Fuller*. New York: Viking, 1971.

Garrett-Davis, Josh. *What Is a Western?: Region, Genre, Imagination*. Norman: University of Oklahoma Press, 2019.

Geltzer, Jeremy. *Dirty Words and Filthy Pictures: Film and the First Amendment*. Austin: University of Texas Press, 2015.

Georgakas, Dan. "They Have Not Spoken: American Indians in Film." In *The Pretend Indians: Images of Native Americans in the Movies*, edited by Gretchen M. Bataille and Charles L. P. Silet, 134–42. Ames: Iowa State University Press, 1980.

Gertel, Elliot. *Over the Top Judaism: Precedents and Trends in the Depiction of Jewish Beliefs and Observances in Film and Television*. Lanham, MD: University Press of America, 2003.

Gilbert, Julie Goldsmith. *Ferber: Edna Ferber and Her Circle, a Biography*. New York: Applause, 1999.

Gillespie, Michael Boyce. *Film Blackness: American Cinema and the Idea of Black Film*. Durham, NC: Duke University Press, 2016.

Girgus, Sam B. *Generations of Jewish Directors and the Struggle for America's Soul: Wyler, Lumet, and Spielberg*. Cham, Switzerland: Palgrave Macmillan, 2021.

Gittell, Noah. "What the Western Means Now." *Atlantic*, June 17, 2014. https://www.theatlantic.com/entertainment/archive/2014/06/the-return-of-the-western/372871/.

Golden, Harry. *Forgotten Pioneer*. New York: World, 1963.

Goldman, William. *Four Screenplays with Essays*. New York: Applause, 1995.

Goldmark, Daniel. *Tunes for 'Toons: Music and the Hollywood Cartoon*. Berkeley: University of California Press, 2005.

Gordon, Karen. "*First Cow*: An Anti-Mythic Tale of the Old West, Fabulous Fritters, Lactic Larceny and Larger Themes." *Original CIN*, March 11, 2020. https://www.original-cin.ca/posts/2020/3/11/first-cow-a-less-than-mythic-tale-of-the-old-west-fabulous-fritters-lactic-larceny-and-bigger-themes.

Gray, Beverly. *Seduced by Mrs. Robinson: How "The Graduate" Became the Touchstone of a Generation*. Chapel Hill, NC: Algonquin, 2017.

Griffiths, Paul. Notes to *Copland: Dance Symphony, El Salón México, Four Episodes from Rodeo, Fanfare for the Common Man*. Polygram, 1982, LP.

Gross, Terry. "The Coen Bros. Reflect on Making a 'Gritty' Western." *Fresh Air*, NPR, February 11, 2011. https://www.npr.org/2011/02/11/133652721/the-coen-bros-reflect-on-making-a-gritty-western.

Gross, Terry. "Mel Brooks Says His Only Regret as a Comedian Is the Jokes He Didn't Tell." *Fresh Air*, NPR, December 7, 2021. https://www.npr.org/2021/12/07/1061836388/mel-brooks-all-about-me.

Grossbach, Robert. *The Frisco Kid*. New York: Warner, 1979.

Gruber, Ruth Ellen. "Heym on the Range." *Tablet*, November 4, 2020, https://www.tabletmag.com/sections/arts-letters/articles/heym-on-the-range.

Gruenwald, Ithamar. "Midrash and the 'Midrashic Condition': Preliminary Considerations." In *The Midrashic Imagination: Jewish Exegesis, Thought, and History*, edited by Michael Fishbane, 7–22. Albany, NY: SUNY Press, 1993.

Gutterman, Leon. "Our Film Folk." *Jewish Press*, January 28, 1949.

"Hal Frayer." *Prabook*, accessed August 12, 2024. https://prabook.com/web/hal.fryar/2327178.

Hamilton, Marsha J., and Eleanor S. Block. *Projecting Ethnicity and Race: An Annotated Bibliography of Studies on Imagery in American Film*. New York: Bloomsbury, 2003.

Hammerman, Shaina. *Silver Screen, Hasidic Jews: The Story of an Image*. Bloomington: Indiana University Press, 2017.

Hamner, M. Gail. "Scorsese as a Critic of Modernity: The Woman Question." In *Scorsese and Religion*, edited by Christopher B. Barnett and Clark J. Elliston, 107–48. Boston: Brill, 2019.

Handlin, Oscar. *Adventure in Freedom*. New York: McGraw-Hill, 1954.

Handlin, Oscar. "New Paths in American Jewish History." *Commentary*, January 8, 1948, 388–94.

Harris, Rachel S. "New Frontiers: Creating a Nation through the Israeli Western." In *Casting a Giant Shadow: The Transnational Shaping of Israeli Cinema*, edited by Lucy Fischer and Dan Chyutin, 80–101. Bloomington: Indiana University Press, 2021.

Harrison, Ben, and Manny Gould, dirs. *Rough Dough*. Columbia, 1931.

Hartman, Geoffrey H., and Sanford Budick, eds. *Midrash and Literature*. New Haven: Yale University Press, 1986.

Haskell, Molly. *Steven Spielberg: A Life in Films*. New Haven: Yale University Press, 2017.

Hearne, Joanna. "The 'Ache from Home': Assimilation and Separatism in Anthony Mann's *Devil's Doorway*." In *Hollywood's West: The American Frontier in Film, Television, and History*, edited by Peter C. Rollins and John E. O'Connor, 126–59. Lexington: University Press of Kentucky, 2005.

Hearne, Joanna. *Native Recognition: Indigenous Cinema and the Western*. Albany, NY: SUNY Press, 2013.

Herman, Felicia. "Jewish Leaders and the Motion Picture Industry." In *California Jews*, edited by Ava F. Kahn and Marc Dollinger, 95–109. Waltham, MA: Brandeis University Press, 2003.

Herscher, Uri D. *Jewish Agricultural Utopias in America, 1880–1910*. Detroit: Wayne State University Press, 1991.

Hertzberg, Michael. "Back in the Saddle." *Blazing Saddles*, directed by Mel Brooks. Warner Bros., 2004. DVD.

Hodes, Laura. "Why We Need to Remember Gene Wilder in 'The Frisco Kid.'" *Forward*, September 2, 2016. https://forward.com/culture/349138/why-we-need-to-remember-gene-wilder-in-the-frisco-kid/.

Hollis, Tim. *Hi There, Boys and Girls!: America's Local Children's TV Programs*. Jackson: University Press of Mississippi, 2010.

"Horses' Collars." *The Three Stooges*, October 3, 2023. https://threestooges.com/horses-collars/.

Howard, Aaron. "The Jewish Comedy of Mel Brooks, Disobedient Jew." *Jewish Herald-Voice*, December 29, 2022.

Hyde, G. W. G., and William Stoddard, eds. *History of the Great Northwest and Its Men of Progress*. Minneapolis: Minneapolis Journal, 1901.

Ivry, Benjamin. "On Bugs Bunny's 80th Birthday, How Jewish Is That Wascally Wabbit Anyway?" *Forward*, July 26, 2020. https://forward.com/culture/449550/on-bugs-bunnys-80th-birthday-how-jewish-is-that-wascally-wabbit-anyway/.

Ivry, Benjamin. "Were the Three Stooges a Lot More Jewish Than We Realized?" *Forward*, July 19, 2022. https://forward.com/culture/510651/three-stooges-jewish-yiddish-nazi-charlie-chaplin-great-dictator-mad-magazine/.

Jacobs, Louis. *A Concise Companion to the Jewish Religion*. New York: Oxford University Press, 1999.

"John Wayne: Playboy Interview." *Playboy*, May 1971, 75–92.

Jojola, Ted. "Absurd Reality II: Hollywood Goes to the Indians." In *Hollywood's Indian: The Portrayal of the Native American in Film*, edited by Peter C. Rollins and John E. O'Connor, 12–26. Lexington: University Press of Kentucky, 2003.

Kael, Pauline. "The Current Cinema: The Street Western." *New Yorker*, February 25, 1974, 100.

Kael, Pauline. *5001 Nights at the Movies*. New York: Holt, 1991.

Kahn, Ava F., ed. *Jewish Voices of the California Gold Rush: A Documentary History, 1849–1880*. Detroit: Wayne State University Press, 2002.

Kahn, Edgar F. "The Saga of the First Fifty Years of Congregation Emanu-El, San Francisco." *Western States Jewish Historical Quarterly* 3, no. 3 (1971): 129–47.

Kalinak, Kathryn. Introduction to *Music in the Western: Notes from the Frontier*, edited by Kathryn Kalinak, 1–17. New York: Routledge, 2012.

Kasden, Margo, and Susan Tavernetti. "Native Americans in a Revisionist Western: *Little Big Man* (1970)." In *Hollywood's Indian: The Portrayal of the Native American in Film*, edited by Peter C. Rollins and John E. O'Connor, 121–36. Lexington: University Press of Kentucky, 2003.

Katz, Mickey, and His Kosher-Jammers. *Haim Afen Range (Home on the Range)/Yiddish Square Dance*. RCA Victor, 1947.

Kaufman, David. *Jewhooing the Sixties: American Celebrity and Jewish Identity: Sandy Koufax, Lenny Bruce, Bob Dylan, and Barbra Streisand*. Waltham, MA: Brandeis University Press, 2012.

Keeping Score. Season 1, episode 3, "Copland and the American Sound." Aired November 16, 2006, on PBS. https://www.pbs.org/keepingscore/copland-american-sound.html.

Keller, Alexandra. "Generic Subversion as Counterhistory: Mario Van Peebles's *Posse*." In *Western Films through History*, edited by Janet Walker, 27–48. New York: Routledge, 2001.

Keller, Alexandra. "Historical Discourse and American Identity in Westerns since the Reagan Era." In *Hollywood's West: The American Frontier in Film, Television, and History*, edited by John E. O'Connor and Peter C. Rollins, 239–60. Lexington: University Press of Kentucky, 2009.

Keshena, Rita. "The Role of American Indians in Motion Pictures." In *The Pretend Indians: Images of Native Americans in Movies*, edited by Gretchen M. Bataille and Charles L. P. Silet, 106–11. Ames: Iowa State University Press, 1980.

Khannanov, Ildar. "*High Noon*: Dimitri Tiomkin's Oscar-Winning Ballad and Its Russian Sources." *Journal of Film Music* 2, nos. 2–4 (2009): 225–48.

Kibler, M. Alison. *Censoring Racial Ridicule: Irish, Jewish, and African American Struggles over Race and Representation, 1890–1930*. Chapel Hill: University of North Carolina Press, 2015.

Kirshenblatt-Gimblett, Barbara. "Sounds of Sensibility." *Judaism* 47, no. 1 (1998): 49–78.

Kitses, Jim. "Introduction: Post-Modernism and the Western." In *The Western Reader*, edited by Jim Kitses and Gregg Rickman, 15–31. New York: Limelight, 1998.

Kitses, Jim, and Gregg Rickman, eds. *The Western Reader*. New York: Limelight, 1998.

Koffman, David S. *The Jews' Indian: Colonialism, Pluralism, and Belonging in America*. New Brunswick, NJ: Rutgers University Press, 2019.

Kotz, Nick. *The Harness Maker's Dream: Nathan Kallison and the Rise of South Texas*. Fort Worth: Texas Christian University Press, 2013.

Kun, Josh. *Audiotopia: Music, Race, and America*. Berkeley: University of California Press, 2005.

Lane, Trevor. "Deadwood: Comparing the Lead Characters and Their Real World Counterparts." *What Culture*, May 20, 2020. https://whatculture.com/tv/deadwood-comparing-the-lead-characters-and-their-real-world-counterparts.

Langman, Larry. *A Guide to Silent Westerns*. Westport, CT: Greenwood, 1992.

Lawrence, John Shelton. "Filmography." In *Hollywood's West: The American Frontier in Film, Television, and History*, edited by Peter C. Rollins and John E. O'Connor, 300–321. Lexington: University Press of Kentucky, 2005.

Leinberger, Charles. "The Dollars Trilogy: 'There Are Two Kinds of Western Heroes, My Friend!'" In *Music in the Western: Notes from the Frontier*, edited by Kathryn Kalinak, 131–47. New York: Routledge, 2012.

Leket-Mor, Rachel. "My Heart Is in the West but I Am on the Eastern Edge: Hebrew Pulp Westerns and the Sabra Cowboy." In *The Western in the Global Literary Imagination*, edited by Christopher Conway, Marek Paryz, and David Rio, 253–77. Boston: Brill, 2022.

Lenburg, Jeff, Joan Howard Maurer, and Greg Lenburg. *The Three Stooges Scrapbook*. Chicago: Chicago Review, 2012.

Leslie, Edgar, Halsey K. Mohr, and Al Piantadosi. *I'm a Yiddish Cowboy ("Tough Guy Levi")*. New York: Barron, 1908.

Lesses, Rebecca. "Lilith." *Jewish Women's Archive*, March 20, 2009. https://jwa.org/encyclopedia/article/lilith.

Levine, Herman J., and Benjamin Miller. *The American Jewish Farmer in Changing Times*. New York: Jewish Agricultural Society, 1966.

Levine, Joseph A. *Rise and Be Seated: The Ups and Downs of Jewish Worship*. Northvale, NJ: Aronson, 2000.

Levinson, Robert E. *The Jews in the California Gold Rush*. New York: Ktav, 1978.

Levy, Beth E. *Frontier Figures: American Music and the Mythology of the American West*. Berkeley: University of California Press, 2012.

Leyda, Julia. *American Mobilities: Geographies of Class, Race, and Gender in US Culture*. Bielefeld, Germany: Transcript, 2016.

Libo, Kenneth, and Irving Howe. *We Lived There, Too: In Their Own Words and Pictures—Pioneer Jews and the Westward Movement of America, 1630–1930*. New York: St. Martin's, 1985.

Lieberman, Mark. "*True Grit* Isn't True." *Language Log*, December 29, 2010. https://languagelog.ldc.upenn.edu/nll/?p=2873.

"The Light of Western Stars (1930) Review, with Richard Arlen and Mary Brian." *Pre-Code.com*, September 9, 2022. https://pre-code.com/the-light-of-western-stars-1930-review-with-richard-arlen-and-mary-brian/.

Limerick, Patricia Nelson. *The Legacy of Conquest: The Unbroken Past of the American West*. New York: Norton, 1987.

Limerick, Patricia Nelson. *Something in the Soil: Legacies and Reckonings in the New West*. New York: Norton, 2000.

Loeffler, James. *The Most Musical Nation: Jews and Culture in the Late Russian Empire*. New Haven: Yale University Press, 2010.

Logie, John. "*Maus* (W)holes: Reflections on (and in) the Digitization of Art Spiegelman's *Maus*." In *Perspectives on Digital Comics: Theoretical, Critical, and Pedagogical Essays*, edited by Jeffrey S. J. Kirchoff and Mike P. Cook, 138–56. Jefferson, NC: McFarland, 2019.

Lomax, John A. *Cowboy Songs and Other Frontier Ballads*. New York: Sturgis and Walton, 1910.

Loy, R. Philip. *Westerns and American Culture, 1930–1955*. Jefferson, NC: McFarland, 2001.

Lund, Carson. "Blu-Ray Review: Samuel Fuller's *Forty Guns* on the Criterion Collection." *Slant*, January 10, 2019. https://www.slantmagazine.com/dvd/forty-guns-bd/.

Lusted, David. *The Western*. London: Pearson Longman, 2003.

Lynam, Robert, ed. *The Beecher Island Annual*. Wray, CO: Beecher Island Battle Memorial Association, 1930.

Magocsi, Paul Robert. "Galicia: A European Land." In *Galicia: A Multicultural Land*, edited by Chris Hann and Paul Robert Magocsi, 3–21. Toronto: University of Toronto Press, 2005.

Maltin, Leonard, Luke Sader, and Mike Clark, eds. *Leonard Maltin's 2009 Movie Guide*. New York: Penguin, 2008.

Manela, Aaron. "Chosen Cowboy Mazl Tov: Tin Pan Alley and the Wild West Cowboy Jew." *Journal of Jewish Identity* 10, no. 1 (2017): 27–59.

Manischewitz Presents the Jewish Cowboy. Manischewitz, 1958. EP.

Marks, M. L. *Jews among the Indians: Tales of Adventure and Conflict in the Old West*. Chicago: Benison, 1992.

Marschall, John P. *Jews in Nevada: A History*. Reno: University of Nevada Press, 2008.

Marty, Martin E. *Righteous Empire: The Protestant Experience in America*. New York: Dial, 1970.

Marx, Groucho, and Richard J. Anobile. *The Marx Bros. Scrapbook*. New York: Darien House, 1973.

Mask, Mia. *Black Rodeo: A History of the African American Western*. Urbana: University of Illinois Press, 2023.

Matheson, Sue, ed. *Women in the Western*. Edinburgh: Edinburgh University Press, 2020.

May, Lary L., and Elaine Tyler May. "Why Jewish Movie Moguls: An Exploration in American Culture." *American Jewish History* 72, no. 1 (1982): 6–25.

Mayer, Egon, and Carl Sheingold. *Intermarriage and the Jewish Future: A National Study in Summary*. New York: American Jewish Committee, 1979.

McBride, Joseph, ed. *Hawks on Hawks*. Berkeley: University of California Press, 1982.

McBride, Joseph. *Steven Spielberg: A Biography*. 2nd ed. Jackson: University Press of Mississippi, 2010.

McDonough, Kathleen A. "Wee Willie Winkie Goes West: The Influence of the British Empire Genre on Ford's Cavalry Trilogy." In *Hollywood's West: The American Frontier in Film, Television, and History*, edited by Peter C. Rollins and John E. O'Connor, 99–114. Lexington: University Press of Kentucky, 2005.

McGrath, Roger D. *Gunfighters, Highwaymen, and Vigilantes: Violence on the Frontier*. Berkeley: University of California Press, 1987.

Medding, Peter Y., Gary A. Tobin, Sylvia Barack Fishman, and Mordechai Rimor. "Jewish Identity in Conversionary and Mixed Marriages." *American Jewish Yearbook* 92 (1992): 3–76.

Memmi, Albert. *The Colonizer and the Colonized*. Boston: Beacon, 1965.

Merlock, Ray. Preface to *Hollywood's West: The American Frontier in Film, Television, and History*, edited by Peter C. Collins and John E. O'Connor, ix–xii. Lexington: University Press of Kentucky, 2005.

Metz, Nina. "The Stream Became a Binge." *Chicago Tribune*, April 21, 2022.

Meuel, David. *The Noir Western: Darkness on the Range, 1943–1962*. Jefferson, NC: McFarland, 2015.

Meyer, Donald C. "Music Cue Archetypes in the Film Scores of Elmer Bernstein." Paper presented at the From Nineteenth-Century Stage Drama to Twenty-First-Century Film Score: Musicodramatic Practice and Knowledge Organization symposium, April 15, 2012.

Meyers, Helene. *Movie-Made Jews: An American Tradition*. New Brunswick, NJ: Rutgers University Press, 2021.

Miller, Cynthia J. "Tradition, Parody, and Adaptation: Jed Buell's Unconventional West." In *Hollywood's West: The American Frontier in Film, Television, and History*, edited by Peter C. Rollins and John E. O'Connor, 65–80. Lexington: University Press of Kentucky, 2005.

Miller, Loren. "Hollywood's New Negro Films." *The Crisis*, January 1938, 8.

Miller, Stephen. "God and Bugs Bunny." *Sewanee Review* 119, no. 2 (2011): 256–68.

Moffat, Riley. *Population History of Western U.S. Cities and Towns, 1850–1990*. Lanham, MD: Scarecrow, 1996.

Monaco, Paul. *A History of American Movies: A Film-by-Film Look at the Art, Craft, and Business of Cinema*. Lanham, MD: Scarecrow, 2010.

Morgan, H. Wayne. *Oklahoma: A History*. New York: Norton, 1977.

Morrison, Kate. "She Lied about Everything, Except Marrying Wyatt Earp." *Messy Nessy*, March 15, 2017. https://www.messynessychic.com/2017/03/15/she-lied-about-everything-except-marrying-wyatt-earp/.

Moss, Joshua Louis. *Why Harry Met Sally: Subversive Jewishness, Anglo-Christian Power, and the Rhetoric of Modern Love*. Austin: University of Texas Press, 2017.

Most, Andrea. "'Big Chief Izzy Horowitz': Theatricality and Jewish Identity in the Wild West." *American Jewish History* 87, no. 4 (1999): 313–41.

Moyer, Donn J. *Cowboy Cliffhangers: A Listing of All Sound B-Western Chapter Plays from A to Z*. Tacoma, WA: Wild West, 1999.

Murchison, Gayle. *The American Stravinsky: The Style and Aesthetics of Copland's New American Music, the Early Works, 1921–1938*. Ann Arbor: University of Michigan Press, 2012.

Nasaw, David. *Going Out: The Rise and Fall of Public Amusements*. New York: Basic, 1993.

Nathan, Hans, ed. *Israeli Folk Music: Songs of the Early Pioneers*. Madison, WI: A-R, 1994.

Nelson, Andrew Patrick. *Still in the Saddle: The Hollywood Western, 1969–1980*. Norman: University of Oklahoma Press, 2015.

"New National Theatre." *Journal of Education* (Boston), August 24, 1911.

The New York Times Film Reviews. Vol. 3, 1939–48. New York: Arno, 1970.

Nolley, Ken. "The Representation of Conquest: John Ford and the Hollywood Indian, 1939–1964." In *Hollywood's Indian: The Portrayal of the Native American in Film*, edited by Peter C. Rollins and John E. O'Connor, 74–90. Lexington: University Press of Kentucky, 2003.

Novak, William, and Moshe Waldoks, eds. *The Big Book of Jewish Humor*. New York: Morrow, 2006.

Noy, Gary. *Hellacious California!: Tales of Rascality! Revelry! Dissipation! and Depravity! and the Birth of the Golden State*. Berkeley, CA: Sierra College Press, 2020.

Nulman, Macy. *The Encyclopedia of Jewish Prayer*. Northvale, NJ: Aronson, 1996.

Ochs, Vanessa L. "Ten Jewish Sensibilities." *Sh'ma: A Journal of Jewish Ideas*, December 1, 2003. http://shma.com/ten-jewish-sensibilities/.

O'Connor, John E. "The White Man's Indian: An Institutional Approach." In *Hollywood's Indian: The Portrayal of the Native American in Film*, edited by Peter C. Rollins and John E. O'Connor, 27–38. Lexington: University Press of Kentucky, 2003.

O'Connor, John E., and Peter C. Rollins. "Introduction: The West, Westerns, and American Character." In *Hollywood's West: The American Frontier in Film, Television, and History*, edited by Peter C. Collins and John E. O'Conner, 1–34. Lexington: University Press of Kentucky, 2005.

Okuda, Ted, and Edward Watz. *The Columbia Comedy Shorts: Two-Reel Hollywood Film Comedies, 1933–1958*. Jefferson, NC: McFarland, 1986.

Ornish, Natalie. *Pioneer Jewish Texans*. College Station: Texas A&M University Press, 2011.

Orquiola, John. "The Ballad of Buster Scruggs: All 6 Endings Explained." *Screen Rant*, March 3, 2023. https://screenrant.com/ballad-buster-scruggs-endings-explained/.

Ortega, Tony. "How the West Was Spun." *Phoenix New Times*, December 24, 1998.

Ortega, Tony. "I Varied Wyatt Earp." *Phoenix New Times*, March 4, 1999, .

O'Sullivan, John. "Annexation." *United States Magazine and Democratic Review* 17, no. 1 (1845): 5–10.

"Paramount, Newark." *Variety*, February 28, 1940.

Pareles, Jon. "Carl Foreman, Producer and 'River Kwai' Screenwriter, Dies." *New York Times*, June 27, 1984.

"The Passing of the Western Subject." *Nickelodeon*, February 18, 1911.

Pearl, Jonathan, and Judith Pearl. *The Chosen Image: Television's Portrayal of Jewish Themes and Characters*. Jefferson, NC: McFarland, 1999.

Pergament, Alan. "'The Last Movie Stars' Is a Creative and Revealing Portrait of Newman and Woodward." *Buffalo News*, July 22, 2022.

Petley, Julian. "Mann of the West." *Movie* 4, no. 53 (1980): 1046–48.

Pippin, Robert B. "What Is a Western?: Politics and Self-Knowledge in John Ford's *The Searchers*." *Critical Inquiry* 35, no. 2 (2009): 223–53.

Pitts, Michael R. *Western Movies: A Guide to 5,105 Feature Films*. 2nd ed. Jefferson, NC: McFarland, 2013.

Plaut, W. Gunther. *The Jews in Minnesota: The First Seventy-Five Years*. New York: American Jewish Historical Society, 1959.

Pogrebin, Abigail. *Stars of David: Prominent Jews Talk about Being Jewish*. New York: Broadway, 2005.

Portis, Charles. *True Grit: A Novel*. New York: Abrams, 2002.

"A Portrait of Jewish Americans." Pew Research Center, October 1, 2013. https://www.pewresearch.org/religion/2013/10/01/jewish-american-beliefs-attitudes-culture-survey/Pew.

Poulos, Christopher N. *Essentials of Autoethnography*. Washington, DC: American Psychological Association, 2021.

Presnell, Don. *Wandering "The Wild Wild West": A Critical Analysis of the CBS Television Series*. Jefferson, NC: McFarland, 2021.

Proehl, Bob. *Flying Burrito Brothers' "The Gilded Palace of Sin."* New York: Bloomsbury, 2008.

Rabin, Shari. "Fact-Checking *The Frisco Kid*: A Historian's Take on a Jewish Classic." *Jewish Book Council*, December 21, 2017. https://www.jewishbookcouncil.org/pb-daily/fact-checking-the-frisco-kid-a-historians-take-on-a-jewish-classic.

Rabin, Shari. *Jews on the Frontier: Religion and Mobility in Nineteenth-Century America*. New York: New York University Press, 2017.

Raphael, Marc Lee. "Beyond New York: Challenges to Local History." In *Jews of the American West*, edited by Moses Rischin and John Livingston, 48–65. Detroit: Wayne State University Press, 1991.

Raymond, Jon. *The Half-Life: A Novel*. New York: Bloomsbury, 2008.

Raymond, Jon, and Kelly Reichardt. *First Cow*. Webster, TX: Filmscience, 2018. https://deadline.com/wp-content/uploads/2021/02/FIRST-COW-screenplay.pdf.

"Report of the Committee on Church and State." *Year Book of the Central Conference of American Rabbis* 21 (1911): 79–81.

"Reviews of the New Films." *Film Daily*, December 11, 1940.

Richler, Mordecai. *St. Urbain's Horseman*. Toronto: McClelland and Stewart, 1971.

Rikoon, J. Sanford. "The Jewish Agriculturalists' Aid Society of America: Philanthropy, Ethnicity, and Agriculture in the Heartland." *Agricultural History* 72, no. 1 (1998): 1–32.

Riley, Michael J. "Trapped in the History of Film: *The Vanishing American*." In *Hollywood's Indian: The Portrayal of the Native American in Film*, edited by Peter C. Rollins and John E. O'Connor, 58–72. Lexington: University Press of Kentucky, 2003.

Rischin, Moses, ed. *The Jews of the West: The Metropolitan Years*. Berkeley, CA: Magnes, 1979.

Robbins, Stephen. Interview by author, telephone, April 18, 2022

Robinson, Forrest G., ed. *The New Western History: The Territory Ahead*. Tucson: University of Arizona Press, 1998.

Robinson, Harry I., and Will J. Harris. *Yonkle the Cow-Boy Jew*. Chicago: Rossiter, 1907.

Rochlin, Fred, and Harriet Rochlin. *Pioneer Jews: A New Life in the Far West*. Boston: Houghton Mifflin, 1984.

Rollins, Sandra Lea. "Jewish Indian Chief." *Western States Jewish Historical Quarterly* 1, no. 4 (1969): 151–63.

Roosevelt, Theodore. *Winning the West*. Vol. 3. Lincoln: University of Nebraska Press, 1995.

Rosen, Jody. "'Cohen Owes Me Ninety-Seven Dollars': Images of Jews from the Jewish Sheet-Music Trade." In *The Song Is Not the Same: Jews and American Popular Music*, edited by Bruce Zuckerman, Josh Kun, and Lisa Ansell, 89–114. West Lafayette, IN: Purdue University Press, 2011.

Rosen, Jody. Liner notes to *Jewface*. Reboot Stereophonic, 2006, CD.

Rosenberg, Joel. "Jewish Experience on Film—An American Overview." *American Jewish Yearbook* 96 (1996): 3–50.

Ross, Steven J. *Hitler in Los Angeles: How Jews Foiled Nazi Plots against Hollywood and America*. New York: Bloomsbury, 2017.

Rosten, Leo. *The New Joys of Yiddish*. New York: Three Rivers, 2001.

Roth, Lane, and Tom W. Hoffer. "G. M. 'Broncho Billy' Anderson: The First Movie Cowboy Hero." In *Back in the Saddle: Essays on Western Film and Television Actors*, edited by Gary A. Yoggy, 11–24. Jefferson, NC: McFarland, 1998.

Rottenberg, Josh. "The Coen Brothers on Their Western Anthology Film 'The Ballad of Buster Scruggs,' Netflix and the Future of Moviegoing." *Los Angeles Times*, November 14, 2018.

Rubin, Barry. *Assimilation and Its Discontents*. New York: Random House, 1995.

Rubinstein, Rachel. "Encountering Native Origins." In *The Cambridge History of Jewish American Literature*, edited by Hana Wirth-Nesher, 62–84. New York: Cambridge University Press, 2016.

Rubinstein, Rachel. *Members of the Tribe: Native America in the Jewish Imagination*. Detroit: Wayne State University Press, 2010.

Runge, Mike. *Deadwood's Mount Moriah Cemetery*. Charleston, SC: Arcadia, 2017.

Salem, Merryana. "'Killers of the Flower Moon' Can't Escape Its Own White Gaze." *Junkee*, October 20, 2023. https://junkee.com/killers-of-the-flower-moon-white-gaze-racism/355061.

Sandweiss, Naomi. "Ethnic Homesteading in the Nineteenth-Century Midwest: A Historiography of Irish Catholic, African American, and Eastern European Jewish Settlements." *Western States Jewish History* 52, no. 1 (2021): 43–54.

Sapoznik, Henry. *The Compleat Klezmer*. Cedarhurst, NY: Tara.

Saricks, Joyce G. *The Readers' Advisory Guide to Genre Fiction*. Chicago: American Library Association, 2009.

Scanlan, Laura Wolff. "Jewish Pioneers." *Humanities* 31, no. 1 (2010). https://www.neh.gov/humanities/2010/januaryfebruary/statement/jewish-pioneers.

Schneider, Paul Miles. "The Best Picture Project: A Film Lover's Journey through Every Oscar-Winning Best Picture in Chronological Order: Cimarron (1930–31)." *Paulmilesschneider.com*, March 20, 2015. www.paulmilesschneider.com/bestpictureproject/cimarron-1930-31/.

Schoenberger, Nancy. *Wayne and Ford: The Films, the Friendship, and the Forging of an American Hero*. New York: Anchor, 2018.

Schulman, Michael. "Mel Brooks Writes It All Down," *New Yorker*, November 28, 2021. https://www.newyorker.com/culture/the-new-yorker-interview/mel-brooks-writes-it-all-down.

Schulte, Janet E. "'Proving and Moving Up': Jewish Homesteading Activity in North Dakota, 1900–1920." *Great Plains Quarterly* 10, no. 4 (1990): 228–44.

Schwarzschild, Steven S. "The Unnatural Jew." In *Judaism and Environmental Ethics: A Reader*, edited by Martin D. Yaffe, 267–82. Lanham, MD: Lexington, 2001.

Scorsese, Martin. Foreword to *A Third Face: My Tale of Writing, Fighting, and Filmmaking*, by Samuel Fuller, xi–xii. New York: Knopf, 2002.

Senensky, Ralph. "*The Wild Wild West*: 'The Night of the Druid's Blood.'" *Ralph's Cinema Trek: A Journey in Film*, accessed August 12, 2024. https://senensky.com/the-night-of-the-druids-blood/.

Shadmi, Koren. *The Twilight Man: Rod Serling and the Birth of Television*. Los Angeles: Humanoids, 2019.

Shapiro, Ann R. "Edna Ferber, Jewish American Feminist." *Shofar* 20, no. 2 (2002): 52–60.

Shein, Debra. "Isaac Raboy's *Der Yiddisher Cowboy* and Rachel Calof's *My Story*: The Role of the Western Frontier in Shaping Jewish American Identity." *Western American Literature* 36, no. 4 (2002): 359–80.

Shepard, Richard F. “Film: Yiddish Cinema.” *New York Times*, April 9, 1985.

“Shimon Wincelberg.” *Variety*, October 1, 2004.

Shoopman, James G. *Patterns of American Popular Heroism: From Roman and Biblical Roots to Modern Media*. Jefferson, NC: McFarland, 2020.

Sidran, Ben. *There Was a Fire: Jews, Music, and the American Dream*. Madison, WI: Nardis, 2012.

Silow-Carroll, Andrew. “In ‘Blazing Saddles,’ Gene Wilder Helped Recall a Fading Black-Jewish Alliance.” *Haaretz*, August 30, 2016.

Silver, Alain, and James Ursini. *What Ever Happened to Robert Aldrich?: His Life and His Films*. New York: Limelight, 1995.

Silver, Steven H. “Jewish Science Fiction and Fantasy.” *Stevenhsilver.com*, accessed August 12, 2024. http://www.stevenhsilver.com/jewishsf.html.

Silverstein, Alan. *Alternatives to Assimilation: The Response of Reform Judaism to American Culture, 1840–1930*. Waltham, MA: Brandeis University Press, 1995.

Simmon, Scott. *The Invention of the Western Film: A Cultural History of the Genre's First Half-Century*. New York: Cambridge University Press, 2003.

Slide, Anthony. *New York City Vaudeville*. Charleston, SC: Arcadia, 2006.

Sinclair, Mick. *San Francisco: A Cultural and Literary History*. Oxford: Signal, 2004.

Singer, Matt. “The Worst Oscar Best Picture Winners Ever.” *Screen Crush*, March 8, 2022. https://screencrush.com/worst-oscar-best-picture-winners/.

Siskel, Gene. “Shootout at ‘Cockeyed Corral.’” *Chicago Tribune*, March 1, 1974.

Sklare, Marshall. *America's Jews*. New York: Random House, 1971.

Slatta, Richard W. *The Cowboy Encyclopedia*. New York: Norton, 1996.

Slotkin, Richard. *Gunfighter Nation: The Myth of the Frontier in Twentieth-Century America*. Norman: University of Oklahoma Press, 1998.

Slutsky, Yehuda. “Cantonists.” In *Encyclopaedia Judaica*, 2nd ed., edited by Fred Skolnik and Michael Berenbaum, 4:437–39. Detroit: Macmillan Reference, 2007.

Smith, David. “‘Hollywood Doesn't Change Overnight’: Indigenous Viewers on *Killers of the Flower Moon*.” *Guardian*, November 3, 2023. https://www.theguardian.com/film/2023/nov/03/indigenous-native-american-review-opinion-killers-flower-moon-movie.

Smith, Steven C. *Music by Max Steiner: The Epic Life of Hollywood's Most Influential Composer*. New York: Oxford University Press, 2020.

Smyth, J. E. “The New Western History in 1931: RKO and the Challenge of *Cimarron*.” In *Hollywood's Indian: The Portrayal of the Native American in Film*, edited by Peter C. Rollins and John E. O'Connor, 37–64. Lexington: University Press of Kentucky, 2003.

Sollors, Werner. *Beyond Ethnicity: Consent and Descent in American Culture*. New York: Oxford University Press, 1987.

Spiegelman, Art. *Maus: A Survivor's Tale*. New York: Pantheon, 1986.

Spiegelman, Art. *Maus II: A Survivor's Tale: And Here My Troubles Began*. New York: Pantheon, 1991.

Spittles, Brian. *John Ford*. New York: Routledge, 2004.

Stanton, Ann Haber. *Deadwood's Jewish Pioneers: A Gold Rush Odyssey*. N.p.: Prairie Hills, 2019.

Steiner, Max. "Scoring the Film." In *We Make the Movies*, edited by Nancy Naumburg, 216–38. New York: Norton, 1937.

Stern, Norton B. *California Jewish History: A Descriptive Bibliography*. Glendale, CA: Clark, 1967.

Stern, Norton B. "Louis Phillips of the Pomona Valley: Rancher and Real Estate Investor." *Western States Jewish History* 16, no. 1 (1983): 54–80.

Stern, Norton B. "Toward a Biography of Isaias W. Hellman: Pioneer Builder of California." *Western States Jewish Historical Quarterly* 2, no. 1 (1969): 27–43.

Stern, Norton B., and William M Kramer. "Anti-Semitism and the Jewish Image in the Early West." *Western States Jewish Historical Quarterly* 6, no. 2 (1974): 129–40.

Stern, Norton B., and William M. Kramer. "The Major Role of Polish Jews in the Pioneer West." *Western States Jewish Historical Quarterly* 8, no. 4 (1976): 326–44.

Stevens, George, Jr. *Conversations with the Great Moviemakers of Hollywood's Golden Age at the American Film Institute*. New York: Vintage, 2007.

Stone, Bryan Edward. *The Chosen Folks: Jews on the Frontiers of Texas*. Austin: University of Texas Press, 2010.

Stratton, Jon. *Coming Out Jewish: Constructing Ambivalent Identities*. New York: Routledge, 2003.

Szasz, Ferenc Morton. *Religion in the Modern American West*. Tucson: University of Arizona Press, 2000.

Tassel, Janet. "Mame-loshn at Harvard." *Harvard Magazine*, July 1, 1997. https://www.harvardmagazine.com/1997/07/mame-loshn-at-harvard.

Thompson, Anne. "Beyond-the-Pale Riders." *Film Comment* 28, no. 4 (1992): 52–54.

Thompson, Jennifer H. *Jewish on Their Own Terms: How Intermarried Couples Are Changing American Judaism*. New Brunswick, NJ: Rutgers University Press, 2013.

Thomson, David. *A Biographical Dictionary of Film*. New York: Morrow, 1976.

Thomson, David. *Warner Bros: The Making of an American Movie Studio*. New Haven: Yale University Press, 2017.

Tobias, Henry J. *The Jews in Oklahoma*. Norman: University of Oklahoma Press, 1980.

"Tobias Schanfarber in Chicago Israelite." *American Israelite* (Cincinnati), August 28, 1913.

Toll, William. "Intermarriage and the Urban West: A Religious Context for Cultural Change." In *Jews of the American West*, edited by Moses Rischin and John Livingstone, 164–89. Detroit: Wayne State University Press, 1991.

Tollerton, David. "Job of Suburbia?: A Serious Man and Viewer Perceptions of the Biblical." *Journal of Religion and Film* 15, no. 2 (2011). https://digitalcommons.unomaha.edu/jrf/vol15/iss2/7.

Tompkins, Jane P., ed. *Reader-Response Criticism: From Formalism to Post-Structuralism*. Baltimore: Johns Hopkins University Press, 1980.

Tompkins, Jane P. *West of Everything: The Inner Life of Westerns*. New York: Oxford University Press, 1993.

Tracy, Sarah J. *Qualitative Research Methods: Collecting Evidence, Crafting Analysis, Communicating Impact*. 2nd ed. New York: Wiley Blackwell, 2020.

"Trappist Monasteries in North America." *GCatholic.org*, accessed August 14, 2024. http://www.gcatholic.org/churches/list/USA-Trappist.htm.

Travers, Peter. "Forty Guns (1957)." In *The B List: The National Society of Film Critics on the Low-Budget Beauties, Genre-Bending Mavericks, and Cult Classics We Love*, edited by David Sterritt and John Anderson, 140–42. Cambridge, MA: Da Capo, 2008.

Turan, Kenneth. "Letting Jews Be Jews: Ethnicity and Hollywood, Its Fall and Rise." In *Jews in the Los Angeles Mosaic*, edited by Karen S. Wilson, 43–56. Berkeley: University of California Press, 2013.

Turner, Frederick Jackson. "The Significance of the Frontier in American History." *Annual Report of the American Historical Association* (1893): 197–227.

Turner, Matthew R. "Cowboys and Comedy: The Simultaneous Deconstruction and Reinforcement of Generic Conventions in the Western Parody." In *Hollywood's West: The American Frontier in Film, Television, and History*, edited by Peter C. Rollins and John E. O'Connor, 218–35. Lexington: University Press of Kentucky, 2005.

Tuska, Jon. *The Filming of the West*. Garden City, NY: Doubleday, 1976.

Tyler, Poyntz, ed. *Television and Radio*. New York: Wilson, 1961.

Uris, Leon. *Exodus*. New York: Doubleday, 1958.

Urwand, Ben. *The Collaboration: Hollywood's Pact with Hitler*. Cambridge: Belknap Press of Harvard University Press, 2013.

Varner, Paul. *The A to Z of Westerns in Cinema*. Lanham, MD: Scarecrow, 2009.

Vider, Stephen. "Riding Shotgun." *Tablet*, May 18, 2005. https://www.tabletmag.com/sections/arts-letters/articles/riding-shotgun.

Vorspan, Max, and Lloyd P. Gartner. *History of the Jews of Los Angeles*. San Marino, CA: Huntington Library, 1970.

Wald, Gayle. "Dreaming of Michael Jackson: Notes on Jewish Listening." In *The Song Is Not the Same: Jews and American Popular Music*, edited by Bruce

Zuckerman, Josh Kun, and Lisa Ansell, 1–8. West Lafayette, IN: Purdue University Press, 2011.

Walker, Jeffrey. "Deconstructing an American Myth: *The Last of the Mohicans* (1992)." In *Hollywood's Indian: The Portrayal of the Native American in Film*, edited by Peter C. Rollins and John E. O'Connor, 170–86. Lexington: University Press of Kentucky, 2003.

Wallin, B. C. "The Delightful Orthodox Representation in 'The Frisco Kid.'" *Hey Alma*, July 27, 2021. https://www.heyalma.com/the-delightful-orthodox-representation-in-the-frisco-kid/.

Waxman, Chaim. *American Jews*. Philadelphia: Temple University Press, 1983.

Wegele, Peter. *Max Steiner: Composing, Casablanca, and the Golden Age of Film Music*. Lanham, MD: Rowman and Littlefield, 2014.

Weil, Abigail. "Revisiting 'An American Tail,' a Deeply Jewish Immigration Story." *Hey Alma*, September 20, 2021. https://www.heyalma.com/revisiting-an-american-tail-a-deeply-jewish-immigration-story/.

Weiner, Hollace Ava. "Frances Rosenthal Kallison, 1908–2004: Cowgirl with a Jewish Conscience." *Western States Jewish History* 48, no. 1 (2015): 3–26.

Weiner, Hollace Ava, and Kenneth D. Roseman, eds. *Lone Stars of David: The Jews of Texas*. Waltham, MA: Brandeis University Press, 2007.

Weinstein, David. *The Eddie Cantor Story: A Jewish Life in Performance and Politics*. Waltham, MA: Brandeis University Press, 2018.

Wex, Michael. *Born to Kvetch: Yiddish Language and Culture in All Its Moods*. New York: St. Martin's, 2005.

Whitfield, Stephen. *The Culture of the Cold War*. 2nd ed. Baltimore: Johns Hopkins University Press, 1996.

Whitmer, Mariana. *Elmer Bernstein's "The Magnificent Seven": A Film Score Guide*. Lanham, MD: Rowman and Littlefield, 2017.

Whitmer, Mariana. "Reinventing the Western Film Score: Jerome Moross and *The Big Country*." In *Music in the Western: Notes from the Frontier*, edited by Kathryn Kalinak, 51–76. New York: Routledge, 2012.

Wilder, Gene. "Back in the Saddle." *Blazing Saddles*, directed by Mel Brooks. Warner Bros., 2004. DVD.

Wilder, Gene. *Kiss Me Like a Stranger: My Search for Love and Art*. New York: St. Martin's, 2005.

Williams, Leah. "How Hollywood Whitewashed the Old West." *Atlantic*, October 5, 2016. https://www.theatlantic.com/entertainment/archive/2016/10/how-the-west-was-lost/502850/.

Wills, Matthew. "Nittel Nacht: The Jewish Christmas Eve." *JSTOR Daily*, December 16, 2020. https://daily.jstor.org/nittel-nacht-the-jewish-christmas-eve/.

Winokur, Jon. *Encyclopedia Neurotica*. New York: St. Martin's, 2005.

Wolin, Penny Diane. *The Jews of Wyoming: Fringe of the Diaspora*. Cheyenne, WY: Crazy Woman Creek, 2000.

Yogerst, Chris. *The Warner Brothers*. Lexington: University Press of Kentucky, 2023.

Yoggy, Gary A. *Riding the Video Range: The Rise and Fall of the Western on Television*. Jefferson, NC: McFarland, 1995.

Zacharek, Stephanie. "Kelly Reichardt's *First Cow* Is a Tranquil Reflection on Masculine Tenderness." *Time*, March 6, 2020. https://time.com/5797867/first-cow-review/.

"Zane Grey on Film: A Listing of Movies Made from Zane Grey's Writings." *Zane Grey's West Society*, accessed August 12, 2024. https://www.zgws.org/zgmovies.php.

Zen, Beringia. "Rod Serling." *Dictionary of Unitarian and Universalist Biography*, September 16, 2001. https://uudb.org/articles/rodserling.html.

Zerin, Edward. *Jewish San Francisco*. Charleston, SC: Arcadia, 2006.

Zicree, Marc Scott. *The Twilight Zone Companion*. 3rd ed. Los Angeles: Silman-James, 2018.

Zierler, Wendy. "Fools on the American Road: 'Gimpel the Fool,' *The Frisco Kid*, and *Forrest Gump*." In *Hit the Road Jack: Essays on the Culture of the American Road*, edited by Gordon E. Slethaug and Stacey Ford, 214–33. Montreal: McGill–Queen's University Press, 2012.

Index

WISCONSIN FILM STUDIES

The Film Music of John Williams: Reviving Hollywood's Classical Style, second edition
EMILIO AUDISSINO

The Foreign Film Renaissance on American Screens, 1946–1973
TINO BALIO

Hollywood's Unofficial Film Corps: American Jewish Moviemakers and the War Effort
MICHAEL BERKOWITZ

Somerset Maugham and the Cinema
ROBERT CALDER

Marked Women: Prostitutes and Prostitution in the Cinema
RUSSELL CAMPBELL

Depth of Field: Stanley Kubrick, Film, and the Uses of History
Edited by GEOFFREY COCKS, JAMES DIEDRICK, and GLENN PERUSEK

Tough as Nails: The Life and Films of Richard Brooks
DOUGLASS K. DANIEL

Making Hollywood Happen: The Story of Film Finances
CHARLES DRAZIN

Dark Laughter: Spanish Film, Comedy, and the Nation
JUAN F. EGEA

Glenn Ford: A Life
PETER FORD

Chai Noon: Jews and the Cinematic Wild West
JONATHAN L. FRIEDMANN

Luis Buñuel: The Red Years, 1929–1939
ROMÁN GUBERN and PAUL HAMMOND

Screen Nazis: Cinema, History, and Democracy
SABINE HAKE

Peerless: Rouben Mamoulian, Hollywood, and Broadway
KURT JENSEN

A Cinema of Obsession: The Life and Work of Mai Zetterling
MARIAH LARSSON

Continental Films: French Cinema Under German Control
CHRISTINE LETEUX

Escape Artist: The Life and Films of John Sturges
GLENN LOVELL

Colonial Tactics and Everyday Life: Workers of the Manchuria Film Association
YUXIN MA

I Thought We Were Making Movies, Not History
WALTER MIRISCH

Giant: George Stevens, a Life on Film
MARILYN ANN MOSS

French Film History, 1895–1946
RICHARD NEUPERT

The Many Lives of Cy Endfield: Film Noir, the Blacklist, and "Zulu"
BRIAN NEVE

Six Turkish Filmmakers
LAURENCE RAW

Jean-Luc Godard: The Permanent Revolutionary
BERT REBHANDL, translated by EDWARD MALTBY

The Cinema of Sergei Parajanov
JAMES STEFFEN

JONATHAN L. FRIEDMANN is a scholar of Jewish music history and the president of the Western States Jewish History Association. He serves as vice president, academic dean, and director of programs at Ezzree Institute; admissions director and associate professor at the International Institute for Secular Humanistic Judaism; director of the Jewish Museum of the American West; and cohost of *Amusing Jews*, an interview show celebrating Jewish contributors and contributions to American popular culture. He is the author or editor of numerous books and articles, most recently *Jewish Historical Societies: Navigating the Professional-Amateur Divide*, coedited with Joel Gereboff.